The
Feasts
of the
Lord

The Feasts of the Lord

Robert Thompson

**Published by
Omega Publications
P.O. Box 4130
Medford, OR 97501**

Scripture source for this book is the King James Version of the Bible.

Published by
Omega Publications
P.O. Box 4130
Medford, OR 97501

Printed in U.S.A.

ISBN #0-931608-18-X
UNILIT #645571
OMEGA #5018

TO AUDREY
MARC AND DAVID

ACKNOWLEDGMENTS

Paul and Mary Dillinger, who have lovingly put forth so much time and effort to help

Walter and Kay Miller, who were among the first to offer encouragement

George and Harriet Gillies, always a source of wisdom and strength

Leroy Cloud, who provided a place to teach

Many friends who have prayed and keep on praying for the ministry of the Word

TABLE OF CONTENTS

PRELIMINARY

The Levitical convocations are listed in the twenty-third chapter of the book of Leviticus in the Old Testament. There are seven of them. Sometimes they are called the "Levitical feasts," or "feasts of the Lord." But in actuality they are not all feasts, as we think of the word *feast*. However, they were all *convocations*, that is, observances in which the Hebrews were called together by the Lord.

TWO GUIDELINES FOR INTERPRETING BIBLE TYPES

Before we go further, let us mention two rules for interpreting Bible symbols, or types, as they are called. Types, such as the Levitical convocations, help us to understand the Lord Jesus and His plan of salvation.

The first rule of interpretation is this: study the symbol, and then ask the Holy Spirit to cause the main truth to rise to the surface. Do not focus too long on the details of the symbol and attempt to force the interpretation. You will get sidetracked. We see Bible truth through a glass darkly, as Paul says in I Corinthians 13, and the Holy Spirit must be the One to throw light on the subject. Usually a type presents one main truth, or line of truth, and the Spirit will give us the understanding.

For example, Christ is the *Lamb* of God. The truth which rises to the surface is that Christ was led away as an offering for our sins, and that we eat His body and drink His precious blood as our Passover. But we can't pursue the symbol further and claim that Christ today is led around helplessly and is a prey for every wolf who appears on the scene. Again, in one setting leaven is a type of sin; in another setting leaven is a type of the kingdom of heaven.

Still another example is this: the Christian church is referred to as the bride of the Lamb. This symbol of marriage indicates to us that we enter into spiritual union with Christ, and are made one with Him. But we can't go on from this and state that Christians are feminine because they are called the "bride," and that the bride is a different group from the sons of God who are male because they are "sons."

It is not a good idea to get too detailed with the types and shadows of the Bible. When a symbol is seen, the Holy Spirit will bring the truth to the surface. But we should not attempt to apply every detail, because the details do not all reveal spiritual truth.

The second guideline for interpreting Bible symbols is this: all interpretation of symbols must be directly taught in the New Testament. For example, the getting rid of sin is portrayed by the removal of leaven during the convocation of Unleavened Bread. Then the New Testament directly teaches us to get rid of sin. First, there is the bringing down to death of our carnal nature through entering into the death of Christ upon the cross, as dramatized in water baptism. The authority of Satan over us is destroyed and from that point on we can choose to serve righteousness. Second, we have the provision of confessing and getting cleansing from the sins which we practice as Christians, as taught in I John 1:7-9.

If we claim that the removal of leaven during the convocation of Unleavened Bread symbolizes the putting away of sin from the Christian, we must be able to turn to the New Testament and find authority for the fact that God indeed has provided grace through the Lord Jesus Christ, through which we can begin to get the victory over sin in our life. Christ has made it possible for us to get rid of the old leaven of the world, Satan, and our own pride and lust of the flesh.

If we are to make a success of interpreting Bible types, we should get the main idea from the Holy Spirit and not press too hard on the details or attempt to force an interpretation which doesn't fit. Also, there must be direct New Testament teaching for whatever applications we make.

ENUMERATION OF THE SEVEN LEVITICAL CONVOCATIONS

1. Passover—"In the fourteenth day of the first month at even is the Lord's passover" (Lev. 23:5).
2. Unleavened Bread—"And on the fifteenth day of the same month is the feast of unleavened bread unto the Lord; seven days ye must eat unleavened bread" (Lev. 23:6).
3. Firstfruits—"Speak unto the children of Israel, and say unto them, When ye be come into the land which I give unto you, and shall reap the harvest thereof, then ye shall bring a sheaf of the firstfruits of your harvest unto the priest" (Lev. 23:10).
4. Pentecost—"And ye shall count unto you from the morrow after the sabbath, from the day that ye brought the sheaf of the wave offering; seven sabbaths shall be complete: even unto the morrow after the seventh sabbath shall ye number fifty days; and ye shall offer a new meat offering unto the Lord" (Lev. 23:15,16).

The word *pentecost* means *fifty*. The convocation of Pentecost derives its name from the fact that it was celebrated fifty days from the convocation of First-fruits. Sometimes Pentecost is referred to as the feast of weeks.

5. Trumpets—"Speak unto the children of Israel, saying, In the seventh month, in the first day of the month, shall ye have a sabbath, a memorial of blowing of trumpets, a holy convocation" (Lev. 23:24).
6. Day of Atonement—"Also on the tenth day of this seventh month there shall be a day of atonement: it shall be a holy convocation unto you; and ye shall afflict your souls, and offer an offering made by fire unto the Lord" (Lev. 23:27).
7. Tabernacles—"Speak unto the children of Israel, saying, The fifteenth day of this seventh month shall be the feast of tabernacles for seven days unto the Lord" (Lev. 23:34).

FOUR AREAS OF INTERPRETATION OF THE LEVITICAL CONVOCATIONS

There are four general areas of interpretation of the Levitical convocations: (1) the Person and work of the Lord Jesus Christ; (2) the redemption of the believer; (3) the perfecting of the church, the body of Christ; and (4) the setting up of the kingdom of God upon the earth. Although there are many points in common among these four areas, it seems to us that it is helpful to look at them separately.

The Person and work of the Lord Jesus Christ. It will take us the next thousand years to begin to understand a fraction of the grandeur, the authority, the power, the love, the holiness, the beauty, the wisdom, the knowledge, the faithfulness of our Lord Jesus, the living Word of the Father from eternity. All the major types of the Bible add to our understanding of the greatness of Christ, of His love, of His work of redemption upon the cross, of the unlimited power and authority of His resurrection life. Truly the fullness of the Godhead dwells in Christ, and he who has seen Christ has seen the Father. It is not that Christ is the Father, but rather that the Father has given of Himself without measure to the Son.

The redemption of the believer.   The fact that there were seven convocations shows us something about the plan of salvation. It shows us that the redemption which is in and through the Lord Jesus has a definite beginning, a definite process, and a definite fulfillment. Redemption is a perfect work. No part of it has been left for chance or for our own ideas. It is of God through Christ from start to finish. Christ is the *Alpha* and the *Omega*. He finishes that which He starts. He is the Author and the Finisher of our faith.

Salvation begins with our Passover experience, when we accept the precious blood of the Lamb of God, and by faith sprinkle that blood upon our own life and upon our household as a protection against the judgments of God. The blood of the Passover is our covering when the Lord passes over and smites the gods of this world. Salvation is brought to consummation when we enter into the fullness of the Father and the Son through the fullness of the Holy Spirit, as Jesus prayed in John 17. The beginning of redemption is of God, the consummation is of God, and everything in the middle is of God. It is God's salvation through Christ Jesus.

When we say that redemption finishes with the convocation of Tabernacles we are not saying that we cannot grow in God after that. We will grow in the image of Christ throughout eternity as we stand before the great throne of God Almighty, behold His glorious face, and serve Him. When we are speaking of salvation having a specific beginning and ending we mean that God's plan of redemption has a beginning and an ending. The day will come when we will be completely redeemed—spirit, soul, and body.

The perfecting of the church.   The third area of interpretation of the seven Levitical convocations is that of the growth of the body of Christ to maturity. The church commences as relatively loose assemblages of believers in Christ. It finishes up as the new Jerusalem, the bride of the Lamb. The seven convocations portray in symbolic form the development of the body of Messiah from more or less undisciplined groups of believers into the army of the Lord which will be revealed with Him at His appearing, bringing judgment and deliverance to the nations of the earth.

The setting up of the kingdom of God.   The fourth way in which we can understand the Levitical convocations has to do with the setting up of the kingdom of God in the earth. The Lord Jesus Christ upon the cross of Calvary was the great kingdom-wide act of God in which the legal basis for the kingdom was established. At the cross the price of redemption was paid for all people, although some reject God's salvation and are lost as a result. The authority of judgment and the ownership of the earth and its peoples were given to Jesus Christ, being paid for by His precious blood. The mortgage was paid for every person—every man, woman, boy, and girl upon the earth. Whosoever will can now pass from the authority of Satan to the authority of Christ just by receiving the blood of the cross by faith. Hallelujah!

We have seen, then, that the seven convocations speak of the Lord Jesus, of the Christian disciple, of the church, and of the kingdom. The Lord Jesus began His work of redemption as the Lamb of God who takes away the sin of the world, and when God is finished Jesus Christ will be upon His throne within the new Jerusalem. The Christian begins upon the cross with Christ, and when God is finished the Christian will be one in the Father and the Son, being filled with the glory and the love of God. The church comes into being as Christ is born in the hearts of the believers in Christ. When God Almighty is finished the church will be the holy city, the bride of the Lamb, the new Jerusalem. The kingdom of God was preached by Christ for three years, but actually began when Christ rose from the dead. When God is finished there will be a new heaven and a new earth, and sin will no longer be found there. Christ in His church will rule, under God, unto the ages of ages, world without end.

PHYSICAL DESCRIPTION OF
THE LEVITICAL CONOVOCATIONS

In our book a great deal is said about the fulfillment of the types of the Old Testament. The things and events of Israel are seen as symbols of spiritual realities, and as being prophetic of things and happenings of the future, in both the spiritual and the natural realms. Because of the heavy emphasis upon symbolism, it is good to keep in mind that the people and events of the Bible actually took place in the real world, among real people. There was a nation of Israel which came out of Egypt and wandered in the desert for forty years. There was an actual Tabernacle of the Congregation. The Levitical convocations were actually practiced—some are still in practice to this very day. Although these things and events reveal spiritual truths to us, and speak of the future in some cases, yet we must understand that they are facts of history, having taken place among flesh and blood human beings.

Our study takes us back in time beyond 1400 B.C. to the land of Egypt, where a prophet named Moses and Aaron, his brother, were speaking the Word of the living God to Pharaoh. Egypt was in the process of being consumed with various plagues, but the worst was yet to come.

PASSOVER

The story of the first Passover is fairly well known to Christians, besides being of the utmost importance to the

Jews. The Passover is still celebrated by Jews throughout the world.

Let us commence reading in Exodus 12:

"And the Lord spoke unto Moses and Aaron in the land of Egypt, saying,"(Exod. 12:1).

The first Passover marked the only occasion upon which any of the seven Levitical convocations were celebrated in the midst of the Egyptians (a type of the world). The lambs were killed; the blood was sprinkled upon the doorposts of the houses; and the flesh was eaten with unleavened bread. All of this took place in Egypt.

The remainder of the convocations were celebrated outside of Egypt. It is believed that the giving of the Law upon Mount Sinai occurred upon the fiftieth day after the first day of the first week of Unleavened Bread. It should be noted from the very beginning of our study, however, that the Levitical convocations in the main were agricultural festivals. Although they were spelled out in detail during the wilderness sojourn, yet they could not be celebrated until Israel entered the land of promise. The Jews in the wilderness had no crops; and Firstfruits, Pentecost, and Tabernacles celebrated the ingathering of barley, wheat, grapes, and the rest of the yield of the land. The fact that the convocations were instituted in the wilderness, and their observance strictly enjoined upon the Hebrews (and yet could not be practiced until the people had entered the land of promise), has great prophetic significance for the church of Christ.

"This month *(Abib)* shall be unto you the beginning of months: it shall be the first month of the year to you" (Exod. 12:2).

Prior to this time the month *Abib* was the seventh month (of the civil year). Now *Abib* was established as the chief of the months, marking the beginning of the ecclesiastical year. *Abib* overlaps our March-April.

The seventh month *(Tishri)* of the ecclesiastical year which commenced with *Abib* was the first month of the civil year, overlapping our September-October. This may seem a bit confusing, but it is quite simple. The Jews had two overlapping years, just as we do today. We have a calendar year which begins in January, and a fiscal year which begins in July. The Jews had an ecclesiastical year which commenced with the month *Abib,* and a civil year which commenced with the month *Tishri. Tishri* was the seventh month of the ecclesiastical year, just as July is the seventh month of the calendar year. But *Tishri* was the first month of the civil year, as July is the first month of the fiscal year. These two overlapping years of the Jews are of the utmost prophetic significance. The first of *Tishri* is the convocation of Trumpets. It is New Year's Day, *Rosh Hashanah,* and typifies a tremendous occurrence in the plan of redemption, and in the history of the church and of the kingdom of God.

The seven Levitical convocations typify the plan of the redemption of the believer in Christ. The plan of redemption commences with the blood of the Passover Lamb. John the Baptist cried, "Behold, the Lamb of God, who takes away the sin of the world!" (see John 1:29). No one gets anywhere at all with God until he or she comes to terms with the precious blood of the Lord Jesus Christ. Therefore, the Lord God announced to His servant Moses that the month *Abib,* formerly the seventh month of the year, would from this time forth head up the year. For God was about to perform one of the most extraordinary acts in the history of the peoples of the earth, an event which portrays as does no other the death of the Lamb of God who was slain for our sins, but who one day will reign in glory with His wife whom He has redeemed with His blood.

"Speak . . . unto all the congregation of Israel, saying, In the tenth day of this month they shall take to them every man a lamb, according to the house of their fathers, a lamb for a house: and if the household be too little for the lamb, let him and his neighbor next unto his house take it according to the number of the souls; every man according to his eating shall make your count for the lamb.

Your lamb shall be without blemish, a male of the first year: ye shall take it out from the sheep, or from the goats" (Exod. 12:3-5).

Notice how careful the Lord is that there be enough for everyone. It is God's will that all be saved and come unto repentance. There is enough grace in Christ for every person in the world. But neither is there to be waste, and so a small family might go together with another family in order that the lamb would be consumed by the participants.

"A lamb for a house"! When one person of a household gets saved, the blessing of the Lord comes upon the home. Hopefully, all the other members will come to know the Lord through the faithful life of the one who has chosen to serve the Lord.

The lamb was selected on the tenth day of the month *Abib* and could be observed until the fourteenth day to make sure there was no blemish in the animal, no defective limb or other imperfection. Our Lord Jesus Christ was examined carefully by the leaders of Jerusalem, and they could find no fault in Him. He is God's Lamb!

"And ye shall keep it up until the fourteenth day of the same month: and the whole assembly of the congregation of Israel shall kill it in the evening. And they shall take of the blood, and strike it on the two side posts and on the upper doorpost of the houses, wherein they shall eat it" (Exod. 12:6,7).

The expression "in the evening" is thought by some to indicate the period of time between sunset and dark—at dusk. The blood protected the entrances of the houses in which the Israelites ate the Passover lamb. This was the very first Passover, and it was established by the Lord. The last Passover established by the Lord was attended by the Lord Himself, and He Himself was pointing the disciples toward the breaking of His body and the shedding of His precious blood. From that point on the blessing of the Lord was upon the Christian communion service rather than the Jewish Passover. What more need is there of a Passover lamb? Behold, God's Lamb has come and has protected us with His own blood!

> "And they shall eat the flesh in that night, roast with fire, and unleavened bread; and with bitter herbs they shall eat it. Eat not of it raw, nor sodden at all with water, but roast with fire; his head with his legs, and with the inward parts. And ye shall let nothing of it remain until the morning; and that which remaineth of it until the morning ye shall burn with fire" (Exod. 12:8-10).

The Passover lamb was not to be undercooked, or cooked by boiling in water. The entire lamb was to be roasted with fire. Whatever was not eaten was to be burned in the fire. This is a picture of our Lord Jesus Christ who endured the judgment of God (the fire) until His being was consumed. There was no part of Jesus which did not endure the trial by God's fire. He had to suffer it all, so that He might be a fit Redeemer for every person, and so that He might lead many sons unto glory. The consumption of the residue with fire shows us the extreme severity and solemnity with which God regards the crucifixion of His beloved Son. The salvation in Christ is not something to play around with as one feels the whim!

The lamb was eaten with unleavened bread and bitter herbs, speaking of the fact that we must put away the world (leaven) when we come to Christ—all insincerity must be put far from us, or what should prove to be a blessing to us will instead become judgment upon us. The bitter herbs remind us of the suffering of the Son of God, and also of the fact that we may suffer tribulation and persecution for His name. There have been many times in history when Christians have had to suffer for the faith, and some are suffering tribulation in our own time. We must through much tribulation enter the kingdom of God.

> "And thus shall ye eat it; with your loins girded, your shoes on your feet, and your staff in your hand; and ye shall eat it in haste: it is the Lord's passover" (Exod. 12:11).

Perhaps most of us have this sense of haste, of pilgrimage, of leaving the world in search of the city of God, when we first get saved. What happens after a while? Do we lose sight of the fact that we are pilgrims and strangers, looking for a city which has foundations? Do we keep our love for Christ burning hot with the expectation of His glorious appearing?

The Israelites, several million strong, were preparing to evacuate the land where they had lived since the time that Jacob and his eleven sons had come seeking relief from the famine which was ravaging Canaan. The people felt the presence of the Lord God of Abraham, Isaac, and Jacob, and they bowed their heads and worshiped. They had seen the Lord smite Egypt by the word of His servant Moses. Still, they had no idea of the terror that would reach into every home in Egypt, except those houses having blood upon the posts of the doors. Even so it is true today that God requires of people that they apply the blood of His Lamb to their lives as a protection against the judgment to come. Had we any idea of the extent of the calamity which is to come, we Christians would have a deeper appreciation of the precious blood which is our protection against the judgments of God.

God was getting His people ready to move. God desires of us today that we maintain that same sense of urgency and expectancy, always looking toward the day of the Lord, and hastening the coming of Christ by our godly living and prayers unto Him.

> "For I will pass through the land of Egypt this night, and will smite all the firstborn in the land of Egypt, both man and beast; and against all the gods of Egypt I will execute judgment: I am the Lord" (Exod. 12:12).

The Passover was a time of redemption for the Israelites, but a time of unbelievable horror for the Egyptians. In the above verse notice that the firstborn of people died, and the firstborn of the innocent animals died. Yet the judgment was against the gods of Egypt.

So it is today! The coming day of the Lord will be a time of horror for the people of the world. The same day will be the day of redemption for every man, woman, boy, and girl who is protected by the blood of God's Lamb, Christ Jesus. Yet, the judgment is against the gods of this world. The battle is always the Lord against the principalities and powers in the heavenlies. The peoples of the earth are either destroyed or redeemed, depending upon what they do with Christ. The destruction comes from God. He is the Lord! He executes judgment against the gods of this world! Let us take care that we are on the Lord's side in this issue (Exodus 12:12,13,23,27,29; Psalm 136:10).

God singled out the firstborn for death because Pharaoh was holding the Lord's firstborn in captivity (Exodus 4:22,23).

> "And the blood shall be to you for a (sign) upon the

houses where (you) are: and when I see the blood, I will pass over you, and the plague shall not be upon you to destroy you, when I smite the land of Egypt" (Exod. 12:13).

The blood of the lamb was for a sign upon the houses. There is no mention made of sin. The Lord God was about to pass through Egypt executing judgment against Ptah, the fire god; Neith, the cow; Re, the sun god (you may remember that Joseph's father-in-law was Potiphar, the priest of On, where Re was worshiped); and the rest of the many gods and goddesses of nature which the Egyptians worshiped. It is not said, in the account of this first most important Passover, that the blood of the lamb covered the sins of the Israelites. Rather, the blood was a sign upon the house so that when the Lord judged Ptah, Neith, Re, Kneph, Amon, and the others, the plague would not be upon the inhabitants of that house.

"And this day shall be unto you for a memorial; and ye shall keep it a feast to the Lord throughout your generations: ye shall keep it a feast by an ordinance for ever" (Exod. 12:14).

The only true Passover was the first one, for on that night God brought His people out of the land of Egypt, out from the house of bondage. The redemption of God's people meant liberty for them, but destruction for Egypt. So will it be when Christ returns to liberate His saints from the bondage of this age. The Christians will be redeemed, but multitudes of earth's peoples will be destroyed as God pours out His wrath upon the gods of this world.

"And it came to pass, that at midnight (the fourteenth of *Abib*) the Lord smote all the firstborn in the land of Egypt, from the firstborn of Pharaoh that sat on his throne unto the firstborn of the captive that was in the dungeon; and all the firstborn of cattle. And Pharaoh rose up in the night, he, and all his servants, and all the Egyptians; and there was a great cry in Egypt: for there was not a house where there was not one dead" (Exod. 12:29,30).

It has never been true before or since that God went into the midst of a nation and took a group out of their midst, destroying that nation in the process. No matter how much thought we give the first Passover, the importance of what happened here can scarcely be grasped. It was on the same scale with Noah's flood, and the overthrow of Sodom and Gomorrah. The crucifixion and resurrection of the Lord Jesus Christ was on this scale, and the next event of such magnitude will be the return of the Lord Jesus with His saints to execute judgment upon the ungodly.

It is the Lord's will that all Israel, Jews and Christians alike, bring to mind the story of the first Passover. There is no clearer picture of our Lord Jesus Christ upon the cross of Calvary.

"And it shall come to pass, when your children shall say unto you, What mean ye by this service? That ye shall say, It is the sacrifice of the Lord's passover, who passed over the houses of the children of Israel in Egypt, when he smote the Egyptians, and delivered our houses. And the people bowed the head and worshipped" (Exod. 12:26,27).

In order to partake of the Lord's Passover (in Christian terms of the communion service), a person must receive Christ as Lord and Savior, believing in His atoning crucifixion and bodily resurrection, and be baptized in water. Faith in Christ and baptism into Him brings the believer under the protection of the new covenant. He who believes and is baptized shall be saved. True faith and conversion to Christ is a circumcision of the heart, so to speak, cutting away the old malice and lust of the present age. To partake of the body and blood of our Lord Jesus, a person must experience this circumcision of the heart.

> "And when a stranger shall sojourn with thee, and will keep the passover to the Lord, let all his males be circumcised, and then let him come near and keep it; and he shall be as one that is born in the land: for no uncircumcised person shall eat thereof" (Exod. 12:48).

UNLEAVENED BREAD

The Passover lamb was slain in the late afternoon of the thirteenth of *Abib*, in preparation for Passover day, the fourteenth of *Abib*, which commenced at sundown on the thirteenth. The Hebrew day goes from sundown to sundown. The first day of the week of Unleavened Bread was the fifteenth of *Abib*, commencing at sundown of the fourteenth. The week of Unleavened Bread was of seven days duration, commencing on the fifteenth and extending through the twenty-first. The first day of Unleavened Bread, the fifteenth of *Abib*, was a very important Sabbath.

Let us continue with our study of Exodus 12:

> "Seven days shall ye eat unleavened bread; even the first day ye shall put away leaven out of your houses: for whosoever eateth leavened bread from the first day until the seventh day, that soul shall be cut off from Israel" (Exod. 12:15).

Leaven as used here is a type of wickedness. Leaven is fermenting dough which raises bread. Without the addition of leaven the baked bread is flat. For one week, under penalty of being cut off from the nation, no Israelite was to eat leavened bread.

If you stop to think about it, this was a remarkable prohibition. Bread is a staff of life, and leaven makes the bread palatable. No doubt the sternness of the injunction had to do with that which leaven typifies: malice and wickedness. God was saying to us that every man, woman, boy, and girl who comes to Him for salvation must put away the former things, and not leave one particle of the spirit of this age in him. It doesn't take much leaven to leaven the whole ball of dough. A little sin in the life keeps working until the whole person is poisoned. "Put it away!" God commands. "Don't let it be seen in your house. Keep away from sin. Remove it from your presence forever."

"And ye shall observe the feast of unleavened bread; for in this selfsame day (fifteenth of *Abib,* a high Sabbath) have I brought your armies out of the land of Egypt: therefore shall ye observe this day in your generations by an ordinance for ever" (Exod. 12:17).

It can be seen that the separation of leaven from the camp of Israel is symbolic of the separation of Egypt from Israel. It is the division between light and darkness. Notice, "I brought your armies out of the land of Egypt." The word *armies* speaks of the fact that people can only be redeemed by means of war, as will be true at the return of Christ. The convocation of Unleavened Bread is identified with water baptism, for it is there that we put away our sins—we wash away our sins in the waters of baptism.

"In the first month, on the fourteenth day of the month at even (that is, at the conclusion of the fourteenth and the beginning of the fifteenth), ye shall eat unleavened bread, until the one and twentieth day of the month at even. Seven days shall there be no leaven found in your houses: for whosoever eateth that which is leavened, even that soul shall be cut off from the congregation of

Israel, whether he be a stranger, or born in the land. Ye shall eat nothing leavened; in all your habitations shall ye eat unleavened bread" (Exod. 12:18-20).

Blood was shed at every one of the seven Levitical convocations. Notice in the following passage that animals were sacrificed during the observance of Unleavened Bread. Reading in Numbers 28:

"And in the fifteenth day of this month *(Abib)* is the feast: seven days shall unleavened bread be eaten. In the first day shall be a holy convocation; ye shall do no manner of servile work therein: but ye shall offer a sacrifice made by fire for a burnt offering unto the Lord; two young bullocks, and one ram, and seven lambs of the first year: they shall be unto you without blemish" (Num. 28:17-19).

The first and last days of the feast (fifteenth and twenty-first) were especially important. Reading from Leviticus 23:

"In the first day ye shall have a holy convocation: ye shall do no servile work therein. But ye shall offer an offering made by fire unto the Lord seven days: in the seventh day is a holy convocation: ye shall do no servile work therein" (Lev. 23:7,8).

The expression "do no servile work therein" teaches us that there are times when God desires that we stop for a moment our attempts to "make a living," and give Him our undivided attention. There is more to life than laboring in the fire for very vanity; man does not live by bread alone. God wants us to devote some of our time to the unhindered adoration and seeking of Him.

FIRSTFRUITS

It appears that the convocation of Firstfruits was celebrated on the sixteenth day of the first month; that is, on the second day of the week of Unleavened Bread. As we said, the first day of Unleavened Bread (fifteenth *Abib)* was a high feast day, a very important Sabbath. It is felt that the expression in Leviticus 23:11, "on the morrow after the sabbath," refers to the day after the high Sabbath, that is, the day after the first day of Unleavened Bread. Since the first day of the week of Unleavened Bread was the fifteenth of the first month, it is believed that Firstfruits occurred on the sixteenth day of the first month.

Thus we have three very important days in a row: Passover on the fourteenth, the very important first day of the week of Unleavened Bread on the fifteenth, and the feast of Firstfruits on the sixteenth.

The feast of Firstfruits was celebrated by the bringing of a sheaf of barley to the priest to mark the beginning of the harvest of grain, barley being the first grain to ripen. Reading in the twenty-third chapter of Leviticus:

"Speak unto the children of Israel, and say unto them, When ye be come into the land which I give unto you, and shall reap the harvest thereof, then ye shall bring a sheaf of the firstfruits of your harvest unto the priest: and he shall wave the sheaf before the Lord, to be accepted for you: on the morrow after the sabbath the priest shall wave it. And ye shall offer that day when ye wave the sheaf a male lamb without blemish of the first year for a burnt offering unto the Lord.

And the meat offering thereof shall be two tenth deals of fine flour mingled with oil, an offering made by fire unto the Lord for a sweet savor: and the drink offering thereof shall be of wine, the fourth part of a hin. And ye shall eat neither bread, nor parched corn, nor green ears, until the selfsame day that ye have brought an offering unto your God: it shall be a statute for ever throughout your generations in all your dwellings" (Lev. 23:10-14).

Notice the expression "when ye be come into the land which I give unto you." The seven Levitical convocations were pointed toward the land of promise; yet, they were enjoined upon Israel with great solemnity while Israel was still in the wilderness. Sometimes one wonders if we Christians are not like Israel in the wilderness, and much of what God has said to us is intended for a future age.

The sheaf of barley was brought immediately to the priest, as soon as the harvest commenced. The priest waved the barley before the Lord, giving thanks unto God for His goodness, and acknowledging the Lord's ownership of the earth and the fullness thereof. None of the harvest was to be eaten until the offering was presented to the Lord. God intends to be first in our lives in everything that we do and everything that we are.

As we noted, animal blood was shed during each of the seven convocations. In the case of Unleavened Bread and Firstfruits, a ram, two young bulls, and seven first-year lambs were offered as burnt (ascending) offerings, for a sweet savor unto the Lord. The whole burnt offering typifies the perfect consecration of the Lord Jesus Christ. The burnt offering also reminds us that we too must present our bodies a living sacrifice, and this total consecration must be true of us from the moment that we accept Christ on through to mature sainthood. We must never, never let up in our daily walk of perfect obedience to the Lord Jesus Christ.

The meat offering which accompanied the offering of the animals speaks of the fact that the works of our hands are to be offered to the Lord. It is not enough that we consecrate ourselves unto the Lord. In addition, all that we do in our daily life must be offered to God. It cannot be true of a Christian that his life is divided into the sacred and secular. There is no sacred and secular with the saint of God. Everything that he does is performed unto the Lord, offered to the Lord, and perpetually kept in trust for the Master's use.

The concept of the firstfruits is an extremely important one in the workings of God, and the term appears several times in the New Testament. The idea of the firstfruits is that of the first part of a larger amount which is yet to come. This concept has wide application in the new covenant. Jesus Christ Himself is the greatest of all firstfruits. The significance of the firstfruits is that if God will accept the firstfruits, then the whole harvest comes under the blessing of God. When we first accept Christ our spirit gains eternal life and ascends to be with Christ in God. Thus our spirit becomes a firstfruits of the redemption of the remainder of our being. The Holy Spirit works with us until our whole spirit, soul, and body becomes obedient to the law of the Spirit of life, in preparation for the great day of redemption which is to come with the appearing of our Lord Jesus Christ from heaven.

PENTECOST

The word *Pentecost* means *fifty*. It comes from the fact that it was celebrated on the fiftieth day, counting from the day of Firstfruits (sixteenth *Abib*) as day number one. It corresponds to our month of May. Pentecost was termed the "feast of weeks" because it occurred after seven weeks from the convocation of Firstfruits. It is believed that the first fiftieth-day (fifty-two days counting from the first Passover) was the day upon which the Lord gave the Ten Commandments to Moses. In any case, to this day the convocation of Pentecost is associated, in Jewish thinking, with the giving of the Law upon Sinai.

The convocation of Pentecost signaled the conclusion of the wheat harvest. Two large loaves, baked with leaven, were waved before the Lord by the high priest of Israel.

"And ye shall count unto you from the morrow after the sabbath, from the day that ye brought the sheaf of the wave offering; seven sabbaths shall be complete" (Lev. 23:15).

The "sabbath" was the first day of Unleavened Bread. The "morrow after the sabbath" was the convocation of Firstfruits. The "sheaf of the wave offering" was the first sheaf of the barley harvest. "Seven sabbaths" is forty-nine days, the fiftieth day being Pentecost. The disciples had to wait until the day of Pentecost came, and then "the promise" of the Father was poured out upon them.

Seven sabbaths is a sabbath of sabbaths, indicating that Pentecost was indeed a high holy day. It was the only one of the seven convocations standing by itself; the remaining six were in two groups of three each. The extraordinary importance of Pentecost is due to the fact that it represents the Person and work of the Holy Spirit; and the Person and work of the Holy Spirit is to be dominant in all areas of the church until the church is presented to the Lamb as His wife. It is our thinking that the Holy Spirit is of far greater importance in the Christian church than is ordinarily thought to be true. We believe that it is time now for Christians to begin to realize the tremendous importance of the Person and work of the Holy Spirit in the body of Christ. We may need to give back to the Holy Spirit the responsibility for building the church of Christ. That is His assignment!

"Even unto the morrow after the seventh sabbath shall ye number fifty days; and ye shall offer a new meat offering unto the Lord. Ye shall bring out of your habitations two wave loaves of two tenth deals: they shall be of fine flour; they shall be baked with leaven; they are the firstfruits unto the Lord" (Lev. 23:16,17).

The two large loaves were waved before the Lord by the anointed priest. It seems strange that they were baked with leaven, after the stern injunction concerning the removal of leaven during the seven days of Unleavened Bread. Our understanding of this seeming inconsistency is as follows: the leaven during the week of Unleavened Bread typifies sin; all sin was to be put out of the camp of the Israelites, symbolizing their separation from the sin of Egypt. But the leaven of Pentecost, we believe, is the new leaven of Christ. The two great loaves represent the anointing of the Holy Spirit upon the church of Christ, and the leaven represents the substance of Christ Himself which is working within the members of His corporate Body. The disciples had not reached perfection at the time that the Holy Spirit was poured out, but Christ had been born in them; and slowly but surely, just as a little leaven works through the whole ball of dough, the substance of Christ was beginning to influence their deeds, words, imaginations, and motives.

God has a way of calling things which are not true as yet as though they had already come to pass. When God looked down upon the early church He chose to see Christ, the new leaven, in them—He saw what they were going to become in Christ.

Christ is the first of the firstfruits of the kingdom of God, being the firstborn from the dead. Next come the saints, the overcomers, who are a firstfruits of the whole church. The entire church itself is a firstfruits of the earth unto God, paving the way for the reign of the kingdom of God throughout the entire earth. The church of Christ is a firstfruits of the harvest of the world; Christ shall yet receive the heathen for His inheritance and the uttermost parts of the earth for His possession.

The wave loaves of Pentecost were of fine flour and

baked, speaking of the fact that the nature of the Lord Jesus Christ was without blemish; then He was "baked" in the fires of judgment. The same must be true of the church, which is His Body. Many of the events of our lives, though we may not appreciate them at the time, are for the purpose of refining the "flour" of our nature, separating the wheat from the chaff. Then the fire of God "bakes" us until we are fine bread, worthy to be consumed by God and man.

> "And ye shall offer with the bread seven lambs without blemish of the first year, and one young bullock, and two rams: they shall be for a burnt offering unto the Lord, with their meat offering, and their drink offerings, even an offering made by fire, of sweet savor unto the Lord. Then ye shall sacrifice one kid of the goats for a sin offering, and two lambs of the first year for a sacrifice of peace offerings. And the priest shall wave them with the bread of the firstfruits for a wave offering before the Lord, with the two lambs: they shall be holy to the Lord for the priest.
>
> And ye shall proclaim on the selfsame day, that it may be a holy convocation unto you: ye shall do no servile work therein: it shall be a statute for ever in all your dwellings throughout your generations" (Lev. 23:18-21).

Again, we have the shedding of blood, for the sins of people can be handled only through blood. We have the burnt (ascending) offering; also a sin offering and two first-year lambs for peace offerings.

Notice also the drink offerings. Wine was poured out in the holy place of the Tabernacle of the Congregation, evidently onto the floor (bare ground) next to the table of showbread, whenever offerings were made on behalf of the nation of Israel. The wine represents the blood of Christ which was shed for many. Some aspects of redemption are ever with us, from the time of our new birth until we stand perfect and complete in all the will of God. Two of these continuing factors are the total consecration of the believer (burnt offering) and the precious blood of Christ (the blood of lambs, bulls, and goats). If you add to these two the anointing of the Holy Spirit, you have the three factors by means of which we overcome the accuser: (1) the blood of the Lamb (the blood of lambs, bulls, and goats); (2) the word of their testimony (the power to witness through the Holy Spirit); and (3) they loved not their lives unto the death (the burnt offering); compare Revelation 12:11.

Deuteronomy 16 speaks of the joy which always accompanies the celebration of Pentecost:

"Seven weeks shalt thou number unto thee: begin to number the seven weeks from such time as thou beginnest to put the sickle to the corn (the feast of Firstfruits).

And thou shalt keep the feast of weeks unto the Lord thy God with a tribute of a freewill offering of thine hand, which thou shalt give unto the Lord thy God, according as the Lord thy God hath blessed thee:

And thou shalt rejoice before the Lord thy God, thou, and thy son, and thy daughter, and thy manservant, and thy maidservant, and the Levite that is within thy gates, and the stranger, and the fatherless, and the widow, that are among you, in the place which the Lord thy God hath chosen to place his name there.

And thou shalt remember that thou wast a bondman in Egypt: and thou shalt observe and do these statutes" (Deut. 16:9-12).

Every Israelite male was to come before God on the feast of Pentecost with an offering taken from that with which the Lord had prospered him. From these offerings the priest was able to perform the ceremonies according to the statutes. Every man was to give "a freewill offering." That which we give to the Lord must be given freely, and with joy. God loves a cheerful giver. That which is extorted or forced is not acceptable. We should give our all to the Lord Jesus with the greatest of abandonment and joy, and break the bottle of the perfume of our life upon His feet, counting it not wasted.

Notice the spirit of generosity and thankful rejoicing which was to go along with the celebration of the end of the wheat harvest. Have you experienced your Pentecost yet? If you have, you perhaps will agree that it was one of the happiest experiences of your entire life. The outpouring of the Holy Spirit of God upon us brings joy unspeakable and full of glory. Yet, through all of this we remember that we were slaves to the Pharaoh of this age until the mighty Redeemer, Christ, set us free.

TRUMPETS

The convocation of Trumpets (Yom T'ruoh, the day of the blowing of the trumpet) occurred on the first day of the seventh month of the Hebrew religious year— the year which began with Passover (Pesach). Today the festival is called Rosh Hashanah. The blowing of the trumpet calls attention to the nearness of the solemn Day of Atonement (the sixth of the Levitical convocations) which occurs on the tenth day of the same (seventh) month. The Day of Atonement (Yom Kippur—in actuality, Yomim Kippurim, the Days of Atonement) is the greatest and holiest day of the Jewish year. Tabernacles (Succoth), the seventh and last of the Levitical convocations, also comes during the seventh month, the month of Tishri (the fifteenth of Tishri).

Trumpets (Yom T'ruoh—there are variant forms of these

anglicized Hebrew terms) falls on the first day of the seventh month. But it is the seventh month of the Hebrew year which begins with Passover (Exodus 12:2). However, this same seventh month *(Tishri)* of the year which begins with Passover is in fact the first month of the Hebrew civil year. And since the convocation of Trumpets falls on the first day of *Tishri*, and *Tishri* is the first month of the civil year, then Trumpets falls on New Year's Day as far as the civil year is concerned. And it is a fact that in America today, *Rosh Hashanah* (synonymous with *Yom T'ruoh*, convocation of Trumpets) is celebrated by the Jews as New Year's Day, and the trumpet is blown in the local temples of worship.

Therefore the Jews have two overlapping years, one beginning on the first month with Passover, and another beginning seven months later with Trumpets. It is true also in America that we have two overlapping years, the calendar year beginning on January first, and the fiscal year beginning seven months later on July first.

It appears that in the Hebrew thinking the Levitical convocations of Trumpets and the Day of Atonement are considered together, more or less.[1]

The Jewish New Year's celebration is *Rosh Hashanah* which seems to correspond most closely with *Yom T'ruoh*, the day of the blowing of the trumpet. It should be kept in mind that trumpets were blown on numerous important occasions. But they were blown "especially loudly and alarmingly on the first day of the seventh month."[2] The familiar *Yom Kippur* is the Day of Atonement. *Rosh Hashanah* and *Yom Kippur* are known as the "Days of Awe." The Hebrew year which commences with *Yom T'ruoh* corresponds to the natural cycle of agriculture.

The concept of the blowing of the trumpet seems to be

---

[1] Hayyim Schauss, *The Jewish Festivals.* New York: Union of American Hebrew Congregations, translated by Samuel Jaffe, 1938.
[2] Schauss, *op. cit.,* p. 159.

an important one in the mind of God, if frequency of mention in Scripture is an index of importance. Trumpets *(shofar, yobel,* and *hasosera* are the Hebrew terms used) were sounded to announce significant events (Lev. 25:9); to assemble Israel (Num. 10:2); to obtain God's help against an enemy (Num. 10:9); to call God's attention to an offering (Numbers 10:10); to announce the Presence of God (II Sam. 6:15); to warn of war and danger (Jer. 4:19); and to play music (II Chron. 5:13,14).

Trumpets are mentioned in the New Testament writings in connection with the return of Christ and the gathering together of His elect (Matt. 24:31); with the resurrection from the dead (I Cor. 15:52; I Thess. 4:16); with signals (I Cor. 14:8); and with significant announcements and events (Rev. 1:10; 8:2).

The Rabbis say that the trumpets ordained by the Lord had three purposes: (1) to raise the dead to newness of life through repentance from sin; (2) to bring to the Lord's mind His covenant with Israel; and (3) to confound the accusations of Satan against the Jews.[3]

Trumpets were blown on the first day of the ancient civil year. *Tishri,* the first month of the civil year, coincides with the latter part of September and the beginning of October. Perhaps we Gentiles get our practice of blowing horns on New Year's Day from this ancient custom.

Reading in Numbers 29:

"And in the seventh month, on the first day of the month, ye shall have a holy convocation; ye shall do no servile work: it is a day of blowing the trumpets unto you" (Num. 29:1).

Here again we see the expression, "you shall do no

---

[3] Victor Buksbazen, *The Gospel in the Feasts of Israel.* Philadelphia: The Friends of Israel, 1954, p. 23.

servile work." The idea of a Sabbath day is that we refrain from occupying ourselves with the numerous and varied tasks of our existence, and turn our thoughts and attention toward the Lord God and His pleasure and purposes. Man cannot live by bread alone; we must have the touch of God in order to make it successfully through this life.

"And ye shall offer a burnt offering for a sweet savor unto the Lord; one young bullock, one ram, and seven lambs of the first year without blemish: and their meat offering shall be of flour mingled with oil, three tenth deals for a bullock, and two tenth deals for a ram, and one tenth deal for one lamb, throughout the seven lambs: and one kid of the goats for a sin offering, to make an atonement for you: beside the burnt offering of the month, and his meat offering, and the daily burnt offering, and his meat offering, and their drink offerings, according unto their manner, for a sweet savor, a sacrifice made by fire unto the Lord" (Num. 29:2-6).

As usual, each Levitical convocation was accompanied with the shedding of blood and with the burnt (ascending) offering of a sweet fragrance unto God. The poured-out wine of the drink offering was included, reminding us of the offering of the precious blood of God's Lamb, the Lord Jesus Christ. What God is saying here is this: as you come into each new season of experience with God, do not forget the body and blood of the Lord Jesus Christ; do not forget that you yourself are an ascending offering, a total consecration unto the Lord; do not forget the meat offering, the presenting of all the works of your hands unto the Lord—do not divide your life into the sacred and the secular, that which God will accept and that which He will not accept; do not forget the sin offering, that is, do not forget to confess your sins to Christ as the Holy Spirit brings you into further light each day (I John 1:7-9).

The following passages from Scripture may give the reader some small notion of the many times in which the trumpet is mentioned in the Bible:

"Speak unto the children of Israel, saying, In the seventh month, in the first day of the month, shall ye have a sabbath, a memorial of blowing of trumpets, a holy convocation" (Lev. 23:24).

"And when the voice of the trumpet sounded long, and waxed louder and louder, Moses spoke, and God answered him by a voice" (Exod. 19:19).

"Make . . . two trumpets of silver; of a whole piece shalt thou make them: that thou mayest use them for the calling of the assembly, and for the journeying of the camps" (Num. 10:2).

"And if ye go to war in your land against the enemy that oppresseth you, then ye shall blow an alarm with the trumpets; and ye shall be remembered before the Lord your God, and ye shall be saved from your enemies" (Num. 10:9).

The preceding passage contains an important principle of the overcoming Christian life. The idea is that of blowing an alarm so that God can hear it. The Lord has written many promises to us. Has He forgotten? It seems so at times. But perhaps God is waiting for us to remind Him of what He has said. It says, "Ye shall be remembered before the Lord your God, and ye shall be saved from your enemies." What would happen if they did not sound the alarm? Very simple. God would not remember them and they would not be saved from their enemies.

And so it is true that we have a Bible full of promises. But many times we do not have the answers to our many

problems. Why not? Because we do not remind God of who
we are and what He has said concerning us. We bear needless
pain because we do not carry everything to God in prayer. In
many cases we are entirely too passive about the things of
God. We need to start blowing the trumpet in God's ears
loudly enough that He can hear, and be sure of what it is we
really desire. When He is persuaded that we mean business
and truly believe what He has promised, then the answer will
be forthcoming. We have not because we ask not.

"Also in the day of your gladness, and in your solemn
days, and in the beginnings of your months, ye shall
blow with the trumpets over your burnt offerings, and
over the sacrifices of your peace offerings; that they
may be to you for a memorial before your God: I am
the Lord your God" (Num. 10:10).

"So the people shouted when the priests blew with the
trumpets: and it came to pass, when the people heard
the sound of the trumpet, and the people shouted with
a great shout, that the wall fell down flat, so that the
people went up into the city, every man straight before
him, and they took the city" (Josh. 6:20).

"And the three companies blew the trumpets, and
brake the pitchers, and held the lamps in their left
hands, and the trumpets in their right hands to blow
withal: and they cried, The sword of the Lord, and of
Gideon" (Judg. 7:20).

"So David and all the house of Israel brought up the ark
of the Lord with shouting, and with the sound of the
trumpet" (II Sam. 6:15).

"It came even to pass, as the trumpeters and singers
were one, to make one sound to be heard in praising and

thanking the Lord; and when they lifted up their voice with the trumpets and cymbals and instruments of music, and praised the Lord, saying, For he is good; for his mercy endureth for ever: that then the house was filled with a cloud, even the house of the Lord; so that the priests could not stand to minister by reason of the cloud: for the glory of the Lord had filled the house of God" (II Chron. 5:13,14).

"And when the builders laid the foundation of the temple of the Lord, they set the priests in their apparel with trumpets, and the Levites the sons of Asaph with cymbals, to praise the Lord, after the ordinance of David king of Israel" (Ezra 3:10).

"God is gone up with a shout, the Lord with the sound of a trumpet" (Ps. 47:5).

"Cry aloud, spare not, lift up thy voice like a trumpet, and show my people their transgression, and the house of Jacob their sins" (Isa. 58:1).

"My bowels, my bowels! I am pained at my very heart; my heart maketh a noise in me; I cannot hold my peace, because thou hast heard, O my soul, the sound of the trumpet, the alarm of war" (Jer. 4:19).

"Also I set watchmen over you, saying, Hearken to the sound of the trumpet. But they said, We will not hearken" (Jer. 6:17).

"Blow . . . the trumpet in Zion, and sound an alarm in my holy mountain: let all the inhabitants of the land tremble: for the day of the Lord cometh, for it is nigh at hand" (Joel 2:1).

"And he shall send his angels with a great sound of a trumpet, and they shall gather together his elect from the four winds, from one end of heaven to the other" (Matt. 24:31).

"For if the trumpet give an uncertain sound, who shall prepare himself to the battle?" (I Cor. 14:8).

"In a moment, in the twinkling of an eye, at the last trump: for the trumpet shall sound, and the dead shall be raised incorruptible, and we shall be changed" (I Cor. 15:52).

"For the Lord himself shall descend from heaven with a shout, with the voice of the archangel, and with the trump of God: and the dead in Christ shall rise first" (I Thess. 4:16).

"I was in the Spirit on the Lord's day, and heard behind me a great voice, as of a trumpet" (Rev. 1:10).

"And I saw the seven angels which stood before God; and to them were given seven trumpets" (Rev. 8:2).

It can be seen from the above selected passages that there are many and varied references to the trumpet in the Bible.

One of the most significant trumpets of the Scripture is that of the year of jubilee.

"Then shalt thou cause the trumpet of the jubilee to sound on the tenth day of the seventh month, in the day of atonement shall ye make the trumpet sound throughout all your land. And ye shall hallow the fiftieth year, and proclaim liberty throughout all the land unto all the inhabitants thereof: it shall be a jubilee unto you; and ye shall return every man unto his possession, and ye shall return every man unto his family" (Lev. 25:9,10).

The year of jubilee is a type of the great day of redemption which is to come at the appearing of our Lord and Savior Jesus Christ. The millennium will be this great Sabbath of Sabbaths, when that which has been stolen and destroyed will be restored to the rightful owners.

DAY OF ATONEMENT

Now we come to the sixth of the Levitical convocations, the most solemn day of the Jewish year. It was observed on the tenth day of the seventh month, *Tishri*. The Day of Atonement was the only day of the year when the high priest of Israel was allowed into the holy of holies. The anointed priest went in before the mercy seat (Propitiatory Cover) and sprinkled blood for his sins and for the sins of the people. Also, a scapegoat bearing the sins of the people, was lead away into the wilderness.

The word *atonement* contains many concepts, including the idea of complete reconciliation to God. There are the ideas of covering over sin, of appeasing the wrath of God, of forgiveness, of annulment of debt, of remission of sin, of reconciliation, of healing—in short, all that is needed for bringing a human being from a state of absolute unfitness and rejection all the way to the throne of glory. There is no lack in God's plan of atonement and redemption in Christ. Every need for body, soul, and spirit is included in the atonement made by Christ Jesus. There is no person who has a need, as far as reconciliation to God is concerned, that has not been completely met in the atonement made by Christ upon Calvary.

The term *mercy seat* may be an unfortunate choice of

words. The cover of the Ark of the Covenant should be called the Propitiatory Cover, or Lid of Atonement. Far more than mercy is involved here. We have not only mercy and forgiveness, but healing, grace, power, authority, reconciliation, wisdom, everything that is needed to conform us to the image of Christ. Also, the cover of the ark was not a *seat.* God dwells between the cherubim, not on top of the ark. He covers the ark with His presence, just as He covered the Lord Jesus Christ, and as He will cover the body of Christ.

There was no other day of the Jewish calendar equal to *Yom Kippur,* the Day of Atonement. The whole success of the year hinged on whether the anointed priest was received of God on that day. If he was, the whole nation rejoiced. But there always remained the possibility that the glory would flare out and the priest would be struck dead because of the wrath of God. And so the nation waited breathlessly to see if the Lord God would be pleased to accept the sprinkling of the blood on behalf of their iniquities of the past year.

Let us turn now to the sixteenth chapter of Leviticus, for the Day of Atonement was carefully described by the Lord so that there could be no chance of an incorrect observance.

> "And the Lord said unto Moses, Speak unto Aaron thy brother, that he come not at all times into the holy place within the veil before the mercy seat, which is upon the ark; that he die not: for I will appear in the cloud upon the mercy seat" (Lev. 16:2).

Aaron had just lost his two sons because they offered incense in a rash manner before the Lord. Now God was warning Aaron that the veil which concealed the Ark of the Covenant and the mercy seat was to remain undisturbed except for the one solemn occasion each year when the anointed priest was allowed to sprinkle blood upon and before the mercy seat. The penalty for rashness was death!

God Himself was given to appearing in the cloud of glory upon the mercy seat. It was no place for proud flesh to be!

"Thus shall Aaron come into the holy place; with a young bullock for a sin offering, and a ram for a burnt offering. He shall put on the holy linen coat, and he shall have the linen breeches upon his flesh, and shall be girded with a linen girdle, and with the linen mitre shall he be attired: these are holy garments; therefore shall he wash his flesh in water, and so put them on" (Lev. 16:3,4).

The beautiful, glittering ephod of the anointed priest was not to be worn on this solemn occasion. Instead, Aaron was to put on the sparkling white linen garments that speak of righteous conduct. The clean, white linen caused a minimum of perspiration, and portrayed the sanctity of the occasion. The priest had to wash in the bronze laver at the door of the Tabernacle before he was allowed inside.

"And he shall take of the congregation of the children of Israel two kids of the goats for a sin offering, and one ram for a burnt offering. And Aaron shall offer his bullock of the sin offering, which is for himself, and make an atonement for himself, and for his house" (Lev. 16:5,6).

Here is one of the great differences between Christ and the Levitical priesthood. The high priest of Israel, being a sinful man like the rest of us, had to make an atonement for himself and for the rest of the priests. But Christ was offered for the whole world, not at all for Himself. He needed no atonement for Himself, being born without sin and living His life without any trace of sin in His Person.

"And he shall take the two goats, and present them before the Lord at the door of the tabernacle of the congregation. And Aaron shall cast lots upon the two goats; one lot for the Lord, and the other lot for the scapegoat" (Lev. 16:7,8).

If there had been only one goat it would have signified that Jesus came only to forgive our sins. But because there were two goats, we realize that Jesus not only forgives our sins but also removes our sins. He saves His people *from* their sins, not just *in* their sins!

"And Aaron shall bring the goat upon which the Lord's lot fell, and offer him for a sin offering. But the goat, on which the lot fell to be the scapegoat, shall be presented alive before the Lord, to make an atonement with him, and to let him go for a scapegoat into the wilderness" (Lev. 16:9,10).

One goat was slain, and one lived. The Lord's goat was slain and its blood shed. It was a sin offering. So Christ was offered for our sins. But the scapegoat lived, and yet an atonement was made with him also. He was let go into the wilderness. This typifies that Christ not only forgives our sin, canceling the guilt, but also removes from us our sins and iniquities. That scapegoat reveals to us that Christ will give us the grace to live a righteous life in this world. Christ will remove our sins from us so that we do not have to keep on sinning.

"And he shall take a censer full of burning coals of fire from off the altar before the Lord, and his hands full of sweet incense beaten small, and bring it within the veil: and he shall put the incense upon the fire before the Lord, that the cloud of the incense may cover the mercy seat that is upon the testimony, that he die not" (Lev. 16:12,13).

The high priest took one of the golden censers from the lampstand, filled it with coals of fire from the altar of incense which stood before the veil, and then picked up some incense from the cups on the border of the table of showbread. Then, passing within the holy veil, he threw the incense upon the glowing coals, causing the holy perfume to completely fill the area. Every single element here, including the composition of the incense, was carefully described in statute. It had to be done just so, and the penalty for carelessness was death.

It is no small matter that a heathen upon accepting Christ can now come boldly before the throne of God. Only a Jew who had once waited in trembling and fear to see if God accepted the anointed priest could ever appreciate what it means for us to rush into the holy of holies with our needs at any time we please. There is only one reason for this unimaginable turn around. It is that the offering of Christ and the interceding presence of Christ are so totally pleasing to the Father that we can now come into a place that once was allowed to only one man in the whole world, and him just once a year. This gives us some idea of the power of the atonement made by the Lord Jesus Christ. How could anyone turn Him away?

"And he shall take of the blood of the bullock, and sprinkle it with his finger upon the mercy seat eastward; and before the mercy seat shall he sprinkle of the blood with his finger seven times. Then shall he kill the goat of the sin offering, that is for the people, and bring his blood within the veil, and do with that blood as he did with the blood of the bullock, and sprinkle it upon the mercy seat, and before the mercy seat" (Lev. 16:14,15).

The blood of the bull was for Aaron and the other priests, and the blood of the goat was for the rest of Israel.

The blood was sprinkled upon the mercy seat, and before the mercy seat, probably upon the ground in order to sanctify the steps of the priest as he approached the living God.

The blood was sprinkled seven times, signifying that God's redemption is perfect and will continue working in the earth until the job is finished—otherwise it would have been sprinkled once or twice only.

The blood of the Lord Jesus Christ was not sprinkled within any earthly tabernacle. It was brought into the heavens and there presented to the Father, to the "mercy seat" in heaven. The blood of Christ is still working, both for the sins confessed by Christians, and also for the newly saved. The blood of the Lord Jesus Christ is the life of the Christian, and it is through His blood that we overcome the accuser.

> "And when he hath made an end of reconciling the holy place, and the tabernacle of the congregation, and the altar, he shall bring the live goat: and Aaron shall lay both his hands upon the head of the live goat, and confess over him all the iniquities of the children of Israel, and all their transgressions in all their sins, putting them upon the head of the goat, and shall send him away by the hand of a fit man into the wilderness: and the goat shall bear upon him all their iniquities unto a land not inhabited: and he shall let go the goat in the wilderness" (Lev. 16:20-22).

What a wonderful sight for the Israelite to see his sins being carried away into the wilderness, never to be remembered against him again. He got the idea that God not only forgave him his sins, but removed them from him. We Christians have that same privilege. When we confess our sins, Christ not only forgives us our sins but also cleanses us from all unrighteousness. The atonement includes both forgiveness of sins and removal of sins. It is the will of God in Christ that through His grace we can live a holy life in the earth, not having to continue in our lust, idolatry, malice, filthiness, or any other evil work. We who belong to Christ have put on Christ, and do not make provision for the flesh to fulfill the lust thereof. This privilege is ours through the atonement which is in Christ Jesus.

Christ was led out of the camp, just as the scapegoat of old, bearing our sins upon Himself. He descended into the heart of the earth; but there the Spirit of God raised Him up in power, free from the load of sin and death which He bore away on our behalf.

> "And this shall be a statute for ever unto you: that in the seventh month, on the tenth day of the month, ye shall afflict your souls, and do no work at all, whether it be one of your own country, or a stranger that sojourneth among you: for on that day shall the priest make an atonement for you, to cleanse you, that ye may be clean from all your sins before the Lord. It shall be a sabbath of rest unto you, and ye shall afflict your souls, by a statute for ever" (Lev. 16:29-31).

Pentecost and Tabernacles were seasons of rejoicing. But the Day of Atonement was a time of fasting, of repentance, of humiliation of soul. It is true that the Christian life is made up of both rejoicing and the enduring of hardness and suffering. There is milk and honey, but also the bitter herbs. A balanced experience in Christ must have its blessings and its trouble, its rain and its sun, its glory and its tribulation. It takes both rain and sun to bring wheat to maturity.

Again we find the injunction to "do no work at all." It is extremely important that we interrupt our busy lives on a regular basis and make the time for waiting upon God and for meditating in His Word. It is a curse upon a person that he or she should get so busy that there is no time left for waiting upon the Lord. One thing in life is needful—that we give time to the pursuit of God. If we do not, then God has His own effective ways of slowing us down where we begin to take the time that we should to communicate with God and to receive of Him the wisdom and strength that we must have if we are to survive. We destroy ourselves when we do not take time for God.

The expression "that ye may be clean from all your sins before the Lord" is enlightening. Sometimes we are taught that the only good accomplished by the Levitical sacrifices, ceremonies, and ordinances was the pointing forward to Christ—that there was nothing of immediate effectiveness in them. It seems, however, that this was not the case.

Of course, there is no comparison between Christ and the law of Moses. Christ is the Lord Himself come to earth, and the Law was a servant that brings us to Christ. Nevertheless, there are numerous passages in the Old Testament which reveal clearly and definitely that if an Israelite walked blamelessly in the Law, and in the ordinances, making the appropriate sacrifices for sin, for thanksgiving, for consecration, paying tithes and giving offerings, then that person was blameless before God and accepted of Him. The believer at that time did not have the spiritual blessings and opportunities which we have under the new covenant, it is true; but the love and blessing of God was upon him, and he was cleansed from his sins through means of the atonement made with the slain bulls, goats, sheep, and birds.

"And the priest, whom he shall anoint, and whom he shall consecrate to minister in the priest's office in his father's stead, shall make the atonement, and shall put on the linen clothes, even the holy garments: and he shall make an atonement for the holy sanctuary, and he shall make an atonement for the tabernacle of the congregation, and for the altar: and he shall make an atonement for the priests, and for all the people of the congregation. And this shall be an everlasting statute unto you, to make an atonement for the children of Israel for all their sins once a year. And he did as the Lord commanded Moses" (Lev. 16:32-34).

The priest "whom he shall anoint" refers to the high priest.

The atonement was made for the holy sanctuary, for the tabernacle of the congregation, for the altar, for the priests, and for all the people of the congregation. Thus Christ has made an atonement for the spirit, soul, and body of the believer, for the church—the body of Christ—and for the entire kingdom of God. Christ made an atonement for the whole world; He paid off the mortgage for every person. The only souls who are lost are those who simply will have none of Christ. Yet He died for them also. It is a shame that a man or woman, boy or girl, should miss out on God's salvation when redemption is there for the receiving. God has made provision for all; our part is to believe, receive, and then to press on to the rewards which go to the overcomer.

"But Christ being come a high priest of good things to come, by a greater and more perfect tabernacle, not made with hands, that is to say, not of this building; neither by the blood of goats and calves, but by his own blood he entered in once into the holy place, having obtained eternal redemption for us" (Heb. 9:11,12).

TABERNACLES

The convocation of Tabernacles (Succoth) was the most joyous occasion of the year. For seven days the Israelites were to sleep out under the stars in booths made of branches. Tabernacles marked the end of the harvest and processing of all the grains, fruits, vegetables, and nuts farmed by the Jews. The Law was read. Water from the pool of Siloam was poured out upon the altar of burnt offering. It was a time of the most extreme rejoicing.

One can imagine a Jew coming out of his house each year and living for a week in a booth made from the branches of trees. Perhaps this was God's way of repeatedly bringing to the attention of the Israelites that their most important contribution among the nations of the earth is not to be in the area of government, economics, or the arts or sciences, as significant as their contributions in those realms may be. The most important and significant gift that Israel brings to the family of mankind is the Law and presence of the living God. Also, living in the booths pointed to the day when God dwells in Israel and Israel dwells in God; God rests in Israel and Israel rests in God. The prophets testified of that day to come, and Jesus and the apostles taught us how God is bringing His plan to pass in human beings.

Reading in Leviticus 23:

"Speak unto the children of Israel, saying, The fifteenth day of this seventh month shall be the feast of tabernacles for seven days unto the Lord. On the first day shall be a holy convocation: ye shall do no servile work therein. Seven days ye shall offer an offering made by fire unto the Lord; on the eighth day shall be a holy convocation unto you; and ye shall offer an offering made by fire unto the Lord: it is a solemn assembly; and ye shall do no servile work therein" (Lev. 23:34-36).

Trumpets was on the first day of the seventh month, *Tishri.* The Day of Atonement was on the tenth day of the seventh month. Tabernacles lasted seven days, from the fifteenth through the twenty-first of *Tishri.* Notice the expression, "the eighth day (twenty-second of *Tishri*) shall be a holy convocation unto you." The eighth day was a very high Sabbath, celebrated with extraordinary rejoicing and exhilaration. The eighth day typifies the first day of the new week of eternity, the week which has no end. The eighth day will find its most complete fulfillment during the new heaven and earth reign of Christ (Rev. 21;22).

Trumpets, the Day of Atonement, and Tabernacles were observed during the seventh month of the ecclesiastical year, the year which began with Passover. But the seventh month *(Tishri)* of the ecclesiastical year was the *first* month of the agricultural year, agriculture being a chief occupation of the nation of Israel. Thus the last three convocations typify the beginning of doing business in the kingdom of God. Do you see that?

The ecclesiastical year, which goes from about March through February of our calendar, typifies the plan of redemption in Christ Jesus—our personal growth in Christ, from total chaos to the throne of glory, and also the creating of the church of Christ upon His body and blood through means of the gifts and ministries of the Holy Spirit.

The farming year, which commenced with *Tishri*, running about September through August of our calendar, typifies the setting up of the kingdom of God upon the earth.

Continuing reading in the twenty-third chapter of Leviticus:

"Also in the fifteenth day of the seventh month, when ye have gathered in the fruit of the land, ye shall keep a feast unto the Lord seven days: on the first day shall be a sabbath, and on the eighth day shall be a sabbath" (Lev. 23:39).

As we mentioned before, the observance of the Levitical convocations was strictly enjoined while Israel was in the wilderness. Yet they could not gather in "the fruit of the land" until they were in Canaan. It appears that we Christians are to learn our lessons carefully now, for they will be useful in the age to come. Much of what God enjoins upon us at this time will have increasing significance throughout our lifetime upon the earth, and even more in the future beyond that.

The celebration of Tabernacles signified the end of the agricultural year, and the beginning of the new. All that had been sown in the land had by this time been reaped and processed. The "fruit of the land" included the following: wheat, barley, lentils, peas, beans, onions, millet, grapes, cucumbers, melons, citrus fruits, and nuts.

"And ye shall take you on the first day the boughs of goodly trees, branches of palm trees, and the boughs of thick trees, and willows of the brook; and ye shall rejoice before the Lord your God seven days. And ye shall keep it a feast unto the Lord seven days in the year: it shall be a statute for ever in your generations; ye shall celebrate it in the seventh month. Ye shall dwell in booths seven days; all that are Israelites born shall dwell in booths: that your generations may know that I made the children of Israel to dwell in booths, when I brought them out of the land of Egypt: I am the Lord your God. And Moses declared unto the children of Israel the feasts of the Lord" (Lev. 23:40-44).

It was the Lord's intention that Tabernacles be a time of great rejoicing. Notice the words of the following passage, reading in Deuteronomy 16:

"Thou shalt observe the feast of tabernacles seven days, after that you have gathered in thy corn and thy wine: and thou shalt rejoice in thy feast, thou, and thy son, and thy daughter, and thy manservant, and thy maid-servant, and the Levite, the stranger, and the fatherless, and the widow, that are within thy gates.

Seven days shalt thou keep a solemn feast unto the Lord thy God in the place which the Lord shall choose: because the Lord thy God shall bless thee in all thine increase, and in all the works of thine hands, therefore thou shalt surely rejoice" (Deut. 16:13-15).

Tabernacles is sometimes referred to as the feast of booths, or the feast of ingathering.

The convocation of Tabernacles was associated with the reading of the law of Moses to the congregation of Israel in solemn assembly..

"And Moses commanded them, saying, At the end of every seven years, in the solemnity of the year of release, in the feast of tabernacles, when all Israel is come to appear before the Lord thy God in the place which he shall choose, thou shalt read this law before all Israel in their hearing. Gather the people together, men, and women, and children, and thy stranger that is within thy gates, that they may hear, and that they may learn, and fear the Lord your God, and observe to do all the words of this law" (Deut. 31:10-12).

The feast of Tabernacles was associated also with water. By the latter part of our month of September, the time of the feast of Tabernacles, the dry season (May through August) is about ended. The early (former) rains are soon to fall. The rivers will begin to flow. The hard clods of earth, baked by the summer sun, will be moistened so that they can be ploughed in preparation for the sowing of seed of the new farming year. So during the celebration of Tabernacles, the Jews were rejoicing not only because of the abundance of the preceding year, but also in expectation of the coming of refreshing rains.

Tabernacles was celebrated for seven days, and then came the eighth day, a high Sabbath, the "great day of the feast." It was the practice, at the time Jesus was on earth, for water to be brought in golden vessels from the pool of Siloam. Then the high priest poured the water into a basin on the altar of burnt offering. On the eighth day, trumpets were blown and Isaiah 12:3 was sung: "With joy shall you draw water out of the wells of salvation." It was on this occasion of fervent thanksgiving and jubilation that Jesus stood in the midst and cried, "If any man thirst, let him come unto me, and drink. He who believeth on me, as the Scripture hath said, out of his belly shall flow rivers of living water" (John 7:37,38).

When we read the twelfth chapter of Isaiah, remembering that this passage was closely connected with the celebration of Tabernacles, we realize that the Holy Spirit is teaching us that Tabernacles has to do with the abiding of God in Christ in us; and that out from the throne of God in us is going to flow rivers of living water, and that these are waters of eternal life which will one day flow out from the church of Christ to the farthest reaches of the earth. "Behold, God is my salvation; I will trust, and not be afraid: for the Lord Jehovah is my strength and my song; he also is become my salvation. Therefore with joy shall you draw water out of the wells of salvation."

The fact that God required His people to live in booths for one week out of the year had to do with the special history and mission of the nation of Israel. The Jews were not like the Egyptians, the Babylonians, or the Philistines. They were a special called-out nation, a kingdom of priests, the elect of God, the recipients of the divine testimony, the Ten Commandments.

If an Egyptian, or an Amorite, or a Hittite went out to live in a booth for a week, there was little of national history and significance that he could contemplate, other than the accomplishments of the wisdom and energy of his race. But the Jew could meditate upon the dealings of God with Abraham, Isaac, and Jacob; upon the provision which God had made for the perpetuation of their family through the events in the life of Joseph; upon the calling of Moses and the judgments of God upon the gods of Egypt; and then upon the unparalleled miracles which brought them safely out of

Egypt and through the wilderness region.

Why would God lay His hand upon one nation of all the nations of the earth, and deal with it after this manner? It was something to think about at night, under the stars, as one lay in his little booth of palm and willow branches. Again we see the injunction of God upon Israel—in the Sabbath day and in the other holy days—that the people cease for a time their grubbing in the earth, and look up in adoration, worship, and thanksgiving to the great God who provides for and is interested in His people.

One of the most important celebration of the convocation of Tabernacles recorded in Scripture can be found in the eighth chapter of Nehemiah. It is significant that the occasion is the rebuilding of the Temple in Jerusalem. It is our understanding that the greatest fulfillment of the convocation of Tabernacles will occur at the descending of the holy city, the wife of the Lamb, upon the great, high mountain of the new earth. At that time there will be the fullest expression of the law of God (the beauty of holiness); eternal water in abundance (the river of life); and the fullness of light (the glory of God shining forth from the throne of God and of the Lamb). This will be the coming of the tabernacle of God among men, so that He may dwell among His children and wipe away all tears.

Reading in Nehemiah 8:

"And all the people gathered themselves together as one man into the street that was before the water gate; and they spake unto Ezra the scribe to bring the book of the law of Moses, which the Lord had commanded to Israel" (Neh. 8:1).

All of the gates of the wall of Jerusalem which were rebuilt under Nehemiah are prophetic symbols of the day of the Lord. In the above verse we see the "water gate," a symbol of the Holy Spirit which will be outpoured upon the earth during the spiritual fulfillment of Tabernacles which is yet to come on a grand scale. Also, it is true in us as individuals that as Christ dwells in us the glory of God flows out to other people.

"And Ezra the priest brought the law before the congregation both of men and women, and all that could hear with understanding, upon the first day of the seventh month" (Neh. 8:2).

The reader may recall that the first day of the seventh month was the convocation of Trumpets. Again, we have the prophetic symbolism of the day of the Lord. The trumpet of God will sound, the glory of God will flow out, and the laws of the kingdom of God will be renewed in God's people; and then, through the saints, those laws will be carried to the ends of the earth until the kingdom of heaven rules the peoples of the earth.

"And the Levites . . . caused the people to understand the law: and the people stood in their place. So they read in the book in the law of God distinctly, and gave the sense, and caused them to understand the reading" (Neh. 8:7,8).

Whenever the fulfillment of Tabernacles comes to us, that is, as Christ grows in us, we gain increased understanding of the ways of the Holy Spirit of God. Our conduct becomes more and more holy.

The next passage presents a concept which is important to the successful pursuit of the overcoming life. The concept is this: if we are to pursue holiness of conduct, under the guidance and enabling power of the Holy Spirit, we are to do so not in grief and gloom but in great joy. We confess our sins before the Lord, and embrace His righteous ways with joy and gladness of heart. With this attitude we become strong in the Lord and are able to go from step to step in the ascent toward holiness of deed, word, motive, and imagination.

"And Nehemiah, which is the Tirshatha (governor), and Ezra the priest the scribe, and the Levites that taught the people, said unto all the people, This day is holy unto the Lord your God; mourn not, nor weep. For all the people wept, when they heard the words of the law. Then he said unto them, Go your way, eat the fat, and drink the sweet, and send portions unto them for whom nothing is prepared: for this day is holy unto our Lord: neither be . . . sorry; for the joy of the Lord is your strength" (Neh. 8:9,10).

As the people who were set upon restoring the glory of Jerusalem studied the Word of God, they found out more about the feast of Tabernacles.

"And they found written in the law which the Lord had commanded by Moses, that the children of Israel should dwell in booths in the feast of the seventh month: and that they should publish and proclaim in all their cities, and in Jerusalem, saying, Go forth unto the mount, and fetch olive branches, and pine branches, and myrtle branches, and palm branches, and branches of thick trees, to make booths, as it is written.

"So the people went forth, and brought them, and made themselves booths, every one upon the roof of his house, and in their courts, and in the courts of the house of God, and in the street of the water gate, and in the street of the gate of Ephraim. And all the congregation of them that were come again out of the captivity made booths, and sat under the booths: for since the days of Joshua the son of Nun unto that day had not the children of Israel done so. And there was very great gladness" (Neh. 8:14-17).

(Remember that Tabernacles had never once been celebrated under Moses, but rather under Joshua. The reason is that Tabernacles can only be celebrated in the land of promise, never in the wilderness. Something to think about!)

"Also day by day, from the first day unto the last day, he read in the book of the law of God. And they kept the feast seven days; and on the eighth day was a solemn assembly, according unto the manner" (Neh. 8:18).

During the time of Jesus on earth it was a custom for the Jews to come in procession to the Temple carrying torches. The combined light from the processional torches and the candlesticks of the Temple lit up the whole area in and around the Temple. In this context Jesus taught:

"You are the light of the world. A city that is set on a hill cannot be hid" (Matt. 5:14).

"Let your light so shine before men, that they may see your good works, and glorify your Father who is in heaven" (Matt. 5:16).

When one studies the traditions which have accumulated around the Jewish celebrations, of which the lights of the convocations of Tabernacles are a beautiful example, one can see the guiding influence of the Holy Spirit. It is a blessed thought to realize that the Jews are so close to the truth of Christ that when God opens their eyes they will move into the worship of God through Jesus Christ in such power and glory that Jerusalem will truly be the joy of the whole earth. Let us never forget, however, that the inheritance of the overcomer is available today, right now, to whoever will move ahead in faith and grasp the fullness of God in Christ. This prospect is open to all, young or old, male or female, Jew or Gentile. Now is the accepted time. Today is the day of salvation.

We can observe the connection between rain (the outpouring of the Holy Spirit), and the observance of Tabernacles (the abiding presence of God in Christ), in the following passage from Zechariah 14:

> "And it shall be, that whoso will not come up of all the families of the earth unto Jerusalem to worship the King, the Lord of hosts, even upon them shall be no rain" (Zech. 14:17).

Since the convocation of Tabernacles is the seventh feast, is in the seventh month, and lasts seven days—a trinity of sevens—we are led to believe that it typifies perfection, or maturity, or consummation, however one wishes to term it. Tabernacles is the "mark" toward which Paul was pressing. The glorious fulfillment of Tabernacles in the kingdom of God was clearly revealed to the mind of Christ when He stood and cried:

> "If any man thirst, let him come unto me, and drink. He who believes on me, as the Scripture has said, out of his belly shall flow rivers of living water.
>
> (But this spake he of the Spirit, whom they who believe on him should receive: for the Holy Spirit was not yet given; because that Jesus was not yet glorified)" (John 7:37-39).

The fulfillment is described in Revelation 21:

> "And I John saw the holy city, new Jerusalem, coming down from God out of heaven, prepared as a bride adorned for her husband. And I heard a great voice out of heaven saying, Behold, the tabernacle of God is with men, and he will dwell with them, and they shall be his people, and God himself shall be with them, and be

their God. And God shall wipe away all tears from their eyes; and there shall be no more death, neither sorrow, nor crying, neither shall there be any more pain: for the former things are passed away" (Rev. 21:2-4).

THREE CONVOCATIONS

The seven Levitical convocations were grouped into three great annual convocations. Reading in Deuteronomy 16:

"Three times in a year shall all thy males appear before the Lord thy God in the place which he shall choose; in the feast of unleavened bread, and in the feast of weeks, and in the feast of tabernacles: and they shall not appear before the Lord empty: every man shall give as he is able, according to the blessing of the Lord thy God which he hath given to thee" (Deut. 16:16,17).

The above are the three holy convocations which occurred annually. Passover, Unleavened Bread, and Firstfruits were termed the feast of Unleavened Bread. Pentecost was termed the "feast of weeks." Trumpets, Day of Atonement, and Tabernacles were termed the feast of Tabernacles. Every Jewish man without exception was to appear before the Lord three times in the year, and he was to come with something in his hand to give unto the Lord: an animal from the flock or herd; some oil or wine, some grain or money—something taken out from the riches with which God had blessed him.

The feast of Unleavened Bread, consisting of Passover, Unleavened Bread, and Firstfruits, occurs about March-April of our calendar. These three ceremonies suggest to us the first level of the process of redemption, that of accepting the Passover blood, entering into water baptism for the washing away of our sins, and the born-again experience of being made alive by the Spirit of God and having Christ born in us.

The feast of Pentecost, about May of our calendar, brings to mind the experience of the baptism of the Holy Spirit which causes us to grow strong in Christ, bear witness in power, lead a holy life, worship God in Spirit-filled adoration, be ministered to and minister, and serve as a priest of God by bringing the blessings of Christ to the peoples of the earth.

The feast of Tabernacles, consisting of Trumpets, the Day of Atonement, the seven days of the week of Tabernacles, and the high Sabbath of the eighth day, takes place in September-October of our calendar. Trumpets speaks to us of God's New Year, of war, of rejoicing, of jubilee, of victory, and of the redemption of our mortal body at the glorious appearing of our Lord Jesus Christ.

The Day of Atonement brings to mind our continual need to bring our sins to Christ for forgiveness and cleansing, under the guidance of the Holy Spirit. Tabernacles portrays to us the coming of the Father and the Son to dwell in us forever; and of the new heaven and earth reign of the Lord Jesus.

The eighth day of Tabernacles is the first day of the new week of eternity, the week which has no end. Complete fulfillment of the eighth day occurs during the new heaven and earth reign of Christ, but is fulfilled also in the moment of our accepting Christ. "I am the resurrection and the life. He who believes in me, though he were dead, yet shall he live; and whosoever lives and believes in me shall never die" (John 11:25,26).

```
Passover          ⎫
Unleavened Bread  ⎬  — March (feast of Unleavened Bread)
Firstfruits       ⎭

Pentecost         ⎬  — May (feast of weeks)
```

Trumpets
Day of Atonement } — September (feast of Tabernacles)
Tabernacles

"Three times in a year shall all your males appear before the Lord your God."

PROCLAIM IN THEIR SEASONS

God has a present truth for every hour. The present truth may vary from place to place. In one city, the present truth may be the good news of salvation by faith, and of being born again. In another city, the good news may be that of divine healing, or of holiness, or of ministries and gifts of the Spirit, or of evangelism and missionary work. Sometimes, the Spirit of God will move in great blessing upon a city, or in warning, just before some calamity. Many of the writings of the prophets of the Old Testament were warnings of impending disaster.

The truth may be different for the same people at different points of time. At the turn of the twentieth century, the Holy Spirit was poured out in the Los Angeles area and the gift of tongues was restored to the Christian church. In 1948 there was another powerful move of the Lord. Around this time the power of God came upon an unknown evangelist holding a revival in southern California, and Billy Graham began to see people converted by the thousands. About the same time another unknown evangelist, also a Baptist, received a most extraordinary ministry of healing. His name was William Branham. The presence of Christ in his meetings cannot be described; one had to have been there to understand. Many other preachers with gifts of healing arose in America soon after Branham.

A quieter spirit seemed to settle upon some of the Pentecostal churches, and the amount of prophetic utterance increased. The message of many of the utterances was that revival was on the way, and that God was going to do a new thing. This message of revival soon to come ran counter to the teaching from the pulpit which was that the church was falling away, and that spiritual life would become weaker and weaker until finally the Lord would remove His bride before her final collapse.

Evidently the prophetic messages were of the Lord, because the charismatic movement has taken place since then, along with mighty revivals in South America, Southeast Asia, Africa, Europe, and other places. An extraordinary restoration of signs and wonders with the gospel has occurred in Indonesia.

God has a present truth for each individual. What is fresh for an individual today will not be as wholesome tomorrow. Yesterday's manna is not suitable for consumption. Every day is to be a new start for us, and the Lord will renew our spiritual life with fresh manna from heaven. It always is the will of the Lord that our contact with Him be current, fresh, warm, living, full of power and glory.

So it is in the feasts of the Lord, the holy convocations. Each must be proclaimed in its season. The minister of God must be aware of the mind of the Holy Spirit so that he will know the present burden. If the Holy Spirit is pressing for Passover, then the preacher should not be on Pentecost. The Holy Spirit will anoint that which is His will for the disciples at a given place and time.

"These are the feasts of the Lord, even holy convocations, which YE SHALL PROCLAIM IN THEIR SEASONS" (Lev. 23:4).

THE AGRICULTURAL YEAR

The agricultural year began in our September-October, with the early (former) rains. This was the time of Trumpets, the Day of Atonement, and Tabernacles. The moistened ground was ploughed up and prepared for the seed in October-November. The seed was sown in November-December. In December-January the winter rains would fall. In January-February the almond trees blossomed. Citrus fruits were harvested in February-March.

The period of March-April is the time of the spring (latter) rains. The barley and flax harvest occurred. Passover, Unleavened Bread, and Firstfruits were celebrated. Most ground moisture of the area comes from the winter rains, but the spring (latter) rains brought the grain to maturity.

In April-May the six-month dry season began, which lasted until the fall rains of September-October. Pentecost was celebrated in May-June, signaling the conclusion of the wheat harvest. But the threshing of wheat could last to the end of August, or later. June-July was the time of the grape harvest; July-August, the olive harvest. August-September brought the harvest of dates and summer figs. By the September-October period the harvest had been completed. The feast of Tabernacles was celebrated with thanksgiving and rejoicing because of the abundance which the land had brought forth, and also in joyful anticipation of the fall (early, former) rains which were at hand, renewing the earth after the half-year drought of summer.

In some parts of Canaan, grapes, cucumbers, and melons could be cultivated during the long drought of summer, the moisture coming from the subsoil and from heavy summer dew.

THE BEST IS YET TO COME

We have just looked briefly at the actual celebration of the seven convocations by the Jews. Some of these occasions are still very prominent among the Jewish people. The *shofar* (ram's horn trumpet) is still blown in the synagogue, for example, and the Passover is kept by the faithful.

There is an astonishing truth which appears right at the outset, and this truth has significance for our whole perspective with which we view the meaning of the Christian life. The truth is as follows: these seven convocations, along with the Law, the Levitical statutes and the ordinances, and the Tabernacle of the Congregation, were given to Israel with great solemnity. The Lord spoke to Moses in detail, and Israel was commanded to keep the feasts faithfully. The extraordinary fact here was that these convocations were to be observed in Canaan—in the land of promise—but they were taught to the Israelites while they were yet in the wilderness. They were given in detail while these ex-slaves of Egypt were wandering in the Sinai wilderness where not a farm was in sight in the whole region. The people were being given elaborate ceremonies to observe in a land they had not seen!

How would you feel if you had just come out of Egypt and had never seen the land of promise, yet you were being instructed in detail about the correct method for worshiping God and for offering to Him the best of the products of your farm? You had no land, no crops; you were wandering in a hot desert, eating manna which came down from the sky each day. You would have to continue pressing on in faith and hope in the promise of God.

Well, all of this is precisely true of the Christian salvation. Much of what has been given to us in Christ we cannot fully realize as yet. We are still in the wilderness. We are in the hot desert of this world. The day of redemption is still ahead of us.

We have been sealed unto the day of redemption, Paul tells us in Ephesians. What we have at this point is an "earnest," a down payment, a first installment, of the Holy Spirit of God. Please do not misunderstand us at this point— the dealings of God are for today, it is true, and most Christians, it appears, are not laying hold upon the fullness of the grace which is available right now. God provides for each step of our journey through the wilderness of this world, just as He provided so well for the Israelites in the desert.

But there is a concept here which must be grasped by hope and faith. The workings of God in you and me are for our "real life" which is yet to come. We are still being created, so to speak. We are struggling in the night as we are being formed by the Spirit of the Lord in the "lowest parts of the earth." In one sense of the word, we have not even seen the light of day as yet.

The day of redemption is ahead of us. As we see the creation groaning and travailing in pain, let us realize that these are the pangs of birth. When we witness the earthquakes, wars, famines, disasters of all kinds, men's hearts failing them for fear, then we are to lift up our heads for our redemption draws near. Our real life is just over the horizon and we will look back upon this brief life of pain and pressure as a dark mold in which our character was formed by the Lord.

The Lord labors over each one of us in loving care as He works through the trials which we have each day. He is preparing us for a better existence, the real purpose of our life, which has hardly begun. How can we compare our sixty or seventy years with the scope of eternity? Christ came from eternity in order to bring us into His kingdom, where we will begin a fuller, more significant career.

Israel was destined to serve the Lord in the land of promise. As real and true as were the lessons of the wilderness, the wilderness was a preparatory school. If you stop to think about it, it would be ridiculous to state that God brought Israel out of Egypt so that His people could inherit the wilderness! The wilderness was one of the greatest schools in history, just as our life in this world is a school. But a school is a school, and it is supposed to prepare us for life!

We Christians are destined to serve the Lord during the millennium, and especially throughout eternity in the new heaven and earth. This present life is a preparatory school, nothing more nor less. Let us make sure that we learn our lessons well now. We will be profiting from them forever and ever.

II

FOUR MAJOR TYPES
OF REDEMPTION

It appears that there are at least four major types of redemption outlined in the Bible. The four types are as follows: (1) the seven days of creation; (2) the journey of Israel from Egypt to Canaan; (3) the Tabernacle of the Congregation; (4) the seven Levitical convocations. By the term *redemption* we are referring to God's plan in Christ for the bringing of human beings from their miserable state of sins, degradation, and death, all the way to the throne of Glory. To redeem a thing or a person is to restore it or him to the rightful and lawful owner. The concept of redemption implies that something has been taken away from where it belongs by legal sale, by forfeiture, or by deceit or force.

In order for redemption to take place someone must come up with the price of redemption. The mortgage must be paid. Sometimes the person holding the mortgaged property will not give up the property even when the price has been paid, which is true of Satan concerning those people whose price of redemption was paid on Calvary. In that case, redemption must be brought about through the use of superior force. The kingdom-wide Day of Atonement which will take place at the appearing of our Lord Jesus Christ will be just such a day of redemption by violence and force.

There are many similarities among the four major types

of redemption, and when they are combined we have available a very helpful and enlightening picture of God's plan of redemption in Christ Jesus.

To begin with, let us take each of the four and enumerate the seven aspects contained in it. Then, as the Holy Spirit helps us, perhaps we can combine the four types and gain some understanding of God's workings in the past, present, and future.

The seven aspects of the seven days of creation can be found in the first chapter of Genesis: (1) the dividing of the light from the darkness; (2) the dividing of the waters by means of the firmament of heaven; (3) the gathering together of the waters under the firmament, the appearing of the land, and the creation of vegetation; (4) the creating of the sun, moon, and stars in the firmament; (5) the creation of fish and birds; (6) the creation of animals, and of mankind in God's image; (7) God rested from all His works.

The seven aspects of the journey from Egypt to Canaan are as follows: (1) judgment upon the Egyptians, the Passover, and the exodus; (2) going across the Red Sea; (3) beginning of the pilgrimage through the wilderness; (4) the Ten Commandments, the statutes and ordinances, the Tabernacle, and the priesthood; (5) organization of Israel into an army; (6) crossing of Jordan and the attack upon Canaan; (7) rest in the land of promise.

The seven aspects of the Tabernacle are summarized in the seven holy furnishings: (1) the bronze altar of burnt offering; (2) the bronze laver; (3) table of showbread; (4) the lampstand; (5) altar of incense; (6) Ark of the Covenant; (7) mercy seat (Propitiatory Cover).

The seven aspects of the Levitical convocations are the feasts: (1) Passover; (2) Unleavened Bread; (3) Firstfruits; (4) Pentecost; (5) Trumpets; (6) Day of Atonement; (7) Tabernacles.

No doubt, if you have some understanding of the Bible and of God's salvation in Christ, you have noticed already what a remarkable set of types we have in these four portrayals of redemption.

THE FIRST ASPECT OF REDEMPTION

Now, let us put these together. The first phase of these seven areas is shown in the dividing of the light from the darkness; judgment upon the Egyptians, the Passover and the exodus; the bronze altar of burnt offering; and the feast of Passover. Can you see in these four types the first step in God's salvation? When we come to Christ we repent of our past life of sin; this is the division between light and darkness. Unlike our previous condition in which we thought we were doing fairly well, we have begun to realize that we actually were lost and undone in the sight of God. We may have thought that God was accepting our profanity, our lying, our stealing, our gossiping, our violent ways, our deceitfulness, our lusting; but now the Holy Spirit has revealed to us that we were heading straight into hell because of our sin. Our conscience had been a light trying to shine in the darkness of our sin, and now God has separated that light from the darkness which is in us so that we can begin to distinguish between right and wrong.

The gods of this world were judged at the cross of Calvary. When we accept the crucifixion of Christ as our personal atonement, the Spirit of God brings us out of Egypt. The legal hold of Satan upon us is destroyed. Our spirit is raised up to sit in heavenly places in Christ. The blood of God's Lamb covers us and our household so that the judgment of God passes over us when God executes His wrath upon the iniquity in the earth.

The bronze altar of burnt offering portrays Christ upon the cross. The bronze altar, by its size, odor, location, and accompanying activity, dominated the outer appearance of the Tabernacle of the Congregation. So it is that the crucified Christ dominates the kingdom of God. God meets man at the door of the Tabernacle, at the altar of burnt offering. We enter into the things of God through means of the cross. Some people are unwilling to get saved because the cross is an offense to them. However, the cross does not hinder a little child. So children enter into the kingdom freely and gladly, while the proud flesh of adults keep them outside.

The feast of Passover brings to our mind that we must first sprinkle the blood of God's Lamb upon our own life and the lives of the members of our household. Then we must eat His body and drink His precious blood. The communion service dramatizes our partaking of the body and blood, although our actual receiving of the body and blood of Christ occurs in the spiritual realm as we keep ourself in the place where Christ can commune with us—in prayer, reading the Bible, in fellowship with our brothers and sisters in Christ, in exposure to the ministry, and so forth.

If we take the first aspect of each of the four major types of redemption, we gain insight into the first facet of salvation. We say facet, rather than step, because salvation has many faces, like a diamond. These seven elements are more like the several faces of a diamond than they are steps on a ladder, or grades in an elementary school. As the diamond turns we see one face, and then another, and another. Soon we return to the first face, but this time we see new light and color, as it were. Redemption is a perfect work and we see it all at once. But the faces are revealed and re-revealed to us as our knowledge works together with the grace of God and our experience, so that salvation actually changes us from glory to glory, by the Spirit of the Lord, until we are transformed into His image.

The first aspect of each of the four types is as follows: the dividing of light from darkness; the exodus; the altar of burnt offering; and the feast of Passover. Taken together they form one complete type of the beginning of our salvation.

THE SECOND ASPECT OF REDEMPTION

The second aspect of each of the four types are these: the dividing of the waters by means of the firmament of heaven; going across the Red Sea; the bronze laver; the week of Firstfruits. Isn't it interesting that three of the four involve water? The New Testament counterpart of these four types is water baptism. How perfect are the workings of God! Since Firstfruits speaks of the putting away of the filth (leaven) of the world and the flesh, we get the general idea that God intends to wash us from our sins and iniquities in this second phase of redemption.

The dividing of the waters by the firmament means, in the literal sense, that there is water surrounding outer space. The firmament mentioned in Genesis 1 is space, commencing at the surface of the earth and extending into outer space. All water is divided into two parts: that which is under the firmament, that is, water within the earth and water on the surface of the earth; and the water which is out beyond outer space, which is the water above the firmament. From the time of the Greeks, scientists have speculated as to the nature of the boundary of outer space. Well, outer space is bound by water. And how far that water extends is not known to us.

What is the spiritual interpretation of the division of the waters? Keeping in mind that all of the people, events, and things of the Bible were real people, real events, and real things, let us remind the reader that the heaven and the earth were created in response to conditions in the heavenlies, which existed at a prior time. Much of the account of the creation, in addition to being a literal, factual account—make no mistake about that—is also an allegory, the meaning of which is understood only in the spiritual realm. Very often in the Bible, God is speaking not only to people on the earth but also to His creatures in the heavenlies. The entire Bible account, from Genesis to Revelation, is one great canvas which portrays the redemption which is in Christ Jesus—a redemption necessary because of the rebellion in the heaven- lies. How great is God? and how great is His power and foreknowledge that He could conceive such a plan and then carry it through to consummation, just as a composer takes a melodic chord and constructs a symphony upon it?

The spiritual application of the dividing of the waters is as follows: when the plan of redemption begins its work in us, the waters of our life, which are both natural and spiritual, are all mixed together, just as the darkness and light in us are mixed together before we receive Christ. After we become willing to receive God's atonement for our sin, the blood of our Lord Jesus Christ, then God puts the firmament of heaven within us, so to speak. He separates our natural life from our spiritual life. Our soulish, natural life is assigned to the cross of Christ, and our spiritual nature is raised up in Christ into newness of life. Before this separation occurs we are a whole person, although lost in sin and death. After this separation occurs we begin to experience a sense of division. Our spiritual nature longs after the will of God while our fleshly nature attempts to pull us back down to serve the lusts of the flesh. The battle is joined! Isn't it so in your life?

Before the exodus was complete, Israel had to go across the Red Sea. Water stood between the Israelites and their freedom. Egypt and the land of promise are divided by two bodies of water, the Red Sea and River Jordan; both have to be crossed.

God divided the waters, and Israel went across without harm. But the Egyptians could not go through. When we go down into water baptism we go down into the death of the cross. Satan follows us down; the world presses hard on our heels. But praise God! Satan and the world cannot come up on the other side. The enemy cannot stand on resurrection ground. The water closes back in and the enemy is destroyed. The water seals off Egypt at our back. Before us is the wilderness, the school of the Holy Spirit. At the end of the trail is a river, and then the land of promise. Are you game to go on?

The bronze laver of the Tabernacle speaks to us of the washing of water by the Word of God. God's Word teaches us concerning righteousness and holiness. Righteousness is equitable living between person and person. Holiness is the embracing of God's ways of doing things, and also the rejection of dirty spirits. Righteousness is square dealing with other people. Holiness is cleanliness toward God. If we will listen to God's Word, and do what it says, we will "do justly, love mercy, and walk humbly with our God." We must wash constantly, through the power of the blood of the cross and through the enabling of the Holy Spirit, keeping ourself clean from the defilement of Satan, the spirit of this age, and the filthiness of our own flesh.

The week of Firstfruits teaches us to put away the leaven of the world, of sin, of malice, of wickedness. We put away sin with fervor, with diligence, even with violence at times. We learn to love righteousness and hate iniquity; that is to say, we get determined about what we are doing in the area of holiness and righteousness. It is a determination to please God and to escape clean away from sin and everything that looks like sin. It is not just a lukewarm, mental assent to Christianity. We need to get excited about our religion!

We have just discussed the first two facets, or phases if you will, of God's plan of redemption in Christ Jesus. In order to gain insight, we have taken a look at the first two elements of each of the four major types of redemption. Does the study of these types help you to get some idea of the nature of salvation?

THE THIRD ASPECT OF REDEMPTION

The third dimension of the seven dimensions of redemption is portrayed by the third aspect of the four types: the gathering together of the waters under the firmament, the appearing of the land, and the creation of vegetation; the beginning of the pilgrimage through the wilderness; the table of showbread; and the convocation of Firstfruits. Do you notice that in three of these four we have the thought of the *beginning* of something? So it is that the third dimension is that of the born-again experience, the beginning of the life of Christ in us. Whereas the first two phases had to do with judgment, protection, sin, and washing, this third phase has to do with the beginning of life—the positive side of redemption.

The waters of our soulish life, now having been separated from our spiritual nature, gather together, as it were, and we begin to feel within ourself that Christ has been born in us. He is being formed in us. The dry land begins to appear, and resurrection power helps us to choose to become the servant of righteousness.

The fruit of the Holy Spirit, love, joy, peace, and so forth, begins to show, as typified by the creation of vegetation.

We stand now on the east shore of the Red Sea, ready to begin our pilgrimage toward the land of promise. We are on resurrection ground. Egypt is walled off behind us by the Red Sea, a portrayal of our death to the world. Serious problems of our customary food and water supply face us as we start to move down toward the wilderness of Sinai. The remembrance of the leeks and garlics of Egypt grows fonder with each passing hour. But we move ahead anyway, and begin to see the miraculous provisions of God. Wasn't it that way when you first got saved? Didn't you wonder if you would be able to stand? How you were going to make it? It was that way with me!

The table of showbread of the Tabernacle of the Congregation represents the body and blood of our Lord Jesus Christ. The body and blood of Christ is the tree of life. There is no other life in the world. Whoever has never eaten of the Lord's body and blood is dead; he has no life. The only life in the world is in the body and blood of God's Son. The older we get in the Lord, the more conscious we become of that fact.

When we eat the body and blood of Christ for the first time, in that moment we partake of eternal life. It is the beginning of our life. We are born again by partaking of Him. We are born of the water of baptism in the sense that we escape the authority of Satan and enter into the authority of Christ and into His kingdom. We are born of the Holy Spirit in that the Holy Spirit renews our contact with the Father; we are cut off no longer from the life which is in Him.

But that which grows within us is neither the water nor the Spirit. Nowhere in the Bible does it say that the Holy Spirit grows within us. It is Christ Himself who is born and grows within us. Christ is the living Word, and the Word of God grows within us. The life of Christ Jesus is in His body and His precious blood. As we eat His body and drink His blood, we have life in us. That life is His life, and if we partake of Him we will live by Him as He lives by the Father.

The church of Christ is the wife of the Lamb. She is the wife of the Lamb because she partakes of the Passover Lamb. She eats Him and becomes one with Him. He is the living bread. His flesh is meat indeed, and His blood is drink indeed (John 7). We are born again "by the word of God, who lives and abides for ever" (I Pet. 1:23).

The Levitical convocation of Firstfruits adds to our understanding of the third aspect of redemption by reminding us that when we are born again a firstfruits of our personality, that is, our spirit, is raised up in Christ. There is still a great deal of our personality yet to be harvested. But the reaping has commenced, and now the firstfruits has been waved before God in joy and thanksgiving. God, with a joy to match our own, graciously accepts our firstfruits. Therefore, the harvest of our entire life has now been accepted. The blessing upon the firstfruits falls upon the whole harvest, of which the firstfruits is a representation. Praise God! We may have just been saved and born again. But God sees us already perfect in Christ Jesus, sanctified, and glorified.

These first three phases of redemption, the atonement, water baptism, and being born again, constitute what we generally refer to as "getting saved." They are the salvation experience. The first three Levitical convocations were grouped together in one week, showing that we are to consider them as belonging together. The first two are in the courtyard of the Tabernacle, and the third brings us in the holy place. "He that believeth and is baptized shall be saved" (Mark 16:16). This is the first of the three great areas of redemption.

THE FOURTH ASPECT OF REDEMPTION

The fourth aspect of redemption has some remarkable characteristics. In terms of the four types, we have the following: (1) the creating of the sun, moon, and stars in the firmament; (2) Mount Sinai, the Ten Commandments, the Levitical statutes and ordinances, the Tabernacle of the Congregation, and the Aaronic priesthood; the golden lampstand; and the feast of Pentecost. The common factor of *light* may be noted. Here we have the concept of the communication of the will and knowledge of God to mankind.

Of the seven Levitical convocations, Pentecost was the only one which stood by itself. The remaining six were divided into two groups of three each. By this God signifies to us that Pentecost is especially important. Four is midway between one and seven, and Pentecost truly is a turning point in our Christian life. It is at Pentecost that we can choose to go on to the fullness of redemption, and to become the servant of the Lord. Of the three orderings of the seven furnishings of the Tabernacle, the lampstand is always number four.

Before we come to the fourth day of creation, our

"firmament" is present, but there is nothing in it, so to speak. It is a clear blue. But on the fourth day God puts in our firmament the sun, moon, and stars, in that order. The first spiritual consciousness which we have is of the "sun," that is, of the Lord Jesus Christ. He gives us light.

The second spiritual consciousness which we have is that of the "moon," that is, the church. The church has no light of its own, but reflects the glory of Christ. Through the church we receive of the ministries and gifts of the Holy Spirit. They build us up until Christ is formed in us.

The third spiritual consciousness which we have is that of the "stars," that is, the overcomers, God's mighty men. It is the business of the church of Christ to travail in birth until the members of the body of Christ become strong in the Lord and in the power of His might. It will never be possible for the Lord to return and for the kingdom of darkness to be overthrown until the church brings forth the overcoming saints.

The Ten Commandments, and the rest of the ordinances revealed to Moses, represent the knowledge of His will which God gives to us. The golden lampstand portrays the head and body of Messiah, the anointed One, the Servant of the Lord, God's Vine. Through Messiah, God is going to fill the earth with His will and His blessings.

During the convocation of Pentecost, two great loaves of fine flour were waved before the Lord. These two loaves are the outpouring of the Holy Spirit upon the church. *Two* in Bible symbolism stands for *power*. The two loaves reveal the fact that just before the coming of our Lord Jesus Christ there will be an outpouring of gospel glory and power that has never been seen upon the earth, not even during the early church. He has kept the good wine until now. The two loaves are the "two witnesses," the double portion of Elijah, through means of which God will prepare the way of the King of kings, the Lord Jesus Christ (Isa. 40).

The fourth aspect of redemption is the outpouring of

the Holy Spirit upon us. There have been outpourings of the Holy Spirit throughout church history, but there has never been anything to compare to that which is ahead. The Scripture teaches plainly that the day will come when the earth will be filled with the Spirit of the Lord. The millennium, for example, will be a Pentecost of Pentecosts. The river of life will be available throughout the earth, under the auspices of Christ. During the new heaven and earth reign of Christ, the water of life will proceed out from the throne of God and of the Lamb.

But even before these unspeakable glories, the Holy Spirit is going to be poured out upon the earth in signs and mighty wonders until the kingdom of God has been demonstrated and taught throughout every nation under heaven.

One reason that God emphasizes the fourth aspect of redemption is that it is the Holy Spirit's mission to prepare the church, the body of Christ, the bride of the Lamb. Hopefully, in the near future, we will be able to work with the Holy Spirit much more successfully than has been true in the past. We must remember, and take it sincerely to heart, that the job of building the church of Christ belongs to the Holy Spirit and to the Holy Spirit alone. The only good we do in this area is that which was wrought through us under the direct wisdom and enablement of the Holy Spirit. We need to learn to walk in the Spirit of God, particularly when we set out to exercise our gift or ministry.

THE FIFTH ASPECT OF REDEMPTION

Now we have come to a phase of redemption with which many of us may be unfamiliar. Most of us understand quite well the first three aspects, for the basics of the plan of salvation have been taught well throughout the Christian church. We also may be familiar with the fourth aspect. The "charismatic" movement which currently has been a blessing to so many reflects the fourth aspect of the plan of redemption. What, then, is the fifth aspect?

Let's think for a moment about the fifth aspect of each of the four major types of redemption: the creation of fish and birds; the organization of Israel into an army; the golden altar of incense; and the convocation of Trumpets. This aspect of redemption should be of interest to charismatics because it is the phase of redemption which stands between the outpouring of the Holy Spirit and the presence of Christ.

The common factor here is that of beginning, of newness of life. It is not life as we have known it, but greatly increased spiritual life.

The creation of fish and birds is the beginning of animal life upon the earth. Prior to this there had been vegetation, but no animal life of any kind whatever. Now God has placed upon the earth the forerunner of the greatest creation—mankind in His image.

The "fish" are symbolic of the fact that after the outpouring of the Holy Spirit there is to be an ingathering of souls into the kingdom of God (see Ezek. 47:9,10). The creation of "birds" is symbolic in that for the first time we become conscious of the interest of the creatures of heaven in the church. Paul, the apostle, was very aware of the role of angels in God's workings, and made many references to them. As we grow closer to the coming of the Lord, we will become much more knowledgeable of the part that angels, cherubim, and other creatures of God are going to have in the ages to come.

After the Israelites had constructed the Tabernacle of the Congregation and had left the Sinai region on their journey toward Kadesh-Barnea, they began to march as an army. Before this they had been a disorganized mass of people following Moses through the wilderness. But as soon as the Tabernacle had been constructed and the Aaronic priesthood set in order, the twelve tribes were organized into a fighting formation with the Ark of the Covenant in the middle. They went out and came in at the sound of silver trumpets. The nearer they got to the land of promise, the more threatening became the environment. Soon they were going to be fighting their way into the land which God had given them, and this would not be possible while the people remained disorganized and undisciplined. The trumpet of the Lord is sounding in the churches in these days; it is getting near the time for the Lord's vengeance against His enemies.

The golden altar of incense stood just before the holy veil, directly in line with the Ark of the Covenant. The altar of incense is the last great move of redemption before Jesus returns and puts in motion the remaining two aspects.

The altar of incense represents man's communication toward God, just as the lampstand represents God's communication toward man. The holy incense is the life of the Lord Jesus Christ worked into the fiber and marrow of every Christian until fervent prayer, thanksgiving, and praise begins to ascend before the throne of God. The altar of incense is the voice of Messiah, calling out in constant communion with the Father.

The altar of incense portrays the finish of the Moses-type ministry, because the holy veil stands for the River Jordan, which is death to our own desires and ambitions, and Moses cannot cross over Jordan.

We have come to a new life, when we arrive at the altar of incense. It is the beginning of our life as kings and priests of God.

Just before Christ comes, the power in prayer of the church of Christ will reach such monumental proportions that the cry which goes up to God will bring back the Lord. The bride will cry, "Come!" So intense, so holy, so loving, so mighty will be that cry in the Spirit that heaven no longer will be able to hold the Lord Jesus. He will return to the earth.

The altar of incense and the feast of Trumpets go together, as we may notice in the eighth chapter of

Revelation. The seven trumpets of God must sound, and then the Lord will return at the seventh trumpet. It is the holy incense coming up from the prayers of the saints that causes the seven trumpets to begin to sound. The coals from the altar of incense before the throne of God in heaven are thrown into the earth. When these fiery coals touch the world there is judgment and destruction. But when they touch the incense of Christ, which is in the saints, the holy perfume comes up before the Lord God as a pleasing fragrance.

The convocation of Trumpets is the beginning of the new agricultural year. The ecclesiastical year began with Passover. The ecclesiastical year is symbolic of the redemption which is in Christ Jesus, that is, the salvation of the individual believer. It begins with the blood of the Passover, and ends with Tabernacles in which the believer is at rest in the Father and the Son, and they are at rest in him. But the civil year which began with Trumpets represents the kingdom of God. The kingdom of God is the rule of God, the observance of His laws. The kingdom of God reaches completion in four stages: (1) in Christ Jesus Himself, who is the King of the kingdom; (2) in the overcomers, the saints of the Lord who press on in Christ until they, through His grace, are able to walk in the Holy Spirit; (3) in the entire church of Christ; and (4) throughout the entire earth. The coming of the kingdom of God is announced by means of the trumpet.

We noticed before that the first three of the Levitical convocations, Passover, Unleavened Bread, and Firstfruits, are grouped together in a period of eight days. They go together, and represent that which we ordinarily refer to as "getting saved." Pentecost stands by itself, representing the work of the Holy Spirit in preparing the bride of the Son.

The final three convocations, Trumpets, the Day of Atonement, and Tabernacles, also are grouped together. They symbolize the kingdom of God working in us. When we get saved we are forgiven our sins, and we are on our way to heaven, being accepted of God. But when we enter into the last three convocations we begin to actually get the victory over our sins. We begin to overcome the accuser, the world, and the flesh. Now we are on our way toward victory in the earth, which includes getting saved and going to heaven, but is much greater, much more victorious, much more freeing. It is a much larger place of rejoicing and liberty.

Trumpets announces the next two feasts, the Day of Atonement and Tabernacles, which are shortly to come. The kingdom-wide fulfillment of Trumpets will occur at the coming of our Lord Jesus Christ. But as far as the overcomers—God's saints—are concerned, the trumpet of God is blowing now, in the spiritual sense. The church of Christ has tarried at Pentecost long enough. It is time now to pack up the Tabernacle and to move on with God. Get the ark set in place in the middle of the column, being wrapped in its blue cloth and lifted up upon the shoulders of the Kohathite Levites. The cloud has lifted up from off the Tabernacle. The Lord God of hosts is taking His journey northward, toward the land of promise. Come on, let's move on with Him! There's nothing here that interests us after the Lord has moved on!

THE SIXTH ASPECT OF REDEMPTION

It was on the sixth day that man was made in the image of God; and, therefore, we might expect that the sixth aspect of redemption would be extremely significant. And so it is! For it is on this day that the crowning work of God is performed, a work for which the preceding five aspects have served as a foundation.

To begin with, let us refresh our minds with the sixth part of each of the four major types of redemption: (1) the creation of animals, and of mankind in God's image; (2) the crossing of Jordan and the attack upon Canaan; (3) the Ark of the Covenant; and (4) the Day of Atonement. The sixth aspect is a time of war, of the presence of Christ the King, and of the formation of sons of God in the image of Christ (Rom. 8:29).

Joshua.   Moses can only take us through five aspects of redemption; Joshua must take us past this point. Moses represents the Lord Jesus Christ as the good Shepherd, leading His flock through the dangers of the wilderness. Joshua represents the Lord Jesus Christ as the Lord of hosts. As we have known the good Shepherd, the Christ of the Twenty-third Psalm, so also will we know the Lord strong and mighty in battle, the Christ of the Twenty-fourth Psalm.

We find in the Twenty-fourth Psalm that the earth belongs to the Lord, and that if we are to ascend into the hill of the Lord (Zion), and stand in His holy place, then we must have clean hands. Joshua represents our ascent into holiness, and the resulting conquest of the earth. The King of glory is about to enter the everlasting doors of our hearts, so let us lift them up in preparation for His conquest of us, and through us His conquest of the whole earth.

The veil.   Between the fifth and sixth aspects of redemption, that is, between the altar of incense and the Ark of the Covenant, hung the holy veil which separated the holy place from the holy of holies. The counterpart of the veil is the Jordan River, which separated the wilderness from the land of promise. Before we can pass from the fifth aspect of redemption to the sixth aspect, we must go past the veil; we must cross over Jordan. Both the veil and the Jordan symbolize our death. But what kind of death? And remember, resurrection always must be preceded by death!

Three deaths and three resurrections.   There are at least five deaths mentioned in the Bible: (1) the death of the body; (2) the second death, which is the lake of fire; (3) our death in water baptism, which is a burial of our old nature upon the cross with Christ and a sharing in His resurrection life; (4) the death we die as the result of our baptism in the Holy Spirit, as the Spirit leads us in the putting to death of the deeds of our flesh; and (5) the giving over to the Lord Jesus Christ of our personal hopes and ambitions in order that the will and purposes of God may be carried out in us without distraction. Since the first two deaths, that is, bodily decomposition and the lake of fire, are fairly well understood by most readers of the Bible, let us dwell for a moment on the other three. The last death listed is the one typfied by the veil and by the River Jordan.

The three deaths under discussion are symbolized by the three hangings of the Tabernacle of the Congregation. The first hanging was the gate of the courtyard. It led into the court of the Tabernacle, in which stood the bronze altar and the laver. This "death" is a very difficult step for the person who has tried hard, whether in observance of the Jewish Law and ordinances, or in conscience and personal code of morality and honor, to lead a life pleasing to God and worthy of His acceptance and of eternal life. To have to forsake all of this effort in order to embrace the blood of the cross, putting one's self down on the same level with thieves and prostitutes, is more than some people can bear. Their personal pride prevents their coming to God by way of the cross. And so they go on attempting to please God, which is a hopeless endeavor, because for one thing they are in need of redemption and they do not have the amount on hand with which to pay the mortgage which Satan has on them. Coming to Christ and forsaking one's own righteousness is death for the well educated and the ignorant, for the wealthy and the poor, for the black person and the white person.

But there is a resurrection which comes after this death. It is the freeing of one's soul from the guilt of sin, and a welcome acceptance by the Father. If we come God's way, we do not have to worry anymore whether we have made the grade. Christ made the grade for us, and we stand before God in His righteousness.

The gate of the courtyard symbolizes death to the natural man, as our carnal nature is brought by faith down to the death of the cross of Christ. This death is explained in the sixth chapter of Romans. It is a death to our own self-righteousness; death to the law of Moses; death to the first creation.

In water baptism we demonstrate that by faith we enter into a sharing of the death of Christ and into a sharing in His resurrection from among the dead. It is a judgment upon the gods of this age, upon our past, ignorant actions in the darkness of the present evil age. At this point we place our own "body of sin" upon the cross, in order that it might be rendered incapable of resistance to our new life of righteousness. By putting the old man on the cross, through the authority of the blood and the power of the Holy Spirit, we become free to choose to serve righteousness. Our spirit is received by the Holy Spirit and our life rises up to be hid with Christ in God. This is real death and real resurrection. It is dramatized in water baptism, and then we see it wrought out in actual experience as we live each day in the faith that we were buried with Him and have risen in Him and through Him.

The death represented by the gate is our crossing of the Red Sea. The hosts of Pharaoh, attempting to follow us, are destroyed by the judgment which closes in upon them.

The death of the gate results in the resurrection of our spirit. It is an instant death, accomplished through our faith, and results in the resurrection of our spirit. Egypt is forever left behind us, being separated from us by the "Red Sea," so to speak. The light of Christ in us has been eternally divided from the darkness of the world.

The death of the gate is typified by the altar of burnt offering, and by the laver—accepting of the blood of the Lamb of God, and water baptism. The end result of this death is that we walk in the righteousness of Christ imputed to us. We are totally free from condemnation through means of the accepting of Christ by faith.

The second hanging was the door of the Tabernacle.

This is the death to the sins which we commit as Christians. We are baptized into this death when we are baptized in the Holy Spirit. It is a death to our sins as the Holy Spirit puts to death the deeds of the body (Rom. 8:13; I John 1:7-9; 3:3; II Cor. 7:1).

When we are baptized into the Holy Spirit we come under the law of the Spirit of life. Through the wisdom and power of the Holy Spirit and the blood of the Lord Jesus Christ, we are enabled to sit in judgment upon the sins in our own life. We judge ourselves so that we should not be judged. We judge the sins of deed, word, imagination, and motive that we are committing as Christians. We do so, not in gloom and introspection, but in joy and strength as the Holy Spirit leads us into such judgment.

The purpose of this death is the destroying of the power of sin over our members—the destroying of the hold of evil upon us. It is a step-by-step overcoming of sin, and a step-by-step movement into a progressively greater obedience to the Holy Spirit.

The lampstand is an important Old Testament symbol of the life lived in the Holy Spirit.

The end result of the death of the door is the resurrection of our soul, and righteous and holy living.

The third hanging was the veil which concealed the holy of holies. This is not death unto sins past or present, but rather the death of that which is lawful but not expedient. The veil represents our becoming the servant of the Lord.

Coming through the gate of the courtyard caused us to die to the opinions of our own proud mind, a mind which is at enmity against God and cannot be made subject to the law of God. By faith we bring down our natural, soulish life and passions to the death of the cross of Christ. It is amazing how effective the cross of Christ is, when it comes to dealing with our own carnal nature. Crucifixion is the best antidote in the world for the natural man—it is just what the doctor ordered. We struggle, kick, and complain as the cross works death in us. But the end is death to the lusts of the soul and life for our new man. We become identified with the cross so that through the cross we might enter into resurrection life.

Coming through the door of the Tabernacle also has to do with the overcoming of sin; but this time the sins which we are doing, such as spiteful words, unforgiveness, unclean deeds, filthy words, jealousy, pride, and so forth, are pointed out by the Holy Spirit. Instead of dealing with the entire natural man with the cross, we are dealing with the deeds, words, motives, and imaginations in a specific manner, and bringing the authority of the blood and the power of the Spirit against them. One by one our sins of conduct and imagination are brought to our attention by the Holy Spirit, and one by one we confess them to the Lord and get His forgiveness and cleansing. Through the Holy Spirit we put to death the deeds of the flesh (Rom. 8:13). In this manner we overcome our sins through the Holy Spirit of God.

Going through the veil is the deepest death of all. Its purpose is to make us the servant of the Lord, one of Christ's warriors. The purpose of the death of the gate was to turn our minds toward God's salvation and to divide the light from the darkness, so to speak. Its purpose also is to destroy the ability of the natural man to keep us living in the passions of the carnal nature.

The purpose of the death of the door is to enable us, through the Holy Spirit, to get the victory over the sins which we commit as Christians, giving us a chance to be recreated in our soul into the image of Christ, and a chance to grow in our ability to communicate with God in adoration and supplication. The holy place of the Tabernacle is the place where we find the blessings which follow the death of the door.

But the purpose of the death of the veil is to enable us to see God and to serve Him. Even the most righteous person is still unable to see God because that person, though righteous, is still filled with his own ways, righteous and holy though his ways may be.

The death of the veil is death to serving God in our own wisdom and power. It is death to self-achievement, even self-achievement in the things of God. Second Corinthians 4 relates how Paul continually was being pressed out of measure and struck down, as he attempted to serve Christ, having the sentence of death in himself that he should not trust in himself but in God, who raises up the dead. God sees to it that we die to our own efforts and abilities to be anything or to do anything. It is a crucifixion of the will—the deepest death of all.

Judgment comes upon us as an individual, followed by rewards for faithfulness in service to God. One of the greatest of the rewards is that of being made in the image of the Lord.

The death of the veil is a protracted death, as God brings us into the sufferings of Christ. We are being transformed into His glory. One of the end results of the death of the veil is the redemption and glorification of our mortal body—the clothing upon with the house which is from heaven (see II Cor. 5).

To enter into the work of judgment with Christ, in the destroying of sin out of the earth and the installing of the kingdom of God, requires the death of the veil. This death was portrayed in the Old Testament by the crossing of Jordan, just prior to the beginning of the destruction of the Canaanites.

The death of the veil brings us into that which is typified by the Ark of the Covenant and the mercy seat. It is fellowship with the Father and with His Son, Jesus Christ. It is a walk in victory as a king, and as the Lord's servant in intercession and ministry as a priest. The end is participation in the rest of God.

To stand in the presence of the Almighty requires more than righteousness and holiness, as necessary as these are. It requires further death. It requires a work of divine fire in us which goes to the core of our being. It penetrates the deepest areas of who we are and what we are, and there it transforms and transfigures. God burns His way into every atom of our personality, spirit, soul, and body. The result is transparent gold, through and through. It is a gold which has been refined in holy fire until there is nothing remaining but the finest, purest gold.

The person who is willing to go this final route cannot be hurt of any death. He is dead, but he is eternally alive because he is living no longer. It is Christ, the living fire of God, who is living in him. This is the final death, and beyond this is a resurrection in God Himself which is so glorious, so holy, so wonderful, so eternal, so incorruptible, that the believer will be able to stand in His presence forever, to see His face, and to serve Him. Such a privilege is so far beyond our comprehension that we can do no more nor less than offer our bodies as a whole burnt offering, an ascending sacrifice, in the sure knowledge that what God has promised He is going to accomplish in us.

Paul states, "I am crucified with Christ; nevertheless I live. Yet it is not I who am living, but Christ who is living in me" (see Gal. 2:20). Paul was a walking dead man, one might say. But he was gloriously alive, because Christ was in every part of Paul's deeds, Paul's words, his motives, and his imaginations.

In order for us to enter into that which is beyond the veil, that is, into the fullness of service as a king and priest of Christ during the millennium, we are going to have to meet the qualifications for the overcomer (Rev. 12). We overcome through means of the blood (the gate of the courtyard); through means of the word of our testimony—which has to do with the manifestation of the Holy Spirit through us (the door of the Tabernacle—we are baptized by the Holy Spirit into the body of Christ, that is, into the holy place); and by loving not our lives unto the death (the veil leading into the holy of holies).

The sixth aspect of redemption has to do with the creation of animals, and of mankind in God's image. Human beings have both a soulish and a spiritual nature. The soulish nature has many of the characteristics of an animal, so much so that many educated people have convinced themselves that people are nothing more than civilized apes. We have much in common with animal life. But when we come to the making of mankind in the image of God we are not referring to the soulish, carnal part of people. The image of God is the image of Jesus Christ. God is in the process of creating us at this time in the very image of His Son—spirit, soul, and, at His coming, in our body as well. Redemption includes the making alive of the mortal body.

The work of the sixth day includes the making of us into the express image of Jesus Christ. First comes the earthly animal image. Then comes the image of the Lord from heaven. People are never animals, of course; although sometimes they act worse than animals. We are referring to the fact that we are categorized as mammals by scientists, and eat, drink, reproduce, have body temperature mechanisms, and so forth, the same as other mammals. But the making of us into His image is a heavenly work, and in no way has to do with animal life on this planet. In the sense in which we are speaking, the sixth day of creation is still going on because we are still being created in the image of God.

The crossing over Jordan under the leadership of Joshua speaks of our death. As soon as Jordan was crossed, the new generation had to be circumcised. The reason for our death and circumcision toward the end of the plan of redemption is as follows: we are getting ready for the battle of the ages, for Armageddon. Armageddon is the war between Christ and Satan. The battle is waged around one issue—sin! If there is sin in the camp, we lose all of our power. Our strength is based squarely upon the extent to which we have grasped the holiness of Christ. If we are still walking in sin, we may be saved and go to heaven through means of the grace of God. But we will never be worth much in the battle of which we are speaking until we are learned in the ways of righteousness. We will not be ready for God's work until we have grown in holiness, having our senses exercised so that we are able to discern good and evil, and are able to reject the evil and cleave to the good.

The war of God has directly to do with sin and righteousness. In no way will the Lord send forth immature believers into the warfare which has to do with the control of the earth and its peoples. God's weak ones will be kept safe and nourished by His goodness, until they too are strong enough to fight in the holy battle. In the meantime, Christ's mighty men, His overcomers, His saints, are preparing to wage the war, preparing for the takeover of the earth by the King of kings and Lord of lords. Up to this point the Christian strategy has been a defensive position, while we learn to stand and hold our ground against the attacks of the evil one. But when Jesus returns we will switch from defensive waiting to the attack. Hallelujah! So we learn now we must be strictly obedient to the Lord Jesus, because He is the Commander-in-chief of this army.

The Ark of the Covenant represents Jesus Christ as the Lord, strong and mighty in battle. The Ark of the Covenant typifies Mount Zion, that is, the Lord's stronghold against the enemy. The ark was removed from the Tabernacle during the days of Eli, the anointed priest. It was never returned to the holy of holies. Instead, King David pitched a tent for the ark in the city of Zion, and the tent was termed "David's Tabernacle." This is symbolic of the coming of Christ. When Jesus comes, it will not be with the whole church, the whole Tabernacle of the Congregation, to speak in a figure. Instead, He is coming with thousands of His warriors, a handpicked group who have proven their prowess in battle. They are the personal bodyguard of the Lord Jesus, just as David had his mighty men who performed exploits in war.

If you wish, you may be in the Lord's army. Just give yourself over to Him in unreserved discipleship; follow Him in all ways that He leads you; love not your life unto the death; present your body to Christ as a whole burnt offering; He will do the rest. Whosoever will can attain unto the first resurrection. But we will have to become strong in the Lord and in the power of His might if we expect to rule with Him during the millennium. There is a fierce battle ahead, and it is not for weak Christians who are barely making it with the Lord.

The altar of incense stood directly in line with the Ark of the Covenant. This alignment portrays the fact that when the prayers and praises of the Lord's people reach sufficient strength and intensity, during the days of trouble which are ahead, the Lord will return, bringing redemption to us. Then He will shine as the sun in the glory of His Father, and the righteous will shine with Him. One of the clearest symbolic portrayals of this moment of revelation occurred on the mount of transfiguration. There stood the mighty Christ, transfigured in glory, having with Him two of His mighty men from the old covenant, and three of His most faithful disciples from the new covenant. This was a picture of the Lord Jesus Christ coming in His kingdom.

The Day of Atonement, *Yom Kippur,* is the most solemn day of the Jewish ecclesiastical year. The Day of Atonement has to do with sin, its remission, and its removal from the camp. When the four types are put together, we get the concept. Through means of war, Christ is going to redeem the earth from sin. The guilt of sin was forgiven upon Calvary, the Lord Jesus Christ now owns the earth and all of earth's peoples, as symbolized by His possession of the keys of hell and death. The authority is His. But Satan, even though he has no more claim upon the earth or anyone in it, still is holding on. The mortgage has been completely paid, but the mortgage holder will not let go. So the earth and its peoples will be taken away from him by force. This is the kingdom-wide fulfillment of the Day of Atonement. Its greatest fulfillment will come during the millennium, and is the reason for and the meaning of the millennium. Redemption will never occur again after the millennium, as symbolized by the lack of silver in the new heaven and earth reign of Christ. Silver stands for redemption. There is plenty of gold in the new earth, but no silver. Redemption ceases at the end of the millennium.

"When you see these things come to pass," Jesus said, "lift up your heads because your redemption draws near" (see Luke 21:28). We can tell from this saying that redemption is yet ahead of us, meaning that the fullness of the Day of Atonement is yet to come. Paul also refers to the coming day of redemption in the eighth chapter of Romans.

But in a very real sense, the Day of Atonement is operating among us right now. Every time an unsaved person receives Christ, the blood avails for him, atonement has been made for his sins.

Also, very importantly, as we Christians go through our daily lives we must learn to confess our sins (I John 1:9). If we are sensitive to the will of God, and are walking in the light of His presence, the Holy Spirit will point out to us sins of deed, word, motive, and imagination which we are committing. As the Spirit shows these to us, we are to confess them as sin. "If we (Christians) confess our sins, he is faithful and just to forgive us our sins, and to cleanse us from all unrighteousness." In this manner the Day of Atonement is at work continually in the Christian life. It is through means of His blood that we are able to keep on washing ourselves from the sins that we commit. We keep on getting forgiveness and cleansing; and, as we draw nigh to God, the Lord helps us to resist the enemy and quit our sinning. Through means of the authority of the blood, and the wisdom and power of the Holy Spirit of God, we are able to get the victory over sinful practices. This is the individual fulfillment of the Day of Atonement.

We see therefore that the Day of Atonement has a great kingdom-wide fulfillment at the coming of our Lord Jesus Christ; and also that there is a current, individual fulfillment as we get saved, and as we confess our sins when the Holy Spirit points them out to us.

The Day of Atonement, through its eternal power and authority in destroying sinful practices out of our lives, is enabling us to grow into the express image of Christ. This is the sixth aspect of the plan of redemption.

THE SEVENTH ASPECT OF REDEMPTION

The seventh aspect of redemption is the consummation, the "mark," the completion of God's work. We have always assumed that redemption, or salvation, is an open-ended process that goes on and on with no certain finish. But such is not the case. God works for six days, and then He rests. God's workings are always clear-cut, decisive, well-planned out and carried through to perfection. God is not vague; He is forthright and precise in all that He does. His work is perfect. Redemption has a specific beginning, a specific program, and a specific conclusion.

There is one area of growth in our lives which will go on for such a long period that its end cannot be seen by us. It is this: as we, who are children of God, are drawn to Him to serve Him, to stand in His presence, to see His face, we will be transformed, as the face of Moses was transformed. The longer and closer is our association with Him, the more we will become like Him. Because of the unspeakable greatness of God, we can say that this program of transformation will go on throughout eternity, as we become more and more like Him in every way. However such transformation is our growth as sons of God, it is not the process of redemption. Redemption has a definite beginning, a definite program, and a definite finish. There is no silver in the new heaven and earth reign of Christ, indicating that redemption has ceased, and the status and role of each of the creatures of God has been determined.

Let us review the four viewpoints of the seventh aspect

of redemption as taken from the four major types: (1) God rested from all His works; (2) rest in the land of promise; (3) the mercy seat (Propitiatory Cover); and (4) the feast of Tabernacles. The "rest of God" is the subject of the fourth chapter of Hebrews, and these four types speak to us of the rest of God. The rest of God is the fullness of the plan of redemption, and is the "mark" toward which Paul was pressing. The knowledge that there indeed is a goal at which we can aim strengthens our desire to press on in Christ. There is a finish line. We are going somewhere!

We find that after God had created the heaven and earth, the vegetation, the heavenly bodies, and the inhabitants of the earth, He pronounced them to be "very good"—a fine, acceptable piece of work. He approved completely of His entire creation. Then God set apart the seventh day as being His own, and He sanctified it. His work was ended, and God rested from all of His work of creation.

Now, God works independently of time. He does not have His being within the boundaries of time as we do. For example, in the first three days of creation there was no way to measure time. There were no bodies in outer space from which to record the passage of time; there were no people, no clock mechanisms, not even the human heartbeat to act as a regular cycle through which the passage of time could be recorded. The first three days of creation were timeless, from our standpoint. Let us suggest at this point that the days of creation were periods of significant accomplishment, and, because of the greatness of God's power, could have taken place in seven minutes, or seven billion years, as we measure time. Time does not enter into the workings of God, because He lives and works and has His being in the past, present, and future, all at the same time. His name is "I am," indicating a state of perpetual presence and awareness. God can see the past, present, and future, all at the same time, and act in them as He pleases.

On the sixth day of creation, God made man in His own

image. Adam and Eve were in the image of God in the sense that they had been begotten of God, and had within themselves the potential to communicate with God and to grow into His image. But, as they existed in the Garden of Eden, they were a far cry from being in the image of God. Therefore, God was speaking of a creative work yet to come.

Then we see Jesus. Here is the Person who is in the image of God! Here is the One to whom God was referring. Jesus Christ is the only Person who lived on this earth in the image of God. All the rest of the descendants of Adam were and are pretty poor excuses for the image of God. But Jesus Christ was in the express image of the Father in every way—in Spirit, in soul, and now in His body. He is the Son of God, the image of the Father in grace and truth.

So when God said His work was completed, and He sanctified the seventh day and rested in it, being entirely pleased with His work, He was acting in a timeless vision. God's way is to call those things which are not as though they were. He has pronounced us glorified in Christ Jesus (Rom. 8:17), and yet we are not glorified as yet. He has called many things about you, dear reader, as being true. Yet in the realm of time they are not true as yet. We found this very principle operating in the fact that God carefully enjoined upon Israel many ceremonies and ordinances concerning agriculture while they were as yet in the wilderness. His way is to do a thing in the spiritual realm, and then rest while it is carried out. The sixth day of creation is being carried out. When you are in the image of God in Christ, then you will enter into His rest. Praise the Lord!

We see Jesus. He is the only Person this world has ever seen who is in the image of God. But there is more to come. God created "them," male and female, in his image. "Male and female created He them"! Therefore, His work of creating man in His image is not complete. In the sense in which we are now speaking, Jesus Christ will not be complete (understand what we say) until the bride has been created in the image of God. "Male and female created He them"!

Jesus Christ came to earth, and was made perfect through the things which He suffered. Then God caused a "deep sleep" (Calvary), to speak in a figure, to fall upon Christ. Out from the Person of Christ God drew His body and precious blood. Upon this body and blood God is constructing the wife of the Lamb. The wife of the Lamb is being constructed from ordinary saved people of the earth, but what is being constructed has nothing to do with the earth, or with our flesh-and-blood, carnal life. What is being constructed is from heaven just as Christ is from heaven. The church is not born from human blood, or from the will of the flesh, or from the will of man. The church is being constructed by the Holy Spirit from the body and blood of Christ. The church is of heaven, just as Christ is of heaven. It is Jesus Christ and His bride who are the fulfillment of God's edict, "Let us make mankind in Our image, after Our likeness."

The work of building up the church into the wife of the Lamb is going on right now. When it is finished, at the new heaven and earth reign of Christ, God will rest in His love. It is true also that as we as individuals come into the image of Christ, God rests in His love in us. We see, then, that the sixth day of creation, in the sense in which we are speaking, is still going on. Our problems of interpretation arise when we try to put the physical limitations of time and place upon the spiritual workings of God. It can't be done. God is always with us, ever present, calling those things which are not as though they were, and bringing His purposes to pass in the earth without hindrance. He is God!

The "rest" of the land of promise is the main type used in the discussion in Hebrews 3 and 4. Joshua was not able to bring Israel into total victory in Canaan, for one thing. For another, the entrance into the land of promise is symbolic of our rest in God—that rest which comes when we are made in His image.

One of the prominent characteristics of the symbolism which accompanies the entrance of Israel into Canaan is that of warfare. We enter into the promised land by means of war. God gives the land to us as soon as we leave Egypt, that is, as soon as we come out of the spirit of this age. But first we have to go through the school of the wilderness, and then we have to fight our way into the land. Unfortunately for us, our land of promise is occupied by very formidable forces; and so we have to fight. Isn't it so?

Down through the centuries of Christianity the church appears to have assumed that heaven is the land of promise, and that the Jordan River symbolizes physical death. Well, in one sense that may be true. Certainly the hope of heaven has served as a goal and an inspiration to countless saints as they have made their way, bearing their cross through the wilderness of this world, following the Lord Jesus Christ. Heaven is a real place, and we look forward to going home to be with the Lord.

But now, as we draw near to the closing of this age, we can begin to see that the land of promise is not as much in heaven as it is in the earth. The inheritance of Christ is in the earth (Psalm 2).

Who is the enemy against whom we are to fight? It is Satan, the god of this world. We wrestle not against flesh and blood, but against the wicked lords of darkness who control the actions of people upon the earth. God's kingdom is settled forever in heaven, but it is the intention of God that His kingdom come to the earth, and that His King, the Lord Jesus Christ, rule upon the earth.

The earth is the land of promise. We are being prepared to serve God as kings and priests in the earth. The millennium, in particular, will see great impetus given to the setting up of the kingdom of God in the earth. Finally, when all rebellion has been put down, the new heaven and earth reign of Christ will come, and the throne of God and of the Lamb will be in the earth rather than in heaven.

Our first and immediate problem is our own self. We have great problems overcoming the enemy in our own house, our own body, so to speak. Isn't it a fact? Our first battle is with the lusts of our own body and soul, with Satan acting to increase the lusts which we are fighting. We learn the ways of the Lord by going to war against our own nature. It is a fact that the great Battle of Armageddon will be nothing more than an earth-wide expression of the individual battle between God and Satan, between good and evil, that goes on within the breast of the disciple of Christ.

If, through the ability which God gives, we can make a success of overcoming in our personal warfare, we will enter into rest, into our own Canaan. Then, when God gets ready for His kingdom-wide moves, we will be all set to enter into the warfare in order to help great numbers of people enter into the rest of God. But if we are not diligent and successful in our own personal battles, then it is a deception to believe that we are going to arise as one of God's mighty men in the day of the Lord. It just doesn't work that way! Our time of proving is right now. If we go to battle in the Lord right now, today, and gain the victory through the blood of the Lamb, through the mighty testimony of the Holy Spirit through us, and through loving not our own lives unto the death, then we will be prepared to be one of the Lord's mighty men, and to be glorified with Him at His appearing in glory with the holy angels.

There is no way to enter into the land of promise, the rest of God, other than through war. The enemy is formidable, as we have said. But our God is more formidable; and if we follow the Spirit of the Lord, we have no fear. Our biggest problem is our own lack of obedience and faith. If we get these taken care of, we will find that Christ is more than a match for the enemy. We don't get all of our victories right away. Even Christ is still waiting for His enemies to be made His footstool.

There is total victory available for the individual Christian, and for the church of Christ—victory over the world, the flesh, and the devil. In the seven days of creation,

God set up the earth as the area of His workings. It is still the earth—God has not changed what He set out to do. God beheld the finished work—all the way to the new heaven and earth reign of Christ; then He said, "It is very good. It is entirely acceptable to Me, a perfect work." Well, we do not see any such thing as yet, but we do see Jesus, the promise of the fulfillment of all that God envisioned and created in Genesis 1.

The term "mercy seat" is somewhat of a misnomer. The word *mercy* should be *propitiation*, or *atonement;* the word *seat* should be *cover*, or *lid*. It is the *Propitiatory Cover*, or *Lid of Atonement*, if you will. It was the lid, or cover, of the Ark of the Covenant. And God did not sit on it; He dwelled between the Cherubim. *Sitting* implies human characteristics of weight and tiredness, and God has no weight nor is He tired. He doesn't rest because He becomes tired; He rests in order to contemplate and enjoy His handiwork.

The Propitiatory Cover was solid gold, speaking of the fact that the seventh aspect of redemption has to do with the possession of God Himself. The goal of the Christian redemption is God Himself, nothing less. Although He gives us joy unspeakable and full of glory in all that He does for us, yet it is He Himself who is the best gift. The closer we get to God, the more we realize that what our soul really cries out for is the possession of Him. He is the end of our redemption; our rest is in Him, and His rest is in us.

The Propitiatory Cover and the two covering cherubim were beaten out of one slab of gold. God dwelled between the cherubim of glory. The cherubim represent the fullness of God's power; the number *two* denotes power in the symbolism of Scripture. The importance of the cherubim and their oneness with God were illustrated by the fact that they were beaten out of one piece of gold with the Propitiatory Cover.

When we come into the express image of Christ, we will have had wrought in us the three basic elements of His nature. The three basic elements of His nature are typified by the three pieces within the Ark of the Covenant: (1) the tables of stone on which were inscribed the Ten Commandments (these were the covenant, the testimony, from which the ark derived its name); the jar of manna; and Aaron's rod which had budded. So then we must have these three elements wrought within us: (1) the moral law of God's righteousness and holiness; (2) the substance of Christ in His body and blood, which is our life; and (3) the resurrection power of the Holy Spirit.

The above three elements constitute the necessary parts of the fulfillment of the Ark of the Covenant in us, and they must have been wrought in us if we are to be ready to go to war with Christ at His glorious appearing. If we are lacking in any one of the three, we will not be ready. We must have a holy nature, we must have Christ within us, and we must be learning to walk, speak, and act in the wisdom and power of the Holy Spirit.

As soon as we have been constructed into the Ark of the Covenant, so to speak, we are ready for the fullness of God to settle down to rest in us. The fullness of God is represented by the solid gold Propitiatory Cover, with its two winged cherubim. This means that as soon as we come into the moral image of Christ, are of the essence of His being, and are moved by the same Holy Spirit which moves Him, then we will receive, as a crown of glory upon us, the fullness of God. The two cherubim speak of the fullness of His divine glory and power. The Ark of the Covenant must be built up within us, as we have said. But the ark will not be complete until the glory of the Lord settles down to rest over it. This is the rest of God.

The seventh aspect of the Levitical convocations is the feast of Tabernacles. Tabernacles represents the fullness of the indwelling of God in us. It is God's purpose to dwell (tabernacle) among the peoples of the earth. God is building the church, the body of Christ, for that very reason—that He might have a dwelling place in which and through which He can abide among the nations of the earth.

The week of Tabernacles was a season of the greatest joy. The Israelites were commanded to dwell in booths. The dwelling in booths typifies the dwelling of God in His people, and their abiding in Him. "Abide in Me," Jesus said. If we abide in Him and He abides in us, we will bring forth much fruit. Abiding in Christ is the meaning of the booths.

Tabernacles was the celebration of the conclusion of the harvest. In the Tabernacles experience, every last particle of our being will have been harvested unto the Lord—body, soul, and spirit. There will be no part of us that has not died and been resurrected. Nothing of the old will remain. Every element of our personality will be able to dwell in the fire of God with no harm, just as was true of Moses' bush, and of Shadrach, Meshach, and Abednego. The term *resurrection* means that something has died, and God has raised it up again. So it will be true of every inch of our person that it has died in the Lord, and has been raised to newness of life by the Lord.

After the seven days of Tabernacles, there was an eighth day, a holy Sabbath. The eighth day was the climax, the consummation of the thanksgiving and rejoicing which celebrated the end of the agricultural year. The eighth day of the convocation of Tabernacles is the first day of the week of eternity, the week which has no end. The kingdom-wide fulfillment of the convocation of Tabernacles is the new heaven and earth reign of Jesus Christ, just as the millennial jubilee is the kingdom-wide fulfillment of the Day of Atonement. During the first part of the new heaven and earth reign of Christ there will be a season of thanksgiving and rejoicing before the Lord, for, "Behold! He has made all things new!"

All things will be of God, in that day. After the season of rejoicing and thanksgiving before the Lord for His wonderful works and His goodness to the children of men, the "eighth day," the week of eternity, will begin. The week of eternity has no end. It extends into the fullness of God, world without end, forever and ever.

We have just discussed the four major types of redemption: the seven days of creation; the journey of the Israelites from Egypt to Canaan; the Tabernacle of the Congregation; and the seven Levitical convocations. Next, we are going to apply the seven Levitical convocations to four areas of interpretation. The four areas of interpretation are as follows: (1) the Person and work of the Lord Jesus Christ; (2) the redemption of the believer (of which we have given the general idea in the preceding discussion); (3) the perfecting of the Church; and (4) the setting up of the kingdom of God.

The seven Levitical feasts were grouped into three holy convocations, three annual occasions during which every Israelite man was to present himself before the Lord: (1) Passover, Unleavened Bread, Firstfruits; (2) Pentecost; (3) Trumpets, Day of Atonement, Tabernacles.

III

THE PERSON AND WORK
OF THE LORD JESUS CHRIST

PASSOVER

Of the seven Levitical convocations, the Lord Jesus Christ is seen most clearly in the Passover lamb. "Behold the Lamb of God who takes away the sin of the world." "Christ, our Passover, is sacrificed for us."

In the book of Revelation, Christ is presented as the slain Lamb, and the church is presented as the wife of the Lamb. We eat Him in the communion service, and we drink His precious blood, just as the Jewish family ate the Passover lamb. By faith we sprinkle His blood upon ourselves and upon our households; therefore God passes over us when judgment comes upon the sin in our land.

Christ is our Lamb of protection, and also our atonement, our reconciliation to God, as we eat Him together and drink His blood. The truest meaning of our relationship to Christ and His relationship to us is found in the fact that we partake of Him to the extent of eating Him.

We Christians are related to Christ as student to teacher, as disciple to master, as redeemed to redeemer, as friend to friend. But our fundamental relationship to Him has to do with our eating of Him and the drinking of His precious blood—our receiving Him into our spirit, into our soul, and into our body. Thus we become one with Him in the deepest and fullest sense of the word. Because of this deep and full relationship, the church of Christ is referred to as the wife of the *Lamb*, never as the wife, or bride of Christ, or of the Word, or of the Lion of the tribe of Judah, or of any other aspect of Christ. The church is the wife of the *Lamb* because she has become one with Him through the eating of Him. Christ is our Passover Lamb.

It was during the Passover meal that Jesus said, "This is My body," and "This cup is the new testament in My blood" (see Luke 22). Christ is our Passover Lamb. By faith we eat His body in the communion bread and by faith we drink His blood from the communion cup. While we are taking the communion our minds and hearts go back two thousand years to that dark, and yet gloriously lighted, hour when the Lamb of God was slain. If it were not for the breaking of His body and the shedding of His blood, no person on earth could hope to escape the wrath of an angry God whose laws and ways have been violated outrageously.

Let us eat that bread, and drink that blood, and praise the Lord for His everlasting mercy and His goodness to us.

The Passover lamb was slain in Egypt, that is, in the world. Our Lord Jesus Christ was taken outside the city of Jerusalem and crucified at the hands of Roman soldiers. Revelation 11:8 mentions "the great city, which spiritually is called Sodom and Egypt, where also our Lord was crucified." Both Sodom and Egypt typify the spirit of the age in which we live—the lust of the flesh, the lust of the eyes, the pride of life, abundance of bread, and fullness of idleness. We Christians are to flee from the "City of Destruction," just as did Pilgrim. The world is no friend of Christ. The spirit of this age crucified the Lord Jesus Christ, and that same spirit is going to slay the testimony of the church in the end time. But God will raise up the church into everlasting life.

The convocation of Passover was celebrated on the fourteenth day of *Abib*. Therefore God made *Abib* the chief of the months, the first month of the ecclesiastical year. So it is that our Lord Jesus Christ is the beginning of the redemption of the world. Even the unsaved recognize this fact, such that our calendar is dated from His birth.

The lamb was selected on the tenth of *Abib*, giving the family who chose it an opportunity to examine it for blemishes; for it was not possible to offer a Passover lamb which had a blemish. Christ was observed thoroughly by the common people and by the priests. Yet they could find no blemish. Pilate, the worldly judge, could find no fault in Him. Neither the priests of the church nor the worldly judge could find any blemish, any fault, any cause of blame in Him.

The Passover lamb was not to be undercooked or boiled in water. The lamb was to be roasted with fire. So the Lord Jesus went through the fire of God until there was nothing left in Him that could be affected by judgment. There was no part of Jesus untouched by the fire. Every desire, every ambition, every thought of self, every feeling of sentiment, of the need for vindication, was thoroughly burned out of Christ. Desires, ambitions, thoughts of self, and so on, are not sin. Christ was not tempted by sin. These feelings and attitudes are not unholy, not unrighteous. But neither are they divine gold—they cannot stand the fire with which God baptizes His closest servants. And so everything in Christ was "roast with fire." When Christ arose from death He had been consumed in the fire of God. All of our sins and sicknesses which He bore upon Himself also were consumed in the fire of judgment.

The bitter herbs of the Passover meal speak of the sufferings of Christ in this world. Truly, He suffered more than any man. He was despised and rejected of men; a man of sorrows, and acquainted with grief. The only truly righteous man who ever lived was treated the worst of all—so great is the evil of the spirit of this age.

The true Passover was the one celebrated in Egypt. The Passover meals which have been celebrated each year since are memorials of that first great Passover, when Moses, the man of God, led Israel out of Egypt.

Christ is our Passover Lamb, and also our Moses. His blood was shed and sprinkled upon each person who will receive Him by faith. Just before He comes again, the judgments of God will begin to fall upon the Egypt, speaking symbolically, of this age. Christ will begin to destroy Egypt with mighty plagues; but the Pharaoh of this world, Satan and his followers, will become increasingly hardened. The wrath of Christ will mount in fury until men will cry out for the rocks and mountains to fall upon them and hide them from the anger of the Lamb of God.

Then, in a furious outpouring of judgment, the heavenly Moses will appear to remove His people from the slavery of Egypt. Pharaoh and his servants will fight, and attempt to resist the exodus of his slaves, of the peoples of the earth who have labored in the fire, as it were, in the hopeless bondage in which Satan keeps his subjects. Certainly the peoples of the world drive themselves into anxiety and nervous breakdowns, attempting to reach goals which are always out of reach. Satan is a hard taskmaster.

But for all of those who will sprinkle the blood of God's Lamb upon their lives and upon their own households, the Lord Jesus will appear and take them out from the miserable servitude to the evil lords of darkness. In so doing, the Lord will leave Egypt in a shambles, and the power of Pharaoh (Satan) completely destroyed. The day of redemption from Egypt is yet ahead of us. Once the judgment begins to fall, the church will be protected, just as Israel was protected in the land of Goshen. No matter how the plagues and curses fall, every member of the true Israel of God, the church of Christ, will be covered with the protection of God's Almighty hand. No part of God's wrath will touch the believer who keeps himself under the precious blood of Christ.

What we have just described is the kingdom-wide fulfillment of the exodus from Egypt. There are lesser fulfillments—lesser in the sense of magnitude. Each one of us as individuals has our own "exodus from Egypt," when we accept the Lord Jesus Christ as our Passover Lamb. We come out of the spirit of this age, applying the blood of Christ to our own life and to our household, by faith. We partake of His body and blood with other Christians. But we can look ahead with great thanksgiving and rejoicing to the day of redemption which is ahead of us, when the Lamb of God will appear and bring His people out of Egypt, out of the world; and the god of this world will be utterly destroyed, and not a hand can save him. His end is coming. Hallelujah!

It is interesting to note the many occasions upon which the book of Revelation refers to Christ as the *Lamb.* No doubt this is because His appearing is the counterpart of the exodus of Israel from Egypt; and also because of His oneness with His wife as she partakes of His body and His precious blood. "Behold the Lamb of God," John the Baptist cried, "who takes away the sin of the world!" In the days which are ahead of us, frightful curses and plagues are going to be poured out upon the earth because of the anger of God which dates back to past eons. All people will need the protection of the blood of the Lamb. Let us be faithful in holding up Christ as the Lamb of God who takes away the sin of the world, so that every man, woman, boy, and girl upon the earth can have the opportunity to be sprinkled with the blood of the Lamb. When the destroyer comes through the earth, he will pass over every person who is protected with the blood of Christ.

UNLEAVENED BREAD

Christ is our Unleavened Bread. He came down from the Father without inherited sin. He was without the leaven of sin in His nature. Of all the billions of people who have lived in this world, the only one who was ever born without the power or authority of sin upon His life was Jesus Christ of Nazareth.

His Father was God. Through the power of the Holy Spirit He lived a life completely free of the leaven of sin, and then was offered as a perfect sacrifice to God, His Father. If Christ had ever been guilty of one sin, even one small infraction, He would not have qualified as our Redeemer. Think of that! He would then have died for His own sins only, and we would have had to die for ours. If He had sinned, He Himself would have had to be redeemed. But, thanks be to God! Jesus Christ was totally free of leaven, totally without sin, and so He was able to redeem us.

Christ is the unleavened bread from heaven who gives life unto the world. There is no leaven of sin in Him. He Himself is our feast of Unleavened Bread. During the whole Passover season, which was the Passover plus the seven days of the week of Unleavened Bread, there was to be no leaven at all seen among the hundreds of thousands of Israelites. Anyone found with leaven was to be cut off from among his people. The curse of God was upon him, just for having leaven in his house.

Through this very strict ordinance God was showing us His utter abhorrence of sin. Christ came without sin, without leaven, so that we also can become, through Him, totally free from sin in our spirit, in our soul, and in our body. There is no leaven of sin whatsoever in Christ; and when He is finished with His church, which is His body, there will be no leaven of sin in it either. The body of Christ is destined to be the new Jerusalem, the holy city, the wife of the Lamb without spot or blemish.

The first three acts of redemption, as performed by the Lord Jesus Christ, took place over a short period of time. The Passover, the week of Unleavened Bread, and Firstfruits took place when Jesus was crucified, descended into the realms of the dead, and then rose again. It appears that immediately upon His resurrection from the realms of the dead, Christ came straightway before the Father in heaven, bringing His own precious blood to sprinkle upon and before the mercy seat in heaven. As soon as the true tabernacle in heaven had been cleansed (Heb. 9:23), the fulfillment of the first three convocations in the Person and work of Christ had been completed.

It is interesting to note that the ascension of Christ into heaven forty days later, as recorded in the first chapter of Acts, was not reflected in the Levitical convocations. The reason is that the ascension of Christ was merely a change in location from one place to another. Although much help comes to us as a result of the ascension of Christ into heaven, the ascension is not an integral aspect of the plan of redemption. Resurrection in the redemptive sense means that a person has been brought into death through the judgment of God, and that God has brought the person back into life—into eternal life. The new eternal life cannot die again; it has been refined and sanctified in the sight of God. Resurrection does not take place in us all at once. First comes the spirit; then the soul, part by part; and finally the body. Today, right now, there is some part of your life that God is bringing down to death in order that He might give it to you again in a refined, sanctified state, after He has delivered you from its hold on you. Abraham offering up Isaac, and Shadrach, Meshach, and Abednego in the furnace are types of the death and resurrection of which we are speaking.

Passover, Unleavened Bread, and Firstfruits are one of the major Bible types of the process of death, judgment, and resurrection. But the ascension has no place among these major types because the ascension is a work of power of the kingdom of God rather than one of the aspects of redemption. It is very important for us to remember that the prize toward which we are pressing is not ascension but resurrection. We already have ascension, in a spiritual sense; we already are at the right hand of the Father in Christ Jesus (see Col. 3). What we are pursuing is the resurrection. We are seeking after eternal life; and the route to eternal life is through death and judgment. Only as we allow God to bring down our life into death and judgment are we able to be raised again by God's power and set free from all our bondages.

The Lord Jesus Christ came onto the scene of history in order that He might fulfill, in the kingdom-wide sense, the Passover, Unleavened Bread, and Firstfruits. Christ became the Passover Lamb. He was chosen, slain, and then roasted in the fires of judgment. He is the spotless Lamb of God. Then His body was broken and His blood shed, in order that we might eat and drink thereof and receive eternal life. At the same time, we have protection from the wrath of God when He executes judgment against the gods of this age.

As soon as He had drunk the cup of suffering and death for every man, He died. *It is appointed unto men once to die, and after that the judgment.* At the moment that Christ died the veil of the Temple was torn in two; the earth shook; the rocks were split. It was an awesome happening. Just prior to this, from noon until three in the afternoon, darkness had fallen upon the land. This was the moment in which the Lord God was destroying the authority of the gods of darkness, establishing the legal basis for the redemptive release of the peoples of the earth, and of the earth itself.

There was a period of three days and three nights, according to Jesus (Matt. 12:40), during which Jesus was in the heart of the earth. Jonah, who was in the belly of the great fish, was a type of the Lord while He was in the heart of the earth. Jesus in the heart of the earth was the fulfillment of the week of Unleavened Bread. Passover, Unleavened Bread, and Firstfruits, were on the fourteenth, fifteenth, and sixteenth of *Abib,* with Unleavened Bread lasting for seven days (fifteenth through twenty-first). Church tradition has it that Christ was crucified on Friday, the Passover; lay in the grave on Saturday, which was a high Sabbath because it fell on the first day of Unleavened Bread; and was raised early Sunday morning, being the feast of

Firstfruits. Since this does not give Christ three days and three nights in the cave of Joseph of Arimathea, then one of three things must be true: (1) Christ was speaking symbolically when He referred to three days and three nights; or (2) the days of Passover were extended at that time leaving that many days between His crucifixion and the Sunday of His resurrection; or (3) the descent of Christ into the heart of the earth commenced prior to His actual death upon the cross.

Christ fulfilled the convocation of Unleavened Bread during the time that He was in the heart of the earth. *It is appointed unto men once to die, and after this the judgment.* As soon as Christ died, whether we are speaking of a spiritual separation from the Father which may have commenced in Gethsemane or even before, or whether we are speaking of the separation of His spirit from His body upon the cross, the judgment of God fell upon Him. He had to drink the cup, as repulsive to Him as it was. He was mocked and scorned. His body was abused. He was crucified. Then, bearing the weight of the sins of the world upon Him, He died. What a test of faith this was! Only the faithfulness of God stood between Christ and eternal death.

We understand something of the physical suffering of Christ in those days, because we humans know what it is to suffer in the flesh. But we know little or nothing at all, most of us, of the spiritual anguish which Christ suffered at that time. No person has ever lived who could have sustained one-tenth of that load of spiritual oppression. We will never be able to grasp what the Son of God endured in Gethsemane, because we do not have the spiritual size and strength which Christ has. He bore a load known only to the Father and Himself. An angel strengthened Him in Gethsemane, and perhaps that angel, one day when we are in a better age, can recount to us some small part of the role he played in assisting the Son of God in His hour of terror.

The task of the Son of God during His fulfillment of the

week of Unleavened Bread, that is, during His hours in the heart of the earth, was to drink the cup of judgment on the behalf of all who would be saved through Him. He had to hold steady in faith, keeping Himself as a whole burnt offering unto the Father, until the time came for the Holy Spirit at the word of the Father to lift from Christ's spirit the crushing weight of the sins of the world. If the Son of man had wavered in His faith and obedience, all would have been lost. Christ Himself would have been saved, but we would have been doomed forever. He had to bear the judgment upon every man, for the Word of God had to be fulfilled. Christ bore away our sins into the heart of the earth. The leaven had to be removed from the camp, and it was removed in Christ.

If we read the prayer of Jonah, we may notice that the prayer is a prophecy; it is the Spirit of Christ in Jonah foretelling His sufferings in the heart of the earth.

"And I said, I cried by reason of my affliction unto the Lord, and he heard me; out of the belly of hell cried I, and thou heardest my voice. For thou hadst cast me into the deep, in the midst of the seas; and the floods compassed me about: all thy billows and thy waves passed over me" (Jon. 2:2,3).

Isn't it interesting that the second aspect of salvation always refers back to water? Do you remember the four major types of the second aspect: the dividing of the waters by means of the firmament; the Red Sea; the laver; and Unleavened Bread? Here we have Jonah finding salvation by a firmament (the great fish) placed in the midst of the waters. This is a type of our Lord Jesus Christ in the heart of the earth, dividing the waters of death from the waters of life through means of Himself, He being the firmament of heaven, to speak in a figure. (He divides the waters in our lives, separating our carnality from the spiritual part of us. Isn't it so?)

But continuing in Jonah 2:

"Then I said, I am cast out of thy sight; yet I will look again toward thy holy temple" (Jon. 2:4).

And now we come to the part where Christ reached the climax of His act of redemption, in bearing upon Himself the heavy load of the leaven of sin of this world—your sins and mine, let us never forget that!

"The waters (of judgment) compassed me about, even to the soul: the depth closed me round about, the weeds were wrapped about my head" (Jon. 2:5).

What a picture of Christ in the Garden of Gethsemane! He was going down into the depths of the earth, where the spirits of the dead were being held, awaiting the judgment of God: some unto redemption and salvation; but some unto the resurrection of judgment. The only assurance He had of returning from that dread region was the promise of the Father. Going down into the heart of the earth (if we were not bearing the sins of the world) would be bearable to us humans, because we live so much of the time in darkness anyway. But the suffering which this caused the Word of God from eternity, we will never understand. The closer we get to God, the more the sin and darkness of the world depresses us and gives us pain.

"I went down to the bottoms of the mountains; the earth with her bars was about me for ever: yet hast thou brought up my life from corruption, O Lord my God" (Jon. 2:6).

It was written of Christ that He would not see

corruption. This was true even to the extent that His earthly flesh, which was in repose in the cave of Joseph of Arimathea, was preserved against the day of resurrection and did not experience the ordinary processes of decay and death. All the while that Christ was in the heart of the earth, His flesh remained intact in the cave. Yet, the Spirit of Christ in Jonah was prophesying of the preservation of the whole Person of Christ—spirit, soul, and body.

> "When my soul fainted within me I remembered the Lord: and my prayer came in unto thee, into thine holy temple" (Jon. 2:7).

At some point in the heart of the earth, as Christ went down to the bottoms of the mountains; as the earth with its bars closed about Him; as the floods compassed Him about; as all of the billows and waves of God's judgment passed over Him; at the given moment, the fragrance of righteousness and holiness which came up before the face of the Lord God Almighty reached the degree of propitiation required for the redemption of mankind. God was satisfied. The cup of judgment had been drunk. Through His obedience, Christ had atoned for the disobedience of Adam and of all men. The Father was satisfied.

His great heart of love and unbounded mercy cried out, "It is finished! My Son has wrought redemption in the earth."

The mighty Holy Spirit of God, watching the scene intently, waiting for the judgment of the Father, flowed down to the heart of the earth. There the Holy Spirit found Christ abiding in hope and trust, with the depth closed round about Him, the "weeds" of utter futility and loss of all things wrapped about His head. Satan, other lords and dignitaries of the fallen angels, and the host of foul demon hordes were breathing out upon Him the foul odors of their obscenities. He had been the crown of heaven, the jewel of the ivory palaces, the light and joy of the Father and of the holy angels. Now there was nothing left but the tender mercies of fallen angels and filthy spirits. Their tender mercies are sharper and more ugly than the most hideous of the nightmares which pierce men until they scream out in the night.

In this blackness of darkness the fullness of the glory of God entered into the Lord Jesus Christ and clothed Him about with heavenly Light. The legions of uncleanness fell back in dismay and terror. The nightmare was over. The Son of God, and Son of man, too, let us remember, was filled with unconquerable power. The significance of that moment for Christ Himself, or all people past and present, and for the elect angels will not be known to us in its entirety until we have had a few thousand years to think about it.

None of us has ever been brought so low, and none of us will ever be brought that high—although Christ has invited us to sit with Him upon His throne in glory. In that supreme moment Christ was changed from the most defeated of all men to the one Person in the universe, under God, with all power and authority in heaven and upon the earth. Can you imagine what it would be like to have total power, not only over the heavens and the earth, and over all creatures, human and angelic, but also over the past, present, and future? Hopefully, the Holy Spirit will bring us to the place of maturity where we can begin to grasp the breadth, the length, the depth, and the height, and to begin to know the love of Christ.

Satan and his followers were completely finished at that point, and the subsequent history of the earth—although it appears that Satan is still in control—is only the inevitable working out of the total victory which was obtained at that moment in the heart of the earth. The leaven had been removed from the creation. The sting of death is sin, and the sin has been removed.

The Man of God, now in possession of all persons and

things, moved out quickly, issuing commands to the legions of heaven, those angels who excel in strength doing the will of God. Christ went to the place where the multitude of people had been confined since the time that God destroyed the earth in the days of Noah. Christ brought the good news of the kingdom of God, in order that those people might have the opportunity to hear and believe.

The great moment was at hand now, and Christ felt the word of the Father directing Him to take up His body, just as Christ had promised His hearers that He would do this when the three days had been completed. Christ stepped back into His body. Eternal life came into that flesh which had been so tired trudging faithfully along the dusty paths of the land of promise, and treated so shamefully by the Jews and the Romans. The whole Man now stood up, leaving the grave-clothes neatly in place—He was returning the borrowed tomb of Joseph of Arimathea in the same condition in which He had found it.

Christ walked to the massive stone which sealed off the tomb. An angel rolled the stone away; not that Christ had need of that, but it gave a note of propriety to the situation. Also, it was God's will that the disciples go inside and bring back to us the report of that which they saw.

The promise of the Father to Christ (Ps. 2:8) is that He will receive the heathen for His inheritance and the uttermost parts of the earth for His possession.

Who did God pick to be the person who would be the first to see the Master of earth and sea and sky? Mary! Why Mary?

What a moment this was for Christ! What a moment this was for Mary! Will there ever again be a similar event? In this scene is contained the whole story of redemption. God did not choose one of the apostles, delegated by the other apostles, to be the first to see Christ, as we might have done, making it an ecclesiastical event. We might have picked Peter, or maybe John. Why Mary?

Mary represented all of that for which Christ had died. The story of redemption is not one of ecclesiasticism, plans, programs, theology, what have you. It is a love story, a romance, if you will (we are not speaking after the flesh, please understand). The story of redemption is a song, a love song, a winning of a bride. Christ loves people. He has friends. He is not primarily the founder of a new sect, a new organization. He is a Person who is interested in and loves other people. He has so much power and resource that His main interest is in us ourselves rather than in what we are going to do for Him.

All of the previous workings, commandments, and ordinances of God had been means to an end. The end is the Man, coming out of death in the fullness of glory and victory, to take to Himself the promise of His Father. Do you know why God chose Mary to be the one to greet the Lord? The answer is simple: she loved Him. God wanted His Son met with love at the point of His greatest triumph. Mary represents all of us who love the Lord Jesus.

Isn't it great that God is this way? The story of Jesus Christ is the greatest story ever told, and it is a love story. After we get through this miserable wilderness, with its complications and endless problems, we are going to find that the end of the matter is that Jesus loves us and will bring us to the place where we can be with Him. It is because He loves us, nothing more, nothing less. It is simply that!

When Christ stepped into His fleshly body, and His body was changed, the feast of Firstfruits was fulfilled in the Person of Christ. He is the firstborn from the dead, the beginning of the harvest of the earth. Because God has received Him, the entire harvest in Him is already sanctified—set apart unto God, and holy.

Many bodies of the saints which slept arose and came out of the graves after the resurrection of Jesus, and appeared to many people. These also were a type of the firstfruits unto the Lord.

We see, then, that in three glorious days and nights the Lord Jesus fulfilled in His own Person the Passover, Unleavened Bread, and Firstfruits.

It is interesting that He spent forty days somewhere, after His resurrection from among the dead, before He ascended into heaven—ten days before Pentecost. What did Christ do during these forty days? The Bible does not say. The thought has crossed our mind that He may have spent those days going through the earth and looking over His property. It may be recalled that Satan had tempted Him by showing Him the kingdoms of the earth and the glory of them. But the obedient Christ would have none of Satan's rebellion and disobedience against God. Now, the Father may have given Christ the opportunity to go to those same kingdoms, to see their glory, with the realization that they all belonged to Him. In the Father's time He would descend to claim them for His own. In the meantime, the body of Christ had to be created, so that Christ could be greatly enlarged in His glory. Those forty days were a vacation and rest for the Man who had been so faithful, so successful in His pleasing of the Father.

Can't you just imagine the Lord relaxing by the Mediterranean; enjoying the beauties of the snow at the poles of the earth without feeling the cold; looking at and enjoying the peoples of the remote areas of the earth; realizing that all this was now His? Haven't you found that when the Lord brings us through particularly trying times that He gives us a bit of rest and relaxation? Perhaps this took place for the Lord Jesus during those forty days. I hope so.

FIRSTFRUITS

Jesus Christ Himself is the firstfruits of the entire creation of God.

"And unto the angel of the church of the Laodiceans

write; These things saith the Amen, the faithful and true witness, the beginning of the creation of God" (Rev. 3:14).

All things are being made new in Christ Jesus. All things begin and end in Christ, and are of Him and through Him.

"I am Alpha and Omega, the beginning and the ending, saith the Lord, who is, and which was, and which is to come, the Almighty" (Rev. 1:8).

He is first in all things:

"Who is the image of the invisible God, the firstborn of every creature: for by him were all things created, that are in heaven, and that are in earth, visible and invisible, whether they be thrones, or dominions, or principalities, or powers: all things were created by him, and for him: and he is before all things, and by him all things consist: and he is the head of the body, the church: who is the beginning, the firstborn from the dead; that in all things he might have the preeminence" (Col. 1:15-18).

The church is referred to as the "church of the firstborn":

"To the general assembly and church of the firstborn, which are written in heaven, and to God the Judge of all, and to the spirits of just men made perfect" (Heb. 12:23).

The Lord Jesus Christ is the first-begotten of the sons of God:

"And again, when he bringeth in the first-begotten into the world, he saith, And let all the angels of God worship him" (Heb. 1:6).

Jesus Christ is the first-born of many brothers:

> "For whom he did foreknow, he also did predestinate to be conformed to the image of his Son, that he might be the firstborn among many brethrens" (Rom. 8:29).

Jesus was declared to be the Son of God, by the resurrection from the dead. Christ is particularly preeminent in the resurrection, being the first-begotten from the dead.

> "And from Jesus Christ, who is the faithful witness, and the first-begotten of the dead, and the prince of the kings of the earth. Unto him that loved us, and washed us from our sins in his own blood" (Rev. 1:5).

Death, judgment, and resurrection is the program through means of which God is bringing to an end His first creation. Sin at some point in ages past was found in heaven, and from that time on God resolved to bring to an end His creation and to make all things new. Heaven itself is going to be made new. When Jesus Christ walked out of the borrowed tomb belonging to Joseph of Arimathea and spoke eternal words to the weeping Mary, He was the first Person in the making of all things new. What Mary beheld was something which can never be witnessed again in quite the same way: the *Alpha* of God's new universe.

The importance and significance of the resurrection of Christ cannot be overestimated or overstated:

> "But now is Christ risen from the dead, and become the firstfruits of them who slept. For since by man came death, by man came also the resurrection of the dead. For as in Adam all die, even so in Christ shall all be made alive. But every man in his own order: Christ the firstfruits; afterward they that are Christ's at his coming" (I Cor. 15:20-23).

The concept of the firstfruits is that if God will accept the waving of the first sheaf of the barley harvest, or the two loaves of Pentecost, then the entire balance of the harvest is sanctified. The firstfruits represents the whole harvest. God understands this, and by accepting the firstfruits He signifies His acceptance of the whole.

> "For if the firstfruit be holy, the lump is also holy: and if the root be holy, so are the branches" (Rom. 11:16).

Because Christ has been accepted so completely, every person who abides in Him and becomes part of Him receives total acceptance. He, the firstfruits of the harvest, represents us. What He is, *we are* in the mind of God. God has received us in Christ.

Our resurrection is tied to His. He arose, and we arose in Him. He ascended, and we ascended in Him. He is the firstfruits, and we are the balance of the harvest.

Christ fulfilled the Passover in His crucifixion. He fulfilled the week of Unleavened Bread in bearing upon Himself the sin of the world into the heart of the earth, thus removing leaven from the lives of those who will accept Him.

Then, the mighty Son of God fulfilled the convocation of Firstfruits by returning to His body and coming forth from the tomb. These three convocations typify the redemption of the peoples of the earth, and of the earth itself. They portray *salvation* in our usual usage of the term. Thus the first three days of creation, so to speak, were fulfilled in the crucifixion, descent into the heart of the earth, and resurrection from the dead of the Lord Jesus Christ.

It is interesting to note that on the third day of creation the "dry land" appeared. Christ is the first appearance of "land" in the new creation of God. The "seas" (turbulence of life) were gathered together, and Christ appeared in the midst as the foundation upon which all men must build.

Also on the third day of creation, vegetation and fruit

trees appeared for the first time. We see in these first signs of life the Lord Jesus Christ. He is the beginning of life. He also is the tree of life, the eating of whom brings eternal life to those who were dead in sin.

The third piece of the holy furnishings of the Tabernacle was the table of showbread. The table of showbread portrays the body and blood (there were cups of wine on the table) of Christ. The body and blood of Christ enters into us as the beginning of life. The "dry land" of Christ appears in us, as the swirling waters of the turbulence of our life part and the firm ground of Christ appears in us. We are born again through means of our partaking of Him. He is born in us. He, the firstfruits of God's new work, becomes the firstfruits of our new personality. "If any man be in Christ there is a new creation. Old things have passed away. Behold, all things have become new, and all things are of God" (see 2 Cor. 5:17).

All things are measured from the Lord Jesus. Every structure, every institution, every military engagement or business venture—whatever is built, in other words—must have a reference point. There must be a cornerstone, an anchor, a standard, a fixed point which is true and immovable; and then everything which is built is referred back to that point which was set originally. Otherwise, the builder can get into serious trouble in the whole undertaking because there is lack of alignment, unity, and integrity in that which has been put together. It is subject to collapse. Christ Himself is our cornerstone, our anchor, our fixed point, our perfect standard. When we get in trouble we draw back to our original position in Him.

God has set Christ first and has made Him absolutely perfect. Christ has overcome the world. Through His obedience we have been made righteous. God has founded all of His efforts upon Christ. Christ is the beginning, the first-born of every creature, the *Alpha*. He is also the ending, the *Omega*. All things originate in Him, refer back to Him, and will conclude in Him.

God's restoration of the heavens and the earth rests solidly upon Christ as upon a mountain of rock, an immovable foundation established so firmly and securely that no power in heaven or upon the earth can budge it in any manner whatever. He is perfect, true, faithful, without sin, absolutely holy. The heart of the Father abides in undisturbed contentment in His beloved Son because the Son meets every requirement of the Father. No other person could come close to meeting every requirement of the Father. But Christ has done it, and always pleases the Father.

Therefore, Christ is our firstfruits, the firstfruits of the harvest of the earth. When Christ died upon the cross He did not say, "I am finished"; He said, "It is finished." Every person and every thing in the entire universe of God was finished when Christ expired, with the exception of Christ Himself. He rose from the dead, the firstfruits of the church and of all peoples upon the earth. From now on, every person and thing in heaven and upon the earth must be measured from Him. He is God's benchmark, God's standard. That which is not measured from Christ will be shaken, removed, and destroyed.

PENTECOST

Christ Himself is the fulfillment of the convocation of Pentecost. The word *Christ (Messiah)* means *anointed with oil.* The Lord Jesus was anointed with the oil of the Holy Spirit by the Father, signifying that He is to serve as King and High Priest before God. In the Old Testament we find that the priests and the vessels of the Tabernacle of the Congregation were anointed with the holy oil. Also, it was the custom to anoint a new king upon his installation to office. The Lord Jesus is the One who has the seven Spirits of God—He has the Spirit of God without measure. Through means of this total anointing God has established the Lord Jesus as Christ the King and Priest whom God has chosen above His fellows.

The Lord Jesus is the fulfillment of the lampstand of the Tabernacle of the Congregation. Through Christ (Messiah) the Spirit of God brings the revelation of God among men. He is the light of the world. One of the main purposes of the hundreds of years which have passed since the resurrection of Christ is the creating and building up of the body of Christ, the fullness of Messiah. The Lord Jesus is the head of Messiah, the anointed Deliverer. But, through means of our partaking of His broken body and precious blood, we Christians are being built up into the body of Messiah, thus greatly enlarging the presence of the Lord Jesus Christ. He is in us, and therefore we are the enlargement of Him, the "fulness of him that filleth all in all" (Eph. 1:23).

When the Lord Jesus stood before John the Baptist, the Spirit of God came down like a dove upon Him. The Spirit of God has never come down to rest as a dove upon anyone other than the Lord Jesus. When the Holy Spirit came down upon the disciples, fifty days after the resurrection of Christ, the Spirit was not in the form of a dove but rather in the form of flames of fire. The reason for the difference is that the peace of God is in Christ, since Christ is without sin; therefore the Holy Spirit can rest gently upon Him. But the Holy Spirit comes down as fire upon the church, because the church has sin and must still undergo the judgment of God.

When Jesus stood up in the synagogue to read, He opened the scroll of Isaiah to the most pointed reference to Messiah in the whole Old Testament. Today we refer to the section as Chapter 61. He began to read:

> "The Spirit of the Lord God is upon me; because the Lord hath anointed me to preach good tidings unto the meek; he hath sent me to bind up the broken-hearted, to proclaim liberty to the captives, and the opening of the prison to them who are bound" (Isa. 61:1).

"This day," He said, "this Scripture is fulfilled in your ears." The anointing of God rests upon Jesus as upon no other person, because He loves righteousness and hates iniquity.

Christ is the anointed Deliverer (Messiah) who is to deliver Israel; who is to sit upon the throne of David, and set up the kingdom of God in the earth. The Jews expect Messiah to restore the glory of the kingdoms of David and Solomon. If a Jew will read the fifty-third chapter of Isaiah carefully, he will find that Messiah must first come as a man of sorrows, and be wounded for our transgressions and bruised for our iniquities. When Messiah comes the second time, then He will come as King of kings and Lord of lords, and will establish His kingdom in visible power and glory in the earth.

The most important ceremony of the Levitical convocation of Pentecost was the waving of the two large loaves of bread before the Lord. The bread was baked from the finest of flour, and signaled the completion of the harvesting of wheat. The number *two* in Scripture stands for *power.* Pentecost is the feast of *power.* The double portion of the Holy Spirit of God rested upon Christ, giving Him power over men and over unclean spirits. Christ was the finest of the flour of the wheat harvest, so to speak, baked into a loaf and waved before the Lord, speaking of His total consecration and sanctification. The fact that there were *two* loaves speaks of the multiplication of Christ through His body; also of the fact that the fullness of the power of Almighty God rests upon Him. The testimony of Christ always must be accomplished through the power of the Holy Spirit. "Ye shall receive power, after that the Holy Ghost is come upon you: and ye shall be witnesses unto me" (Acts 1:8). Where Christ is there is power to release people from the bondage of Satan, in spirit, soul, and body.

So total and complete was the fullness of the Holy Spirit upon the Lord Jesus that it was impossible for the disciples to receive the Spirit themselves. They had to wait until Jesus ascended to the Father before the Spirit who abode upon Jesus could be poured out upon His disciples. When the Lord took of the Spirit which was upon Moses and gave it to the seventy elders, they "prophesied, and did not cease" (Num. 11:25). When the Holy Spirit came from Jesus down to the waiting disciples, they also prophesied and did not cease. When we Christians get enough of the Holy Spirit we will prophesy and not cease.

Christ is the fullness of the Holy Spirit in bodily form, and He lived among men. Now He has ascended to the Father, and the Holy Spirit has been shed abroad upon all who receive the atonement made through the blood of God's Lamb, and who enter into the water of baptism in His name. By the one Holy Spirit we all are baptized into the body of Christ.

The convocation of Pentecost is associated with the giving of the Law upon Mount Sinai. It is believed that the first date of Pentecost, that is, the fiftieth day counting from the sixteenth of the month *Abib* during which Israel came out of Egypt, was the very day upon which God gave Moses the Ten Commandments. Of course, the Levitical convocation of Pentecost could not be observed at that time because Israel was in the wilderness and had no wheat to harvest. Therefore, it is believed that God gave the Law as an observance of the date. To this day the Jews associate the giving of the Law with the convocation of Pentecost. Pentecost is known to Jews as "The Season of the Giving of the Law," and the birthday of Judaism, because Judaism is founded upon the giving of the Law.

Interestingly enough, the new covenant fulfillment of Pentecost, as recorded in the book of Acts, marks the birthday of the Christian church. Although the fact is not always stressed, the giving of the Holy Spirit to the Christian church is the giving of God's law to the Christian church. The Holy Spirit is the law of the Spirit of life in Christ Jesus. It is God's will that each and every Christian walk in the strictest obedience to the Holy Spirit. The Holy Spirit is the Christian counterpart of the law of Moses.

Nowhere is the association between the Holy Spirit and the law of God seen more clearly than in the Person of the Lord Jesus Christ. Christ observed perfectly every last jot and tittle of the law of Moses, and also every particle of the law of the Spirit of life. The law of the Spirit is the law of the kingdom of God, which can be kept only through the ability which the Spirit Himself gives. It is much more penetrating and demanding than the law of Moses, as anyone can observe by reading the fifth through seventh chapters of the Gospel of Matthew. Anyone who entertains lust in his heart toward a member of the opposite sex is guilty of adultery, whereas the law of Moses dealt only with the act itself.

Jesus Christ lived a holy, righteous, blameless life. He did so in the power and wisdom of the Holy Spirit of God. He therefore is the perfect fulfillment of the giving of the Law upon Sinai. The Holy Spirit is the *Holy* Spirit, and He always leads into holiness. The new Jerusalem is the *holy* city. The new Jerusalem will be the perfect fulfillment of the law of God. The beauty of holiness is the measure of God's law filled to the brim. Christ lives in the beauty of holiness.

Pentecost, as we said earlier, is to be a season of rejoicing. There is great joy and happiness associated with the Lord Jesus Christ. No doubt there have been few men who have had to live with the continual obstinance and perversity which He endured continually, and no man has ever had to bear the load of responsibility and oppression which was borne by Christ. He lived with the cross always before His face. Yet, there is a tremendous joy about the Lord Jesus.

Jesus was a man of happiness, peace, joy, contentment. To be around Him was always a thrill, a time of uplift and delight. Have you ever noticed that when He draws near to you in these days that His coming is always with joy and blessing? It is true that we are called upon to endure hardness as good soldiers of Jesus Christ, but these tribulations are as nothing when He is around. Christ is God's joy, God's song, God's season of rejoicing in the earth. Sin is always accompanied sooner or later by gloom, despair, and the piercing pangs of remorse and grief. But the Lord Jesus is always accompanied by uplifting joy, a song of the soul and spirit that lifts us up until we are walking in days of heaven upon the earth.

The Lord Jesus is our joy. He breaks every chain that keeps us down. In Him we mount up and soar with eagle's wings; we walk with hind's feet. In the darkest of night, on the stormiest and deepest of turbulent waters, we dance on, singing in happy trust, skipping toward the city that radiates light in a rainbow of heavenly colors.

TRUMPETS

The Lord Jesus Christ is the trumpet of God. Through Christ, God has announced His purposes in the earth. Men see their sins, because in Christ God has sounded the trumpet of the Divine warfare against unclean spirits. Christ is the King of the kingdom of God, the Commander of the armies of heaven. He is the Lord of hosts, that is, the Lord of the mighty armies of angels who excel in strength, doing the will of God. When Christ moves, the whole camp of Israel moves. He announces the presence and will of the ancient of days, His Father, who is revered and blessed by all.

The coming of Christ has announced the coming of the kingdom of God to the earth, and also the coming of the day of judgment. Men can never claim to be ignorant of the will of God once they have seen the works of Christ and have heard His Word. God has revealed His will through the Lord Jesus.

The coming of Christ has announced the coming of the millennial jubilee, in which all men who obey God will be able to be redeemed and return to their inheritance in the earth. Christ is the trumpet of God. He is drawing near to the earth in the days in which we live and is warning us to prepare for the coming conflict of the ages, the great flowering of sin in the earth and the abundance of the hideous fruit thereof. Christ is telling us also, in these days, that through Him there is abundant power and provision so that we will be able to stand, and stand in abundance and glory, no matter what develops in the earth.

Christ is the Day Star (II Pet. 1:19). He rises in our hearts, proclaiming the day of the Lord, the millennium, which is just over the horizon.

The *trumpet* is found in the Bible in a variety of usages. One of the primary associations of the trumpet in Scripture is with war. The trumpet must give a certain sound, and then we can prepare ourself for the battle, Paul teaches. (See I Cor. 14.)

We are sick of war in these days, but we Christians are just now getting ready for the greatest war of all—the dispossession of Satan and his hordes from the earth. During the last several hundred years of church history, God may have not raised the question of His war, to any great extent. But in the days which are ahead of the church, one of the predominant burdens of the Holy Spirit will continue to be that of war. It is only through war that the Lord Jesus Christ can come into His inheritance in the earth. At the present time, the Lord Jesus is waiting until His enemies be made His footstool.

The contrast between the Twenty-third and the Twenty-fourth Psalms shows two important aspects of the personality of the Lord Jesus. In the familiar Twenty-third Psalm, we see the Lord as the gentle Shepherd who leads His lambs beside the still waters. If we have never learned to know the good Shepherd, if we have never followed Him through the valley of the shadow of death, nor had Him lead us beside the still waters or prepare a table for us in the midst of our enemies, then we have not been made ready for His revelation to us in the Twenty-fourth Psalm.

In the Twenty-third Psalm Christ is our heavenly Moses. He, the Shepherd of the flock, leads us through the wilderness. But Moses can never lead us across Jordan and into the land of promise. That takes Joshua! And so, in the Twenty-fourth Psalm, Christ comes to us as Joshua.

The Twenty-fourth Psalm starts out with reference to the earth, because the kingdom of God is to be set up in the earth. Christ has come in the anointing of the Holy Spirit to break the bondage of sin and death in the earth. The creation awaits His revealing so that the creation itself may be brought into the glorious liberty of the children of God (see Rom. 8).

Then, the psalm goes into the question of sin. Today, as the Holy Spirit brings to us the good news of the coming kingdom of God, and the fact of its being set up in the earth, the central issues becomes one of sin and righteousness. It is impossible to ascend into the holy hill of Zion, the fortress of God, with unclean hands and an impure heart. The issue today is that of holiness and righteousness, through the enabling power and wisdom of the Holy Spirit.

As soon as we receive the blessing which comes as a result of cleanness of hands and purity of heart, then we are ready to lift up the everlasting doors of our heart to the Lord. And how does He come into us? As the good Shepherd? Not at all! He comes into us as the Lord of armies; as the Lord, strong and mighty in battle; as the King of glory.

When the trumpet is blown, in the sequence of the Levitical convocations, it announces the new year of doing business with God. That is why the Twenty-fourth Psalm commences with a reference to the earth. The convocation of Trumpets is always followed by the Day of Atonement. That is why the Twenty-fourth Psalm immediately gets into the issue of sin, which is the issue of the Day of Atonement.

As soon as the sin has been pardoned—the warfare has been accomplished—the next convocation is Tabernacles. Therefore, the Twenty-fourth Psalm goes directly to the abiding of God in His people. But He comes as the Man of war, because as soon as the heart of the saint has been made pure, then it is the Lord's intention to enter into the pure heart, setting up His fortress. And from here He will go forth to battle against the power of Satan in the earth. This battle will continue until every breath that is drawn in the earth will be breathing the praises of Christ Jesus, the Son of God. Unto Him every knee shall bow, and every tongue shall confess that Jesus Christ is Lord, to the glory of God the Father.

We have known the Lord Jesus as the good Shepherd. Now it is time to learn of Him as the Lord of hosts, the Commander of the armies of God. There is a warfare to be accomplished before peace can be established in the earth. There is a warfare to be accomplished before peace, dear reader, can be accomplished in my heart and your heart!

The Lord of hosts is going to descend from heaven with a shout, with a word of command, with the voice of a chief angel, and with a trumpet of God. This is the kingdom-wide fulfillment of the convocation of Trumpets. Paul informs us that we shall be changed during the last trumpet. The word *last* implies that there are trumpets which precede the trumpet which announces our change and the raising of the dead into incorruptibility (I Cor. 15:52). And so there are! There are, in fact, seven trumpets.

The seven trumpets commence in the eighth chapter of Revelation, and we are raised during the seventh, as Paul says. We find in Revelation 8 that the altar of incense is associated with the sounding of the seven trumpets. The reader may recall that the altar of incense is number five of the seven holy furnishings of the Tabernacle of the Congregation; the convocation of Trumpets is number five of the seven Levitical convocations. The number *five* is the number of *beginnings.* The last kingdom-wide act of God was the outpouring of the Holy Spirit on the day of Pentecost, as recorded in Acts 2. Pentecost is convocation number *four,* and four is the number of God's communication toward men—His light. But *five* represents the beginnings of God, and, in this case, the advent of the Lord of hosts who is going to establish the kingdom of God in the earth.

When the "seventh seal" was opened (Rev. 8:1), the seals being the concealing of the wisdom and purposes of God, there was silence in heaven for about thirty minutes. This silence results from the solemnity and enormity of the occasion; because that which is about to happen is the beginning of day of the Lord—that great day which struck terror into the unclean spirits whenever Jesus approached. It is the day of which the prophets spoke.

The seven angels were given seven trumpets. Then, still another angel came and began to minister at the altar of incense which stands before the throne of God Almighty in heaven. It is interesting that an angel should minister here, because the offering of incense in the Tabernacle of the Congregation was one of the most important and distinguishing acts of the high priest of Israel.

The ministering angel was given "much incense." The holy incense of the Tabernacle was compounded from stacte, onycha, galbanum, and frankincense, the whole tempered or seasoned together with salt. This incense typifies the very essence of Christ who is the substance of God. When some of the holy incense was poured upon the glowing coals in the altar of incense, the holy perfume billowed forth in the face of the holy One of Israel who dwelled between the cherubim covering the mercy seat.

The ministering angel held a golden censer (a pan for holding hot coals) in his hand. He poured the holy incense over the coals. Then the angel brought the prayers of all saints mingled with the holy perfume and offered the mixture before God Almighty. This mixture represents the essence of Christ mingled with the supplications and thanksgivings of the saints.

Before the face of the Almighty come two things: the fragrance of His beloved Son and the fervent supplication, "Your kingdom come, Your will be done in earth as it is in heaven." The bride is calling, "Come, Lord Jesus!" God hears the pleas of His holy ones; He "smells" the fragrance of His beloved Son. The opening of the seals has caused such trouble in the earth that the prayers of God's saints have grown in strength and insistence. The nature of Christ has been "beaten into" and "salted together" with the personalities of the saints.

The combination of the supplications, pleas, intercessions, praises, adorations, mingled together with the fragrance of His beloved Son reaches the level at which the Father is compelled in His boundless love to act. He gives the awful *word.* He authorizes the blowing of the seven trumpets, the last of which will change the bodies of the saints and bring them into perfect union with the Lord Jesus. The end of all things is now at hand. The mighty Lord of hosts, the Lord Jesus Christ, stands before the everlasting doors. The kingdoms of this world are about to become the kingdoms of our Lord and of His Christ.

Then the ministering angel filled the censer with fire from the altar of the God of the whole earth, and cast it into the earth. The result was "voices, and thunderings, and lightnings, and an earthquake" (Rev. 8:5). The seven angels lifted up their trumpets. The first angel sounded, and the result was terrible destruction upon the earth. This is the beginning of the plagues upon Egypt, so to speak. By the time the last angel sounds, Egypt (the spirit of this age) will be reeling under the destruction which comes from the hand of the Lord God. Then will come the great kingdom-wide exodus of Israel (the seed of Abraham, those who are in Christ) from the bondage of Pharaoh, to speak in a figure.

The fire which the ministering angel casts into the earth does two things: it brings forth the holy perfume of Christ from the saints who are in the earth; it also causes judgment and destruction upon sinners in the earth. It is always true that God's fire brings forth righteousness and blessing to the saints, and destruction and death to those who hate God. The same fire which burned up Nebuchadnezzar's mighty men burned the bonds of Shadrach, Meshach, and Abednego. The jawbone of Samson slew the enemies of Israel, but provided refreshing for Samson. The same cloud which protected the fleeing Israelites confused the Egyptians. The same waters which buoyed up Noah and his household killed every other living thing upon the earth. The saint who is walking in Christ Jesus will find only profit in the fire of God, the fire which comes from His altar in heaven. But that same fire is terror and judgment to the enemies of the Lord.

God's saints never have been, are not now, nor will they ever be, destroyed by the wrath of God. But the saints very often have to go through the fire of God. In fact, we must be baptized with fire. The fire of God is a good thing, no matter how much it may seem to hurt us. Children scream with fright when mother comes with the iodine, or the doctor with a shot. But these are temporary hurts which are administered in love. We saints have to be vaccinated with fire until we become fireproof. But the same fire is destruction and eternal death to those who are dwelling in sin. The mercy of God brought Israel into the land of milk and honey, and at the same time killed the Canaanites. That is the way it has to be when there are enemies and rebels against the truth of God.

Notice in the following verses from Psalm 136 how the mercy of God appears when seen from the point of view of God's enemies:

"To him that smote Egypt in their firstborn: for his mercy endureth for ever. . . .

But overthrew Pharaoh and his host in the Red sea: for his mercy endureth for ever. . . .

To him which smote great kings: for his mercy endureth for ever: and slew famous kings: for his mercy endureth for ever:

Sihon king of the Amorites: for his mercy endureth for

ever: and Og the king of Bashan: for his mercy endureth for ever" (vs. 10,15,17-20).

We see, then, that the fire from the altar of God brings voices, thunderings, lightnings, and an earthquake. There will be two kinds of voices: one preaching the gospel of Christ with unprecedented power, and the other advocating the rule of the wisdom of mankind. It is so even now. When the judgment of God hits our life there are two voices in us: one tells us to put our faith and trust in the Word of God; the other voice counsels us to flee from God and take our chances with the world. Also, there comes into our own lives "thunderings, and lightnings, and an earthquake." Isn't it so? Everything in our life that can be shaken is shaken and removed, and only the work of Christ stands. But to the works of Satan, unclean spirits, the spirit of this age, and our own flesh, the voices, thunderings, lightnings, and the earthquake create confusion and a tearing down of what has been built up.

The coming down of the fire of God into the earth is the beginning of the end for the works of iniquity. The seven trumpets will sound, one at a time. During the sounding of the last trumpet, the Lord Jesus will descend with a word of summons, with the voice of a chief angel. "Come up here," the Lord will command. And we will be caught away in clouds to meet the Lord in the air and shall be with Him evermore. Then will be poured out upon the inhabitants of the earth the frightful wrath of God which has been reserved unto this day.

The seventh angel sounds the trumpet which heralds the coming of that most solemn of all days, the Day of Atonement!

DAY OF ATONEMENT

Next to the Passover, Christ is seen most clearly in the

Day of Atonement. First of all, He is our great High Priest. He entered past the veil and stood before the holy of holies. Unlike the high priest of Israel, Christ did not offer the blood of a young bull for Himself and His household, and then the blood of a goat for the sins of the rest of the people of Israel. Christ entered into heaven itself, and with His own precious blood, through the eternal Spirit, purified the holy furnishings of the true tabernacle of God in heaven. The heavenly things were purified through means of the sprinkling of His own blood. It was not possible that the blood of young bulls and of goats should take away sins. But through the offering of the body and blood of Jesus Christ we have been made holy forever, provided we truly apprehend the grace of God, and do not neglect our salvation.

Without the shedding of blood there is no remission, no cancellation, of sin. Life must go for life. Through the blood of Christ, and only through His blood, has the mortgage which Satan holds on us been paid. Christ's blood has now been sprinkled before the Father, atonement has been made, and it is sufficient for every man, woman, boy, and girl upon the face of the earth if they will just accept it. The authority and guilt of sin was destroyed by the blood of Christ, and now Jesus holds the keys of hell and death. He, and only He, has the power and authority. He is the eternal judge whom God has appointed. When Christ declares us guiltless and legally free from the kingdom of darkness, it is His precious blood which backs up the declaration. God has said that the blood of Christ has paid the price. There is no other payment which God will accept for our sins.

During the Day of Atonement the iniquities of Israel were confessed by the high priest and put upon the head of a living goat. The living goat was then sent away, by the hand of a waiting and prepared man, into the wilderness. So Christ, who knew no sin, became sin for us and was led away out from the nation of Israel, bearing our iniquities upon Himself. He was then made to suffer the death of the cross, the turning away of the face of the Father, and the mockeries of the unclean spirits of hell. Christ was burdened beneath the indescribable burden of the sins of mankind. He carried them away into the heart of the earth. He became our scapegoat, and thus our sins of unrighteous and unholy attitude and conduct were separated from us.

Thanks be to God! That part of Christ's suffering is finished. Now it is up to human beings to please God and Christ by taking advantage of God's unspeakably great gift and accept the atonement which Christ has made for us. How foolish a person would be to throw away this opportunity for reconciliation with God. The price has been fully paid for each one of us. Now we have only to accept our redemption and to enter into eternal salvation.

On the sixth day of creation, God made man in His own image; male and female made He them. Adam was in the image of God, and was fashioned from the dust of the ground. Eve was fashioned from the substance of the man, and was made for him, being herself in the image of God. Adam and Eve, taken together, are the "man" whom God made in His image.

Christ, the second Adam, is the only person who ever appeared on earth in the full image of God. Adam indeed was a very rough and immature image of the living God. But Christ was in His express image. The church, the bride of Christ, is being fashioned from the substance of Christ, and is being made for Him. The members of the body of Christ are themselves, as individuals, in the image of God. Christ and His wife, taken together, are the complete fulfillment of the declaration of the sixth day: "Let us make man in our image."

In the Day of Atonement, Christ ministers as the great counterpart of Joshua. He brings His followers through Jordan, that is, through the final death to self and the desires of self that is required for spiritual warfare. Each member of the body of Christ must go through a new circumcision of the heart, because the war of God against His enemies requires absolute holiness and sanctification on the part of each member of His army.

Christ at Calvary paid the price of redemption; He paid the mortgage. But Satan will not release his prisoners. Therefore the mighty Christ will go forth as the Lord of hosts to take His inheritance by force. The battle will be joined, and every spirit in the earth that resists the rule of Christ will be destroyed. This is the day of redemption, of which Christ spoke. Redemption is past, in the sense that we were legally absolved at Calvary. But redemption is yet ahead of us in the making alive of the mortal body. Also, we are to go forth and release the natural creation from the curse of sin. That is the destiny of the church of Christ. It is going to be a battle, because the wicked inhabitants of our land of promise, speaking symbolically of Satan's control of the earth, must be overcome through the force of the Spirit of God. Reader, do you have a heart to fight? That is what it is going to take if we are to follow Christ Jesus in the conquest of the earth.

The Ark of the Covenant was the sixth of the holy furnishings of the Tabernacle of the Congregation. The Ark of the Covenant represents the Lord Jesus Christ as the Commander-in-chief of the hosts of heaven. The golden altar of incense stood directly in line with the ark, signifying that as soon as the prayers of the saints reach the required strength, and have been tempered together with the substance of Christ, then the Lord Jesus will return. He will come as the Redeemer, "Unto those who look for Him He will appear the second time without sin unto salvation" (Heb. 9:28).

What a time of glory! The coming of Christ and the setting up of the kingdom of God was typified by the Tabernacle of David. The ark was removed from its resting place in the holy of holies, and was put in a tent in Zion. This was the Tabernacle of David, and it speaks of the time of the end when the Lord Jesus returns with His fighting men to bring the kingdoms of this world under the rule of the Lord Jesus.

The ark represents war! When the ark goes forward it is God arising, and His enemies are scattered before Him. The ark leads the way across Jordan. The ark encompasses Jericho. The ark is the presence of God. When Israel moved, the ark moved in their lines of march—always eastward! Always toward the land of promise! That is God moving toward His enemies. When we Christians lift up the everlasting doors of our heart and allow the Lord of hosts to have His way in us and with us, we are moving the Lord God toward His inheritance, toward His enemies.

Man cannot be made completely in the image of God until the last traces of sin have been removed, the last bondages broken. Christ is going to accomplish these final acts of redemption at His coming. When He appears, we will be like Him, and we shall see Him as He is. This is that which is perfect, and it is coming. It is the Lord Jesus Christ, returning to finish His work in us so that we are in His express image.

Christ Himself is our Day of Atonement. All that the word *atonement* signifies, and it is an exceedingly broad term, is found in Christ Himself. For the word means propitiation, covering, pacifying, reconciliation, release, remission, forgiveness—in short, all that is required to bring us all the way to the throne of glory from our total slavery to darkness. All this is included in the concept of atonement. The complete redemption and salvation of our spirit, soul, and body is included in the atonement made by Christ. It is all included in Him. Let us not be like unbelieving Israel. Let us have faith in Christ, our Commander-in-chief, and follow Him into our land of promise until every last enemy, great and small, without exception, is completely, totally, utterly demolished—every trace of darkness, its power and its results.

The second coming of the Lord Jesus Christ will be a consuming fire upon all works of unrighteousness:

"For, behold, the day cometh that shall burn as an oven; and all the proud, yea, and all that do wickedly, shall be stubble: and the day that cometh shall burn them up, saith the Lord of hosts, that it shall leave them neither root nor branch" (Mal. 4:1).

But that day will bring blessing and edification to those who fear the Lord:

"But unto you that fear my name shall the Sun of righteousness arise with healing in his wings; and ye shall go forth, and grow up as calves of the stall" (Mal. 4:2).

That same day, the day of the Lord, the fulfillment of the Day of Atonement, the millennium, if you will, shall prove to be a time of joy and gladness, and restoration, for God's Israel, which is the church of Christ. Also, the millennium, will be the jubilee of deliverance and restoration for the peoples of the earth who do not resist Christ and His saints when they are revealed. The trumpet announcing the year of jubilee is blown on the Day of Atonement, proclaiming the fact that in the atonement made by Christ there is not only forgiveness of sins but also total deliverance from the power and effects of sin.

"Then shalt thou cause the trumpet of the jubilee to sound on the tenth day of the seventh month, in the day of atonement shall ye make the trumpet sound throughout all your land. And ye shall hallow the fiftieth year, and proclaim liberty throughout all the land unto all the inhabitants thereof: it shall be a jubilee unto you; and ye shall return every man unto his possession, and ye shall return every man unto his family" (Lev. 25:9,10).

Christ Himself is the millennium. He is the peace of

God; the rule of God; the King of the kingdom of God. As Christ grows within us and brings into subjection every single one of our deeds, words, motives, and imaginations, one might say, in this sense, that the millennium is growing within us. This is a personal millennium, not the kingdom-wide millennium which will commence with the coming of the Lord Jesus. It becomes true in our heart that the tame beast can lie down in safety with the wild beast, and the child can play on the adder's den. It is true within us that there is nothing which hurts or destroys. It can be truly said of each person of whom such inner peacefulness has been established, that he or she is a firstfruits of the millennium.

Unfortunately, Satan is able to stir up the peoples of the earth so that they consistently refuse to accept the peaceful ways of the Lord Jesus. Therefore, He is coming, in the fulfillment of the Day of Atonement, to crush Satan under the feet of the church and to destroy sinners out of the earth. No power in heaven or upon the earth can prevent the Lord Jesus from taking over at the appointed hour of the Father. God is in the process of bringing into subjection to Christ all of His enemies.

The work of subjugation is going on now in the hearts of the saints. When that work has been done to the satisfaction of the Holy Spirit, the Lord Jesus is going to descend in such an awesome display of God's power and wrath that no creature, physical or spiritual, will be able to resist. Christ is coming at the head of His army. The defenses of devils and men will evaporate like water in an oven. The Lion of the tribe of Judah will be as a grizzly with her cubs. Those who are in rebellion against His will shall be sought out and destroyed. The Head of the church will make His appearance as King of kings and Lord of lords, and those who resist will scream in terror and anguish for the mountains of rocks to fall upon them and hide them from the wrath of God's Lamb. Every particle of wickedness will be crushed under the feet of the church, which will glow as bronze in the furnace.

He is Lord! He has made an atonement for every person. All who choose to do so may come under His protection. But for those who refuse His rule there is a fate worse than physical death; it is eternal death in the lake of fire. The Lord Jesus is the good Shepherd of the Twenty-third Psalm. The Lord Jesus is the Lord strong and mighty in battle of the Twenty-fourth Psalm. As we have known the good Shepherd we shall also know the Lord of armies. The good Shepherd exemplifies all that we look for in a shepherd: He is gentle, kind, watchful, wisely guiding us into green pastures and beside still waters. The Lord of armies exemplifies all that we look for in a commander of warriors: He is mighty, cunning, fierce, tireless, and a terror to His enemies whom He destroys until every trace of resistance has been demolished.

In the Lord Jesus Christ is contained all that is signified by the Day of Atonement, the sixth of the Levitical convocations.

TABERNACLES

Finally, Christ is our convocation of Tabernacles. He is our feast of consummation and rejoicing. Christ is the tabernacle of the Father. The Father dwells in Christ in His fullness. Christ is eternally in God, and God is eternally in Christ. Christ is the temple, the dwelling place of God. He who has seen Christ has seen the Father, because the Father dwells in His fullness in Christ.

During the celebration of Tabernacles, the Temple area in Jerusalem was filled with light from the torches of the worshipers. Christ is the light of the world. Also during Tabernacles water from the pool of Siloam was poured out upon the altar of burnt offering by the anointed priest, while the twelfth chapter of Isaiah was chanted. Christ is the water of life.

The Law was read during the feast of Tabernacles. Christ is the law of God, the holiness of God brought to absolute perfection and beauty.

All of the harvest and processing of the foods grown by the Jews had been completed by the time of Tabernacles. In Christ we can see what we will be like when the Spirit of God has completed His workings in us. All of the glorious joy and blessing of the convocation of Tabernacles is in the Lord Jesus Christ.

Tabernacles was a time of the most outstanding rejoicing and thankfulness for the goodness of God during the past year. Christ is our praise and thanksgiving before God; and as we adore the Father, the Lord Jesus adds His own praise and thanksgiving to ours, so that the whole chorus ascends to God as a holy perfume. Christ sings praise in the midst of the church.

The arrival of Tabernacles meant that the long summer drought was over and the fall (former, early) rains were at hand. The fall rains soften the clods of dirt baked hard by the long summer, preparing the ground for the plowing and planting of the next harvest. Christ is our hope of a new planting, a new life, a glorious life beyond our dreams in the ages to come.

God made man in His image on the sixth day, and on the seventh day He rested. He rested because His work was finished, and it was very good. In Christ, God's work is finished. And it is very good! Christ is the rest of God; and, as we abide in Him, we enter into that rest. The creation of God is begun and finished in Christ. When we enter into Christ, making such entering the first business of every day of our life, we enter into that finished work.

We have to *labor* to enter into that rest, as Hebrews 4 informs us. Why do we have to labor to enter into rest? It sounds like a contradiction. We have to labor because of the opposition of our own flesh, of Satan and his accomplices, and because of the spirit of the age in which we live. These three forces do everything in their power to keep us out of the rest of God; to keep us in an uproar in body, soul, and spirit; to keep us in a desert wilderness where we cannot enjoy the good things which God has promised us.

There are enemies in the land of promise!—surprisingly enough. We have to cross over Jordan, under our heavenly Joshua, the Lord Jesus, and drive them out. There are enemies in your land and my land, and it is going to take the Lord in order for us to drive them out. They are comfortable there and do not let go at our request. It is good to know that our enemies, in this respect, are also God's enemies. And if we will follow the Holy Spirit, God will enable us to drive out every trace of the enemy. It is impossible to tabernacle in peace with God while there is a "Canaanite" in the land. Sooner or later trouble comes, and our rest is destroyed. The righteousness of God is often hard to acquire, but it brings rest and peace. Sin is often attractive, fun, and easy to fall into. But sin brings commotion, unrest, grief, and despair. Where there is confusion, sin is not very far away. But God's ways are ways of peace, rest, and joy.

The seventh Levitical convocation is Tabernacles. The seventh of the holy furnishings of the Tabernacle of the Congregation was the mercy seat. By comparing these two we see that the feast of Tabernacles is associated with holiness, in that the mercy seat was in the most holy place. He who would dwell in Christ in God must be on the road toward holiness. The mercy seat was beaten from pure gold, teaching us that in order to tabernacle with God we must have the gold of His nature "beaten" into us through means of the circumstances of life. God required that the mercy seat be beaten out of pure gold. The Israelites were skilled in the art of casting metal, and they could have cast a hundred mercy seats in the time required to fashion one by beating it into shape with a hammer. So it is today that people are hoping for a sudden experience that will transform them into the image of Christ. But there is no way this can be done. The only way in which the mercy seat, the image of the glory of Christ, can be formed in your life or my life, is by thousands of precisely aimed hammer blows. Have you been hammered on a bit lately? It doesn't feel so good, but the end is glory!

The two covering cherubim, which overshadowed the

mercy seat with their wings, represent the power and glory of God Almighty. The way to power and glory is through abiding in Christ. We do not gain the power and glory of God by any amount of strivings, no matter how well intentioned. The path to glory and power is through the *rest* of God. As we enter into His rest and tabernacle with Him, and absorb His righteousness and holiness until our conduct is affected, then His power and glory can *rest* upon our life.

Entering into the rest of God, into the abiding in Christ, is not a passive affair. It is an everyday get-up-and-at-'em operation. In fact, it takes those who are full of life and desire for God who are able to press through into the kingdom in these days. The kingdom of God is entered into by the forceful ways of those who mean business. But it is not a wrenching of the situation, or personal ambition, of which we are speaking. God will soon burn up false motives with His fire. Yet we have to covet earnestly the best gifts. We find God only when we seek Him with the whole heart. As we move toward God with all the concentration of which we are capable, then God teaches us how to rest in Him. In this manner we *labor* to enter into the *rest* of God.

The most complete fulfillment of the convocation of Tabernacles will occur in the new heaven and earth reign of Christ (see Rev. 21 and 22). The tabernacle of God, who is Christ (Head and Body), will be the "booth," the dwelling place of God Almighty, among the peoples of the earth:

> "And I heard a great voice out of heaven saying, Behold, the tabernacle of God is with men, and he will dwell with them, and they shall be his people, and God himself shall be with them, and be their God" (Rev. 21:3).

Christ is the sanctuary of God, and we are to be part of that sanctuary:

"If a man love me, he will keep my words: and my Father will love him, and we will come unto him, and make our abode with him" (John 14:23).

Christ is the chief cornerstone of the Temple of God, and the bride of Christ is the fullness of the building:

"And are built upon the foundation of the apostles and prophets, Jesus Christ himself being the chief corner stone; in whom all the building fitly framed together grows unto a holy temple in the Lord: in whom ye also are builded together for a habitation of God through the Spirit" (Eph. 2:20-22).

Perhaps the greatest expression in the Bible of the tabernacling of God in Christ can be found in the Gospel of John. Several times we find such expressions as:

"If I do not the works of my Father, believe me not. But if I do, though ye believe not me, believe the works; that ye may know, and believe, that the Father is in me, and I in him" (John 10:37,38).

"Believest thou not that I am in the Father, and the Father in me? the words that I speak unto you I speak not of myself: but the Father that dwelleth in me, he doeth the works" (John 14:20).

We also find in John that through Christ we also will become part of the tabernacle of God:

"Neither pray I for these alone, but for them also which shall believe on me through their word; that they all may be one; as thou, Father, art in me, and I in thee, that they also may be one in us: that the world may believe that thou hast sent me" (John 17:20,21).

We see then that the Lord Jesus Christ is the fullest expression of the feast of Tabernacles. Christ Himself is the seventh aspect of redemption, the *Omega* of salvation. He is the end of our quest, the "mark" toward which Paul was pressing with such single-mindedness of purpose and concentration. Salvation is not a thing; He is a Person! Jesus *is* the resurrection. Jesus *is* the way. Jesus *is* the truth. Jesus *is* the life. He doesn't only bring these blessings. He Himself *is* them. He brings Himself. Jesus Christ is healing, eternal life, peace, joy, revelation, wisdom, righteousness, power, knowledge, atonement, redemption—all that people need and hope and can imagine. Jesus Christ Himself is all these realities and blessings to us.

The following passage was chanted by the Jews during the feast of convocations. Can you see why the Holy Spirit would inspire them to do so?

"Behold, God is my salvation; I will trust, and not be afraid: for the Lord Jehovah is my strength and my song; he also is become my salvation" (Isa. 12:2).

THREE HOLY CONVOCATIONS

We mentioned previously that the seven convocations were divided into three groups: (1) Passover, Unleavened Bread, Firstfruits; (2) Pentecost; (3) Trumpets, Day of Atonement, Tabernacles. These three groups correspond in general to the courtyard, the holy place, and the holy of holies of the Tabernacle of the Congregation. This division into three groups, or areas, helps give us insight in the Person and work of the Lord Jesus Christ.

The first group represents Jesus Christ as the great High Priest of God, who ministers at the altar of burnt offering, so to speak. Through means of His own blood He forgives us our sins and cleanses us from all unrighteousness. Whoever would come to God must come by means of the priestly ministry of the Lord Jesus Christ. Only Christ can present a person acceptably to the Father. After our acceptance, our priest in heaven continues to make intercession for us. There is but one mediator between God and men; it is the man Christ Jesus.

The second group (Pentecost, and the holy place) represents Jesus Christ as the great Prophet of God. First through His own personal ministry, and then through the church which is His body, He testifies to the world of the will of God. Through means of mighty signs and wonders, the Lord Jesus bears witness that what the church says is of Him, and is the Word of the Father. The Lord works with the church, confirming the Word with signs following. Christ in the church is the light of the world. The Holy Spirit empowers the church to bear witness of Christ: to bear witness of the Christ of Calvary; of the present Christ; and of the coming of the King to set up His kingdom. Thus the Christ, Head and Body, serves God as a priest in the reconciling of men to God; and as a prophet, by announcing the salvation and judgment of God, and the laws of the kingdom of God.

The third group (the holy of holies and the last three convocations) represents Jesus Christ as the King of kings. It may be true that the Christian church is more familiar with the priest and prophet roles of Christ. That is because the third role of Christ, that of King, is still ahead of us, in the kingdom-wide sense. When the last trumpet sounds, the Lord Jesus will descend in flaming power, with the holy angels, taking vengeance upon His enemies and bringing righteousness and eternal life to His own. That is yet ahead of us.

But in a very real sense, it is time now for the saints of God to begin to lay hold upon this third role of Christ. The saints are a firstfruits of God's kingdom, and we do not have to wait until His appearing to begin to enter into a knowledge of Christ as Lord and King. Of course, the magnitude of the experience at this time is not as great as that which is coming.

But the quality is here now. A large part of the responsibility is ours. If we choose to come as far as the charismatic experience and stop, that is our choice. But if we choose to press on to the third role of Christ, that will please the Lord greatly. It is in the third aspect that the Lord Jesus is fully vindicated in all that He has done thus far. It is in the demonstration of kingdom power that He shall see the travail of His soul and be satisfied.

If you have been saved and filled with the Spirit, do not take the attitude that Christ has nothing more for you until He returns. The best part is ready for us right now. The Holy Spirit is inviting us to begin to know the Lord Jesus as King of kings and Lord of lords. To know Christ in this way we will have to offer our bodies as a burnt offering to the Lord (Rom. 12:1,2). We will have to accept Him not only as Savior but also as Lord.

If we are willing to follow the Lord Jesus into death itself—if need be, giving all to Him—then He will begin to lead us against the enemies who hinder us from a greater realization of the blessings of God. All sin has to go, as the Holy Spirit brings us against our sins one at a time. When the Spirit points out a sin we are committing, whether in word, deed, or continual daydreaming, fantasizing and imagining, then we are to confess our sin and, through the ability which the Holy Spirit gives us, quit doing it. We are to draw near to God and to resist the devil.

The same thing is true in physical sickness. We can't heal ourself, no matter how much positive thinking we do. But we can take a hostile attitude toward our sicknesses instead of passively accepting them, and stand upon God's Word that He "will put none of the evil diseases of Egypt" (Deut. 7:15) upon us; "He heals all our diseases" (see Matt. 4:23). Let us believe Christ for healing with the same fervency that we believe Christ for salvation.

As we take an attitude of conquest and militancy toward every spirit that would hinder our possession of the good things of God, under the direction of the Holy Spirit, the Lord Jesus will become unto us the Lord of armies. He will lead us on. He loves those who are intense in their love of righteousness and intense in their hatred and rejection of all of the works of the devil. The Lord loves those who fight the good fight of faith against the enemy. The Day Star (Christ) will arise in our hearts, and thus we will prepare ourself for His coming as King of kings and Lord of lords. But if Satan, the world, and our own flesh overcome us at every turn, we are weak. We will not be prepared spiritually to ride behind the banner of Him whose appearing will strike mortal terror into the hearts of the enemies of God. Christ is King, and we are being formed now, in these days, into His army. Do you hear the trumpet of God sounding in your spirit?

IV

THE REDEMPTION
OF THE BELIEVER

So far in our book we have discussed the literal observances of each of the seven convocations as they were, and still are in some cases, observed by the Jews. Next we have shown that the Person and work of the Lord Jesus Christ, the Lamb of God, is clearly set forth in each of the seven convocations.

Now we have come to another application of the symbolism associated with the feasts of the Lord. It is the plan of the redemption of the believer. The redemption of the believer includes the movement of the individual Christian from his initial reconciliation to God through the cross of Christ all the way to his becoming one in Christ and in the Father, being filled with all the glory and love of the Father.

It is true also that the Levitical convocations portray the development of the Christian church from a relatively loose assemblage of people gathered around the foot of the cross all the way to the mature body of Christ, the body of Christ being the judge and deliverer of God's creation, and the wife of the Lamb. The development of the individual Christian and of the whole church are closely related, in that the church is made up of individual Christians, and the perfection of the whole depends upon the perfection of each part. However, the growth of the individual Christian, the overcoming disciple, may not be on the same time schedule as the church. The church is moving along many fronts today, and a good number of people have come as far as the convocation of Pentecost, although even more are still milling around in the first principles of salvation.

But it is entirely possible for individual Christians today to go on with God, whatever the rest of the church does. We find this to be true in Revelation 2 and 3, where Christ addresses the seven churches as a whole, and then speaks to each overcomer as a single person. A little later on in Revelation we see that these "overcomers" who give their all to Jesus will be in a position to help the rest of the church come into their own inheritance in the Lord, just as Joseph helped his family. If we become strong in the Lord, through His grace, then we ought to help the weaker brothers and sisters come into their inheritance.

As we outline the fulfillment in the individual Christian of the seven feasts of the Lord, please keep in mind that God's love in Christ has directed that we are to look steadfastly to Christ, walking before Him continually, so that the Holy Spirit may bring us to maturity in Christ. The role of the Holy Spirit is similar to that of Eliezer of Damascus who brought the fair Rebecca away from her home and took her on a journey through a territory unknown to her, until finally she arrived in the presence of Isaac, the son of Abraham. Isaac is a figure of the Lord Jesus Christ who Himself is the end of our quest.

The pattern of the seven feasts indicates that the Christian redemption is not a once-for-all happening. Although the beginning of salvation in a person's life is clear-cut and decisive, salvation is a continuously dynamic process, a growth to maturity.

The covering Passover blood is the initial revelation, the acceptance of which is the first step of the person approaching salvation. The convocation of Tabernacles, the last of the convocations, signifies the consummation—the indwelling of the Father and the Son through the Holy Spirit. Thus salvation has a definite beginning and a definite ending, an *alpha* and an *omega*. Redemption has an ending in the sense of a coming of age, a maturing. Maturity is a goal worth reaching for (Eph. 4:13).

Now let us associate briefly the seven convocations with their New Testament counterparts:

1. Passover—Christ on the cross; eating the Lord's Supper; protection from judgment through the blood of Jesus.

2. Unleavened Bread—Christ in the heart of the earth; water baptism; death to the world; crucifixion with Christ; sincere repentance.

3. Firstfruits—Christ raised from the dead; resurrection with Christ; the born-again experience.

4. Pentecost—Christ sends to us the Holy Spirit; latter rain; baptism with the Holy Spirit; the law of the Spirit of life; gifts and ministries.

5. Trumpets—Christ, the King, returns; the day of the Lord; rulership of Christ over the earth; Christ wages war against evil spirits; the Christian overcomes the enemy; the New Year.

6. Day of Atonement—Christ forgives and cleanses all who come to Him; the Holy Spirit deals with sin in the disciple; confession of sins; putting to death the deeds of the body; judgment of evil spirits; the Christian is transformed into the image of Christ; year of jubilee; cleansing of God's Temple—the body of Christ.

7. Tabernacles—Christ and the Father dwell in the Christian; the "rest" of God; redemption of the mortal body; the

consummation of salvation; the new Jerusalem; the fullness of the presence and glory of God.

It is interesting to note that the Pentecostal, charismatic speaking in tongues experience (call it what you will) is at the halfway point, so to speak. This may inspire us who have spoken in tongues to press on to the fullness of God's plan. Some of us who have been camping at the "tongues" experience need to get back up on our spiritual feet and begin to fight onward toward the good things which God has for us.

The following exposition of the seven Levitical assemblings suggests that they are types of the progressive nature of the working of God in the Christian life. However, the seven assemblings should be considered as portraying seven dimensions of the one redemption, not as seven ordered steps which God follows precisely and in sequence with each individual. In a sense, these all take place at once when an individual accepts Christ, because Christ is the fulfillment of the seven feasts. Yet, there is another sense in which these seven facets are expanded upon as we press on in Christ Jesus.

PASSOVER

"This month shall be unto you the beginning of months: it shall be the first month of the year to you. Speak ye unto all the congregation of Israel, saying, In the tenth day of this month they shall take to them every man a lamb, according to the house of their fathers, a lamb for a house" (Exod. 12:2,3).

"And thus shall ye eat it; with your loins girded, your shoes on your feet, and your staff in your hand; and ye shall eat it in haste: it is the Lord's passover. For I will pass through the land of Egypt this night, and will smite all the firstborn in the land of Egypt, both man and beast; and against all the gods of Egypt I will execute judgment: I am the Lord.

"And the blood shall be to you for a token upon the houses where ye are: and when I see the blood, I will pass over you, and the plague shall not be upon you to destroy you, when I smite the land of Egypt" (Exod. 12:11,12,13).

"And he said to them, With desire I have desired to eat this passover with you before I suffer" (Luke 22:15).

"Purge out therefore the old leaven, that ye may be a new lump, as ye are unleavened. For even Christ our passover is sacrificed for us" (I Cor. 5:7).

Passover symbolizes the protection from God's judgment and wrath, which we have through the blood of Christ. Because the sentence of death overshadows the gods of this world we apply by faith the blood of Jesus to ourself and to our household. When the divine executioner approaches us he sees the blood of the righteous Jesus, which, in obedience to God, we have sprinkled by faith over our lives. The executioner, seeing that we have appropriated the blood of Jesus, "passes over" us without harming us, and continues on his way carrying out the sentences of God. In the same spirit of obedience we "eat of the Passover Lamb" (I Cor. 5:7).

The Passover convocation teaches us of the great importance which God places upon the blood of Christ as a covering for our many sins. We can see in our own times the judgments of God in the land—the turmoil, and the distress of nations. Our refuge from the destroying storm is the blood of Jesus applied to our household by faith, in obedience to the Word of God.

The Passover marks the "beginning of months" to the

Christian (Exod. 12:2). When an unsaved person approaches God he is confronted with Christ upon the cross. God meets man at the cross. Just as the Hebrew approaching the Tabernacle of the Congregation encountered first the altar of burnt offering (Exod. 27:1), so the man or woman, boy or girl, who would enter the Christian salvation must first accept God's offering—the Lord Jesus Christ. Thus the point in time at which we accept by faith the blood of Calvary's cross becomes to us a "beginning of months." It signals the start of a wholly new life. Our existence prior to the cross is of little consequence. Our true life begins on the second that Jesus Christ becomes our personal Passover.

Notice that it is a "lamb for a house" (Exod. 12:3). The words of Paul are brought to mind, "You shall be saved, and your house" (see Acts 16:31). When a person accepts Christ the entire household comes under the protection of the blood (I Cor. 7:14). The believer then should pray for the members of the family that God will grant them repentance unto life; that each one will accept Christ for himself.

The Passover was to be eaten "in haste." We Christians must never lose sight of the fact that Jesus has commanded us to live "with your loins girded, your shoes on your feet, and your staff in your hand" (Exod. 12:11). "Watch therefore; for ye know neither the day nor the hour wherein the Son of man cometh" (Matt. 25:13). We work as diligently as we can while we are in this world, but in our hearts we are strangers and pilgrims!

The Passover blood was for protection during the judgment against "all the gods of Egypt" (Exod. 12:12). So it is today. The Holy Spirit reproves (convicts) the world of judgment, "because the prince of this world is judged" (John 16:11). The Lord will not tolerate the worshiping of demons. In His own time and manner He will destroy utterly the demons and those who worship them. The Passover blood is our protection during the time that God executes judgment upon the works of Satan.

"No uncircumcised person shall eat thereof" (Exod. 12:48). Only Christians can take advantage of the protection from judgment provided by the blood of Christ. No person can escape the judgment of God merely by associating himself with the Christian churches. One's name on a church roster, while it is useful in the administration of a church, is of no value whatever when it comes to protection against the judgment of God. A person must be "circumcised," that is to say, he must through faith obtain a work of Christ in his own heart. Otherwise he cannot avail himself of the protection of the Passover blood.

UNLEAVENED BREAD

"Seven days shall ye eat unleavened bread; even the first day ye shall put away leaven out of your houses: for whosoever eateth leavened bread from the first day until the seventh day, that soul shall be cut off from Israel" (Exod. 12:15).

"In the first month, on the fourteenth day of the month at even, ye shall eat unleavened bread, until the one and twentieth day of the month at even" (Exod. 12:18).

"Thou shalt eat no leavened bread with it; seven days shall thou eat unleavened bread therewith, even the bread of affliction; for thou camest forth out of the land of Egypt in haste: that thou mayest remember the day when thou camest forth out of the land of Egypt all the days of thy life" (Deut. 16:3).

"Your glorying is not good. Know ye not that a little leaven leaveneth the whole lump? Purge out therefore the old leaven, that ye may be a new lump, as ye are unleavened. For even Christ our passover is sacrificed for us: therefore let us keep the feast, not with old

leaven, neither with the leaven of malice and wickedness; but with the unleavened bread of sincerity and
truth" (I Cor. 5:6-8).

"A little leaven leaveneth the whole lump" (Gal. 5:9).

Paul anchors our interpretation of the convocation of
Unleavened Bread with his words in I Corinthians 5:6-8.
Leaven is portrayed as "malice and wickedness" and unleavened bread is shown as "sincerity and truth." In effect,
leaven in the Scripture symbolizes sin. Just as a little yeast
affects a whole ball of dough, so a little sin affects a whole
human life.

God issued a clear command concerning the use of
leaven during Passover week: "And there shall no leavened
bread be seen with you" (Exod. 13:7). This command is
repeated in the Old Testament until the spiritual message
comes across: Purge yourselves from sin and the old nature!
Sincere repentance and a cleansing from the spirit of the
age—the lust of the flesh, the lust of the eyes, and the pride
of life—must accompany the acceptance of Christ, our
Passover.

The sacrament of water baptism dramatizes the fact that
the believer has turned his back upon sin, has died to the
world and the lust thereof. A gospel that does not require the
convert to turn from sin and lead a new life of righteousness
is not the Christian gospel. The "feast" (accepting the Lamb
of God as our personal Passover) must be kept with
"unleavened bread" (sincerity and truth).

"Know ye not," asks Paul, "that so many of us as were
baptized into Jesus Christ were baptized into his death?
Therefore we are buried with him by baptism into death:
that like as Christ was raised up from the dead by the glory
of the Father, even so we also should walk in newness of life"
(Rom. 6:3,4).

The phrase "newness of life" is associated with the

meaning of unleavened bread. Paul says, "Purge out therefore the old leaven, that you may be a new lump." The new life in Christ is free from the leaven of sin.

In water baptism, the leaven of our old nature is portrayed as dying with Christ on Calvary. The crucifixion of our soulish nature is, as we know from Scripture and experience, a theoretical position which we are to accept by faith. Yet, though it may be theoretical and ideal, the adoption of this attitude—that our first personality died with Christ and now we are walking in resurrection life—is essential to the way we regard our own state of being, and is the necessary point of view for the overcomer.

If we do not daily maintain the overcoming point of view, which is that our soulish natural man *now* is crucified with Christ and our new spiritual man *now* is in the heavenlies with Christ—a dual position—then either we will slip carelessly back into a sinful life or else we will wrestle ineffectively with sin in order to gain a position which Christ already has secured for us and which we are to seize by faith and maintain by faith. If our faith is the genuine article and not a silly head belief, we will begin to see our theoretical and ideal position of simultaneous crucifixion and resurrection transformed into physical reality right here in this wicked age in which we live. Our faith, which is a gift from God, transforms the promises of the Bible into solid fact.

> "Then Peter said unto them, Repent, and be baptized every one of you in the name of Jesus Christ for the remission of sins, and ye shall receive the gift of the Holy Spirit" (Acts 2:38).

Water baptism is the provision which God has made in order that a person by faith may dramatize the putting out of his life the old corrupt nature. Here is the new covenant fulfillment of Passover Week, the week of Unleavened Bread. Water baptism portrays burial and resurrection, the beginning of a new life for anyone who accepts God's Passover Lamb, Jesus Christ, who was "slain from the foundation of the world" (Rev. 13:8).

The convocation of Unleavened Bread means to us that every trace of the old life, the old "leaven" of this world, is to be removed from us. Every "Egyptian," to speak in a figure, is to be "left in the Red Sea." To repent is to turn away from the old leaven of sin and to enter into the kingdom of God as a little child.

In water baptism we enter into the death of the cross, and we also enter into the resurrection life of Christ. We enter into the death of the cross so that every trace of Satan's authority over us may be destroyed. From now on we are free to choose to serve God. Before our entering into the death of Christ we were not free to choose to be servants of righteousness. We were bound in the kingdom of darkness. But now we are loosed from that kingdom, through the authority of Christ, and are free to choose to obey the Spirit of God. This is the meaning of the sixth chapter of Romans, and the fulfillment in the Christian of the convocation of Unleavened Bread.

FIRSTFRUITS

"Speak unto the children of Israel, and say to them, When ye be come into the land which I give unto you, and shall reap the harvest thereof, then ye shall bring a sheaf of the firstfruits of your harvest to the priest" (Lev. 23:10).

"And not only they, but ourselves also, which have the firstfruits of the Spirit, even we ourselves groan within ourselves, waiting for the adoption, to wit, the redemption of our body" (Rom. 8:23).

"But now is Christ risen from the dead, and become the firstfruits of them that slept" (I Cor. 15:20).

"But every man in his own order: Christ the firstfruits; afterward they who are Christ's at his coming" (I Cor. 15:23).

"Of his own will he begat us with the word of truth, that we should be a kind of firstfruits of his creatures" (Jas. 1:18).

"These were redeemed from among men, being the firstfruits unto God and to the Lamb" (Rev. 14:4).

The convocation of Firstfruits is the resurrection of Jesus Christ, and our entrance into His resurrection life. We are "born again," meaning that a new life, the life of Christ, has been born in us. This is the beginning of the harvesting of our life. Our spirit at the moment of receiving Christ is raised up to sit with Christ in the heavenlies. Our spirit is the firstfruits of our personality unto God. There is a great part of us which has not been harvested, as we can tell by the way we act sometimes, the things which we do, and the battles which we have. But the remaining part of us, that part which gives the problem, has been accepted of God upon the basis of His accepting that part of us which has been born again.

Our soul has to go through many experiences with God before it is completely harvested. Our body will be harvested last of all. But we rejoice in God because we know that what He has begun in us He will finish. Our spirit has been accepted as a firstfruit of our whole personality. Therefore God will transform our soul and body through His grace, and then the harvest of our life will be completed.

The harvest of the Christian church will be completed as soon as each member has been fully harvested; and then the church will come down as the holy city, the new Jerusalem, upon the new earth (Rev. 21 and 22).

Calling those things which are not as though they were. " . . . God, who quickeneth the dead, and calleth

those things which are not as though they were" (Rom.
4:17).

There is an extraordinary fact connected with the seven
convocations: it is that the ordinances governing their
celebration were issued in detail while the Hebrews were
wandering in a *desert*. And these were *agricultural* festivities!
Firstfruits, Pentecost, and Tabernacles were formal announcements of distinct phases of the harvest season, given
when the Hebrews had no farms.

That they were all *harvest* ceremonies is arresting in
itself because it shows that God regards the entire Christian
era, commencing with Christ's death and resurrection during
Passover Week, as being a harvest of that which had been
sown in the earth by the Lord (John 4:35). In other words,
the Christian church is the fruit of sowing which has been
going on from the time of Abraham (Gal. 3:6-18).

But the extraordinary fact of which we are speaking is
that precise regulations for harvest rituals were given to
former slaves who did not own a square foot of land (except
by faith in God's promise). At the time that the Levitical
convocations were enjoined upon the Hebrews they were
wandering in the Sinai Desert. They were following a cloud
by day and a pillar of fire at night through as barren and
desolate a furnace of a countryside as can be imagined. Yet
the Lord insisted on furnishing them with a list of detailed
instructions for the observance of ceremonies celebrating the
ingathering of barley, wheat, olives, nuts, etc.

This way of doing things is characteristic of God who
"calleth those things which be not as though they were"
(Rom. 4:17). Does the Holy Spirit of God do that to
us—speak to us about spiritual realities which are not a fact
of our physical or spiritual environment? Indeed He does!
And it is the grasping of the promises of God by resolute and
unswerving faith that brings the victory in the overcoming
Christian life.

Our death with Christ on the cross and our ascent with

Him into the heavenlies are two examples of this pattern of divine operation. The positive assurance of the possession of the good things of God's Word provides an anchor and direction for our faith, and creates the substance of the reality. We lay hold upon our land of promise when objective evidence testifies that we are not as yet in possession of it.

When the Holy Spirit makes a promise of God real to us, or even if we just read the promise in the Scriptures (taking due note of the attendant conditions), we then can lay hold upon the promise by faith. We gain possession of various aspects of our land of promise by seeking them out by faith: sanctification, healing, the indwelling of the Father and the Son, the gifts and ministries, etc. Faith in God's promises creates value where none exists, or where evil exists.

> "And we desire that every one of you do show the same diligence to the full assurance of hope unto the end: that ye be not slothful, but followers of them who through faith and patience inherit the promises" (Heb. 6:11,12).

> "But without faith it is impossible to please him: for he that cometh to God must believe that he is, and that he is a rewarder of them that diligently seek him" (Heb. 11:6).

> "These all died in faith, not having received the promises, but having seen them afar off, and were persuaded of them, and embraced them, and confessed that they were strangers and pilgrims on the earth" (Heb. 11:13).

A warning is necessary at this point. There is a trap into which we can fall that is related to the business of possessing the kingdom by faith. There is a light head belief which is not overcoming faith. We may know of someone who prayed a brief prayer, or who even strove in prolonged prayer, and who then claimed that he had the answer because of his mental grip upon the letter of the Bible promise. Yet nothing happened! There is a great difference between making plays upon the promises of Christ, or mental striving, and gaining ground with God through overcoming faith.

We cannot force God to do anything, no matter how much we "believe." We cannot walk on a broken leg, unless and until God evidences to us that He is cooperating with us in the act of faith. It takes experience in the ways of God to be able to walk successfully within the line drawn between presumption and aggressive faith.

The Hebrews would have been regarded as demented by the surrounding tribes if they had gone through the motions of reaping nonexistent crops in the desert, thinking that thereby they were honoring the God who had given them agricultural holidays to celebrate.

True faith gains a vision of God's promise, lays hold upon God through prayer in the Spirit and obedience, and is sensitive to God's schedules. Faith eventually obtains the knowledge of the mind of the Spirit of God. Faith is a real walk in the Spirit and produces concrete results in the physical world.

It is a fact that we secure our inheritance by maintaining unswerving faith in the promises of God, and some of these promises are fantastic. The doing of "greater works," the resurrection of the body into immortality, the powers of the world to come—these are incredible dreams. But these glories and others like them, raised to the millionth power in quality and quantity, will some day be solid reality for the Christian who maintains to the end an unchanging trust in the Lord Jesus Christ.

In God's time the Hebrews had to fight a bloody war to obtain their land of milk and honey. In God's time we Christians are going to have to fight fierce spiritual battles if we intend to transform our spiritual desires into permanent possessions. Let us therefore lay hold upon the promises of Scripture. Let us maintain in rock-like faith that we "have" the promises. And then let us follow the Spirit of Christ as He leads us in spiritual warfare to accomplish the dislodging of Satan. Now back to our consideration of the convocation of Firstfruits.

The concept of *firstfruits* is prominent in God's plan of salvation. For example, Romans 8:23 informs us that we Christians have "the firstfruits of the Spirit." We have a firstfruits, or *first installment,* of the Holy Spirit at the present time. (Imagine what the receiving of the balance of the Holy Spirit is going to be like!) If we "hold the beginning of our confidence steadfast unto the end" (Heb. 3:14), we shall come to the day when we shall reap the remainder of the harvest—the fullness of the Holy Spirit permeating every part of our being, just as is true of Jesus.

Sanctifies the whole harvest. Another dimension of the Firstfruits convocation is that the sanctifying of the firstfruits sanctifies the entire harvest. "For if the firstfruits be holy, the lump is also holy" (Rom. 11:16). This principle explains how it can be that we are without condemnation in Christ even though we still may observe sinful tendencies in our body. Our will already has been reaped (Rom. 7:18) and we delight in the law of God after the inward man (Rom. 7:22).

Our life (the inner spiritual life) "is hid with Christ in God" (Col. 3:3). Thus a firstfruits of our life already has been "waved" (Lev. 23:11) before the Lord. And our "members which are upon the earth" (Col. 3:5), the "body of this death" (Rom. 7:24), are sanctified through the fact that the inner spiritual life, having been waved as a firstfruits before the Lord, has been sanctified by our receiving of the sacrifice of Christ upon the cross. The day will come when our mortal body also will be harvested (Rom. 8:23), thus completing the reaping of our entire being by the Spirit of God unto everlasting life (Gal. 6:8).

We see the principle of the firstfruits operating in the resurrection of Jesus Christ from the dead. "But now is Christ risen from the dead, and become the firstfruits of them that slept" (I Cor. 15:20). Because He (Jesus) was "waved" as a holy offering before the Lord, we also, the harvest of the earth, are sanctified in the sight of God. And we too shall be raised from the dead. "But every man in his own order: Christ the firstfruits; afterward they that are Christ's at his coming" (I Cor. 15:23).

The saints are the firstfruits of the kingdom of God. James 1:18 presents an interesting thought: "Of his own will begat he us with the word of truth, that we should be a kind of firstfruits of his creatures." This verse is in harmony with the idea that God's working in the earth during the church era includes the construction of a temple, a living house from which He can communicate with the rest of His creation. The concept of a group selected out from the totality of His creatures can be observed in Romans 8:19: "For the earnest expectation of the creature waiteth for the manifestation of the sons of God."

The sin and confusion of the old creation was exemplified by Adam's inability to observe one simple prohibition; and the old creation was judged and finished on Calvary. The new creation began with the resurrection of Christ. He is the firstfruits of the new creation—a whole new working of God. And the sons of God, since they are one with Christ in His death and resurrection, can also be considered as a firstfruits of the new creation. The world of nature is waiting expectantly to see these sons of God who already have in themselves the firstfruits of the Spirit of God—the substance of eternal life.

Revelation 14:4 refers to those who are "firstfruits unto God and to the Lamb." Let us, like Paul, "follow after" so that we may grasp that for which we have been "apprehended (grasped) by Christ Jesus" (Phil. 3:12). Let us press toward participation in the first resurrection that we may be firstfruits to God and to the Lamb. "Blessed and holy is he that hath part in the first resurrection: on such the second death hath no power (authority), but they shall be priests of God and of Christ, and shall reign with him a thousand years" (Rev. 20:6).

Notice how clearly the Passover, Unleavened Bread, and Firstfruits convocations portray the crucifixion, descent into the heart of the earth, and resurrection of the Lord Jesus. The Levitical convocations are symbolic of events in the life of Christ, and therefore have direct reference to our own spiritual experience because of our close relationship with Him in His crucifixion and resurrection.

Our book, up to this point, has been reviewing doctrine which is fairly well known to Christians. The remainder of *The Feasts of the Lord* will bring us into waters which may be unfamiliar to some of us; although the next feast, Pentecost, is becoming much more widely understood through the current "charismatic" movement. By the Lord's help, we are going to follow the divine pattern of the Levitical convocations to the climax of the Christian experience—the *omega* of salvation.

PENTECOST

"And ye shall count unto you from the morrow after the sabbath, from the day that ye brought the sheaf of the wave offering; seven sabbaths shall be complete: even unto the morrow after the seventh sabbath shall you number fifty days; and ye shall offer a new meat offering to the Lord" (Lev. 23:15,16).

"Seven weeks shalt thou number unto thee: begin to number the seven weeks from such time as thou beginnest to put the sickle to the corn. And thou shalt keep the feast of weeks unto the Lord thy God with a tribute of a freewill offering of thine hand, which thou shalt give unto the Lord thy God, according as the Lord thy God hath blessed you" (Deut. 16:9,10).

"And when the day of Pentecost was fully come, they were all with one accord in one place. And suddenly there came a sound from heaven as of a rushing mighty wind, and it filled all the house where they were sitting. And there appeared to them cloven tongues like as of fire, and it sat upon each of them. And they were all filled with the Holy Ghost (Spirit), and began to speak with other tongues, as the Spirit gave them utterance" (Acts 2:1-4).

There are amazing differences between the Hebrew assemblings and their new covenant counterparts. The old covenant celebration of Pentecost (feast of weeks) was an important annual agricultural ceremony. But the new covenant fulfillment of the feast of weeks is an extraordinary spiritual occurrence which has affected to a great extent the subsequent course of mankind upon the earth.

The record of Acts speaks for itself concerning the meaning of the Hebrew festival of Pentecost. Jesus had said, "Wait for the promise of the Father"; and again, "But you shall receive power after that the Holy Spirit is come upon you: and you shall be witnesses to me." (See Acts 1:4,8.)

"But you shall receive *power*"! The book of Acts is a record of divine power working in the lives of Christians. Speaking in tongues and the miraculous healing of the sick were, and still are, two of the prominent results of the outpouring of the Holy Spirit of God.

The law of the Spirit of life. Pentecost (feast of weeks) is associated with the giving of the law of Moses on Mount Sinai. And so it is in the new covenant—that the "law" is given at Pentecost. For the law of the Christian is "the law of the Spirit of life" (Rom. 8:2). We Christians are not under the law of Moses, except during such times as we choose to live in the flesh. The law of Moses governs us when we are living "in the flesh" (Rom. 7:5). By *living in the flesh* we mean living in the understandings and appetites of the body, mind, and soul of the natural man, rather than living by the guidance and discipline of the Holy Spirit of God.

But when we "die" to the flesh and to the lusts thereof, and choose instead to live under the guidance and power of the Holy Spirit, we come under a law different from the law of Moses. Our new law is the law of the Spirit of life. It is the law which rules Christians who are "not in the flesh, but in the Spirit" (Rom. 8:9).

We are not "adulterers" though we have left the law of Moses to be married to Jesus Christ, because we were released from the law of Moses through means of our death with Christ on the cross (Rom. 7:2-4). We Christians are not without law. Rather we are playing under the rules of a different game. We are ruled by the Spirit of God whose voice we are to obey at all times. Living in the flesh brings some fun and satisfying of fleshly lusts, and a tremendous amount of mental, bodily, and soulish grief, remorse, confusion, and eventually eternal separation from God and everlasting punishment. On the other hand, strict obedience to the law of the Spirit of life brings some self-denial and delayed gratification, and a tremendous amount of peace, health, certainty, and eventually release and glory and the fullness of the presence of God in Christ throughout eternity. On top of all this, the Spirit of God *helps* us obey the law of the Spirit of life!

Harvest rain. The harvest (spring; latter) rain (Joel 2:23; Zech. 10:1) began, as we understand it, with the events recorded in the book of Acts. The Pentecostal "harvest rain" has been available to all Christians since the days of the first apostles of the Lord Jesus Christ. It is regrettable that the early Christians rejected the leadership and manifestation of the Holy Spirit in favor of a human-directed church, as soon as the original apostles passed from the earth. In fact, there is evidence in Paul's writings that while he yet was ministering, his own converts were rejecting the teachings which the Lord Jesus had presented through him (see Gal. 3—5, for example).

People seem to find it difficult to be willing to live under the rulership of the Holy Spirit of God.

History of the harvest rain. The history of the outpouring of Pentecostal "rain" upon mankind is a fascinating and inspiring story. The miraculous effects of the workings of the Holy Spirit are described in the book of Acts. Since that time there have been powerful manifestations of the Spirit of God whenever and wherever Christians have met God's conditions; and also in times and places selected sovereignly by the Lord Jesus according to His own purposes. Some of the outpourings of the Spirit are on record; no doubt there were many of which we are ignorant. The names of Luther, Wesley, Fox, Finney, Howells, for example, are associated with manifestations of the harvest rain—the fulfillment of the convocation of Pentecost.

If it is true, as we have suggested, that the harvest (latter) rain has been available throughout the entire Christian era, then we would expect similar manifestations throughout the whole period. A study of past revivals indicates that this has been the case. Speaking in tongues and miraculous healings, two prominent characteristics of the outpouring of the Spirit of God recorded in the book of Acts, consistently have followed the anointed preaching of the gospel from the first century to the twentieth.[4]

Speaking in tongues and miraculous healings are graces which every Christian should expect to accompany his life in Christ Jesus. Both of these signs are readily available to each Christian believer. It does not require a profoundly mystical experience in order for a person to speak in tongues or to be healed by the Spirit of God, or to pray with success for the

[4]See, for example, Chapter XXIII, "Pentecostal Outpourings in History," Stanley Howard Frodsham, *With Signs Following.* Springfield, Mo.: Gospel Publishing House, 1946, pp. 253-62.

healing of others. These are the normal, business-as-usual privileges of everyone who follows Jesus. Tongues and healing both are at hand, indeed very close to us, when we accept the lordship of Christ in our daily life.

If we ask the Lord for the ability to speak in tongues, and thank Him in advance for the answer, we soon will find ourselves speaking in tongues. *We* do the speaking, under the gentle prompting of the Spirit, and the Spirit gives the words. The same is true of divine healing. If we ask the Lord to heal us, or to heal another person, and thank Him in advance for the answer, He will come and heal us. How could it be otherwise? The Bible is the Word of God and God does not and cannot lie. Tongues and healings are as effortless as eating and breathing, and do not require much more faith than do eating and breathing on the part of the person who daily is following the Lord Jesus in a devout and obedient manner.

Pattern of the outpouring. A study of Christian revivals from the time of Martin Luther to the present day points up some facts about the outpouring of the Holy Spirit, the "harvest rain." The promises of the Scripture plus the historical pattern of the outpouring of God's Spirit prompt us to believe that there has been a gradual increase of the Spirit during the period of time from Luther until now, and that the "latter rain" will increase in volume until there is a worldwide downpour of glory. One of the features of the moving of the Spirit has been a restoration of understanding of the writings of the first apostles—of the entire Bible, for that matter. The book of Joel has some important things to say about the convocation of Pentecost. On the day of the celebration of Pentecost, the Holy Spirit announced through Peter: "This is that which was spoken by the prophet Joel" (Acts 2:16). The message of Joel is that there is to be a time of desolation and famine, followed by restoration and fruitfulness. This, we believe, is the pattern of the spiritual harvest rain: a period of desolation, followed by an abundant restoration of the things of God.

It appears that the dark ages of Western civilization were paralleled by a dark age of the Christian church in which, with some notable exceptions, the presence of the Spirit of God and the understanding of the Scriptures were diminished greatly from that which had been true of the ministry of the first apostles. But there seems to have been since the time of Luther an incoming tide of restoration of the Spirit and the Word of God. Of particular interest here is Joel 2:23,24 which suggests that the end of the Christian era will experience a visitation of God's Spirit upon the earth, the like of which never has been witnessed from the time of Adam to the present day.

During the last three hundred years there have been mighty manifestations of the Holy Spirit in Europe, Asia, and America, and in other places throughout the world. The outpouring of the Holy Spirit in America during the opening years of the twentieth century has been of particular interest to the writer, perhaps because of his good fortune in having been acquainted with some people who either were active during the early days, or who were associated with Pentecostal pioneers of that period. Their testimony carried a savor of divine grace and power that could not be denied.

One of the American Pentecostal pioneers of the early twentieth century was Frank Bartleman (not one of those known to us personally). An abridged version of a book authored by Frank Bartleman describes the Azusa Street outpouring.[5] Bartleman's account is an excellent resource for anyone who is interested in examining the nature of the new covenant counterpart of the feast of weeks (Pentecost) and in seeking to understand the significance of the Azusa Street outpouring in its relationship to the whole of church history.[6]

[5] Frank Bartleman, *What Really Happened at Azusa Street.* Northridge, Calif.: Voice Christian Publications, Inc., edited by John Walker, 1962.

[6] Also see Carl Brumback, *Suddenly . . . from Heaven.* Springfield, Mo.: Gospel Publishing House, 1961.

Frank Bartleman's narrative abounds in inspirational moments. But some disquieting facts emerge. As one reads the book the impression is gained that the church leaders and people were so anxious to return to a conventional form of worship that they fairly drove the Holy Spirit of God from their midst. Bartleman's record of people driving away the Holy Spirit by resisting the patterns of worship, prayer, and ministry taught to them by the Spirit of God is nearly unbelievable. But one need look no further than Holy Writ to discover that Israel always resists the Holy Spirit.

The writer believes that the Pentecostal (latter; harvest) rain has been available during the entire Christian church age, and that the reason the Holy Spirit of God is present in small amounts in our assemblings is because that is the way we want it. It is possible that our understanding of the Christian assembling (church service) and our patterns of church behavior do not go along with the desires and actions of the Holy Spirit.

It is the writer's conviction that an abundant and continual outpouring of glory is available to any and every group of Christians who will allow the Holy Spirit to rule their activities. It is useless, we believe, to pray for and to expect an outpouring of God's Spirit unless and until we are willing, under the guidance of the Spirit of Christ, to change the patterns of our individual and corporate behaviors until they line up with the wishes of the living and present Christ.

The significance of "tongues." It may be true that the divine meaning and intent of Azusa Street, and similar outpourings, has not been understood clearly. What is the purpose of "tongues," for example? Since speaking in tongues seems to be associated with the outpouring of the latter rain, what significance does it have for us Christians other than the fluency which it gives to our individual worship and supplications?

Speaking in tongues is more than an interesting phenomenon to append to our business-as-usual church life.

Speaking in tongues signals a new way of obeying God—the way of the law of the Spirit of life. "Tongues" is the key which opens the door to a new life for the Christian. It appears that the churches involved in the Azusa Street outpouring, not understanding the significance of what was going on in their midst, moved off the course which the Holy Spirit was setting for them.

Isaiah 28:9-13 aids our understanding of the significance of the speaking in tongues experience:

"Whom shall he teach knowledge? and whom shall he make to understand doctrine? them that are weaned from the milk, and drawn from the breasts. For precept must be upon precept, precept upon precept; line upon line, line upon line; here a little, and there a little:

For with stammering lips and another tongue will he speak to this people. To whom he said, This is the rest wherewith ye may cause the weary to rest; and this is the refreshing: yet they would not hear. But the word of the Lord was unto them precept upon precept, precept upon precept; line upon line, line upon line; here a little, and there a little; that they might go, and fall backward, and be broken, and snared, and taken."

The meaning of speaking in tongues, its role in determining our Christian experience, is contained in this passage from Isaiah. Tongues, the Holy Spirit is saying here, is a means which God has selected to guide us into the life in the Spirit. Speaking in tongues builds us up and helps us toward the "rest" of God—the refreshing for those who are weary from trying to please God in their own strength. Notice in Isaiah 28:11 that the stammering lips and other tongue are presented in context with growth in the understanding of doctrine and the receiving of knowledge.

The emphasis is upon "line upon line; precept upon

precept." And the purpose of it all is "that they might go, and fall backward, and be broken, and snared, and taken." The passage portrays the "taking" of the person by the Spirit of God. A Christian is the flesh being made the Word of God, just as Jesus was the Word made flesh. And the process of transforming of the Christian into the Word of God is "precept upon precept, precept upon precept; line upon line, line upon line; here a little, and there a little." It is a daily transformation as we keep our eyes steadfast upon Christ. Little by little the strength of the believer's self-life is destroyed and divine resurrection life takes its place. Here is a picture of the rulership of the Holy Spirit gradually increasing in power in the life of a Christian (think about II Cor. 3:18).

This then is the purpose behind the speaking in tongues. It is a means through which God brings people from the power of the rule of the flesh to the power of the rule of the Spirit of life. Speaking in tongues teaches the Christian how to yield to the dominion of the Holy Spirit instead of acting from the lusts of the flesh. The end result of the Pentecostal experience, and of all other divine programs, is the complete submission of the believer to the Spirit of Christ.

At Azusa Street the Holy Spirit attempted to instruct the church in the doctrines of the Lord: the life in the Spirit, the oneness of the body of Christ, the need for heart holiness. But the Christians, after having experienced some of the manifestations of the Spirit of God, returned to their denominational forms. They reconvened in the Methodist, Episcopal, Presbyterian, Baptist, etc., manner. The denominational form was renamed "Pentecostal," since speaking in tongues had been added to the church activities. But it appears that they were not as yet ready to be ruled by the Spirit of God and to be led wholly by the Spirit of Christ individually and in the assemblings.

"To whom he said, This is the rest wherewith ye may cause the weary to rest; and this is the refreshing: yet they would not hear." Speaking in tongues teaches us how to rest in the Lord—how to cease from our own works (Heb. 4:10). The life in the Spirit is a rest and a refreshing for those who are worn out from trying to please God by their own fleshly methods and strength (Matt. 11:28-30). The greater part of the anointed people of God from the time of Joshua to the present day have not been able, because of unbelief, to enter into the "rest" of God—life lived under the rulership of the Spirit of Christ. Therefore there yet remains a rest to the people of God (Heb. 4:9).

A symbolic portrayal of a believer entering into the life in the Spirit of God can be found in Chapter 47 of Ezekiel, starting with the third verse:

"And when the man that had the line in his hand went forth eastward, he measured a thousand cubits, and he brought me through the waters; the waters were to the ankles. Again he measured a thousand, and brought me through the waters; the waters were to the knees. Again he measured a thousand, and brought me through; the waters were to the loins. Afterward he measured a thousand; and it was a river that I could not pass over: for the waters were risen, waters to swim in, a river that could not be passed over."

When we first come to Christ it is as though the waters of the Holy Spirit are "to the ankles." That is to say, we can walk at our own will although we have been saved from wrath and are in contact with the life of God.

If we go a bit deeper in the things of Christ the waters of the Holy Spirit's rulership come up "to the knees." The "water" is not as easy to churn through; it slows us down. More of our being is in contact with and affected by the Spirit of God. The powers of the natural self-life are beginning to be diminished and the life from God is beginning to affect our words and deeds. We can at this point turn around and walk back to dry land, back to the life lived in the lust of the flesh, the lust of the eyes, and the pride of life. Or we can choose to go yet deeper with God in the process of death to self and the laying hold upon resurrection life.

"Again he measured a thousand, and brought me through; the waters were to the loins (hips)." By now our walk has been influenced very greatly. We are controlled in our motions by the water to a much greater extent than is the believer who is splashing about in ankle-deep water.

Notice how the illustration of the "water" parallels that of "precept upon precept; line upon line." The Spirit of God, always with our consent and eventual cooperation, gradually extends His holy rulership over our deeds and words and thoughts. What was once an experience of the manifestation of the Spirit, an addition which we have attached to our regular church life, has now become an important part of our Christian life, a source of enablement to us as we pray in the Spirit. The fullness of the giving over of our life to the Spirit of Christ is a joyful attraction to us.

"Afterward he measured a thousand; and it was a river that I could not pass over: for the waters were risen, waters to swim in, a river that could not be passed over." It is a sad day for the flesh of man when finally he comes to something that is too big for him. But the fullness of the life in the Spirit is as a river which cannot be mastered.

The entire being of the beliver—imaginations, motives, words, and deeds—comes under the dominion of the Spirit of Christ. The "shore line" has been cut. The believer's life has been given over to God without reservation. In the words of Isaiah, the Christian has been "broken, and snared, and taken." He is experiencing the knowledge of Christ, and the power of the resurrection of Christ, and the fellowship of the sufferings of Christ. At the coming of Christ, the sufferings will cease and the faithful disciple will be immersed in the fullness of the Holy Spirit, the river of God, for evermore.

Resurrection life will extend completely into the body, soul, and spirit of the overcomer.

We humans are unable to measure the quality or the quantity of the Spirit of God. But mankind has seen one Person who walks eternally in the fullness of the Holy Spirit. The Son of man has the Spirit without measure, and He came that we also might have the Spirit without measure. Will we, like Esau, trade the inheritance of the life lived in the fullness of the Spirit of God for the fleshly pleasures of this age?

Here then is the dimension of the Pentecostal outpouring that we have not understood. The latter rain is the law of the new covenant—the law of the Spirit of life. We are to be brought under the governing power of the Spirit of God. The manifestation of the Holy Spirit is a means given by God to bring us to the goal of redemption, which is complete union with, and conformity to the express image of, the Lord Jesus Christ.

Loaves offered with leaven.   The convocation of Pentecost came at the end of the wheat harvest. Two large loaves made from wheat flour were "waved" before the Lord. The harvesting of grain had been completed.

The loaves contained leaven. We have noticed previously in our study that the Levitical convocations started off with Passover, during which unleavened bread was eaten; and then moved to a seven-day period of time, the week of Unleavened Bread, during which there was to be "no leaven found in your houses" (Exod. 12:19). The prohibition was very strict: "for whosoever eateth that which is leavened, even that soul shall be cut off from the congregation of Israel, whether he be a stranger, or born in the land" (Exod. 12:19). Leaven typifies sin, in the symbolism of Passover Week. We learn from this that God is exceedingly strict concerning the sincerity of our repentance and turning away from sin when we accept Christ and enter into water baptism. The disciple must be "crucified" with Christ so that the old leaven of sin can be destroyed (Rom. 6:6).

But now we find the Pentecostal bread, loaves which were waved before the Lord as a sign that they were intended for His use alone, being baked with leaven!

When we first come to Christ we must repent and turn away from all sin (leaven) of which we are aware. We identify ourself with Christ upon the cross in order that the body of sin in us might be rendered powerless. At the same time we identify ourself with His resurrection so that we can give our attention to walking in newness of life with Christ. Through means of this double identification, with His death and with His resurrection, we become free to choose to be servants of righteousness and to live righteously.

So, we are to consider the old leaven as being gone permanently, having been left by faith in the waters of baptism. Such is our position in Christ. In actual experience, we have to deal with the actions of the flesh. The Holy Spirit leads us in the putting to death of the deeds of our body (Rom. 8:13). The Day of Atonement, the sixth of the Levitical convocations, portrays the provision which God has made for forgiving our sins and cleansing us from all unrighteousness (I John 1:9).

But now there is a new leaven working in our life. The new leaven is the substance of Christ within us. A little leaven will work in a loaf until the whole has been affected and rises into the shape and texture which we desire. When we first come to Christ a *piece of Him* is placed into our nature (Luke 8:15). As we move along in our discipleship we come into situations where it seems that we are surrounded by never-ending problems and getting nowhere. Yet, though we may not be aware of it, the substance of Christ is working as leaven within us and governing the new creation which is being formed in us.

The two wave loaves of the convocation of Pentecost represent the church of Christ, which is a firstfruits unto God of the harvest of the earth. The loaves are two in number because the church is going to receive a double portion of His power and glory (Joel 2:23-32). The resurrected Christ is the first of the firstfruits. Then comes the church, which is His body. His body is leavened with Himself. Then will come the "nations of them which are saved" (Rev. 21:24). This pattern is revealed in the three areas of the Tabernacle of the Congregation: the holy of holies; the holy place; and the courtyard. There also is a "firstfruits unto God and to the Lamb," a "Tabernacle of David" if you will, which is being born through the travail of the church in these days (Acts 15:15; Rev. 12:5; 14:4).

Pentecost was not the last feast of the harvest season. There was more to the agricultural season after the grain had been harvested. The oil, nuts, fruits, and wine still had to be gathered and processed. It was the feast of booths (Tabernacles) coming at the very end of the agricultural year that announced the completion of the harvest season. The person who has received the baptism of the Holy Spirit has been partially harvested, in a manner of speaking. There remains much of his personality, including his mortal body, which has not as yet been harvested by the Lord.

A "halfway point."   Of the seven Levitical convocations, Pentecost is number four. Since four is halfway between one and seven we might infer that the person who has "arrived" at Pentecost is at a critical point in his spiritual journey. He is about to pass the "point of no return" (Heb. 6:4-6). He will still feel the world pulling him back, and he always must keep his body under discipline and guard himself with vigilance against deception. And yet there is an ever-deepening yearning in his heart to pass on to the richer joys of the Spirit of God. God has spoken plainly to this situation: "If any man draw back, my soul shall have no pleasure in him" (Heb. 10:38).

Anointing for priestly service.   Another aspect of the outpouring of the harvest rain is the anointing for priestly service.

"And thou shalt anoint Aaron and his sons, and

consecrate them, that they may minister unto me in the priest's office. And thou shalt speak unto the children of Israel, saying, This shall be a holy anointing oil to me throughout your generations. Upon man's flesh shall it not be poured, neither shall ye make any other like it, after the composition of it: it is holy, and it shall be holy unto you" (Exod. 30:30-32).

There are certain spiritual responsibilities attached to the anointing of the Holy Spirit who is upon and within the Christian disciple. Note the great importance of the ideas contained in the following statements:

"Then said Jesus to them again, Peace unto you: as my Father hath sent me, even so send I you. And when he had said this, he breathed on them, and saith unto them, Receive ye the Holy Ghost (Spirit): whosesoever sins ye remit, they are remitted unto them; and whosesoever sins ye retain, they are retained" (John 20:21-23).

"But ye shall receive power, after that the Holy Ghost (Spirit) is come upon you: and ye shall be witnesses unto me both in Jerusalem, and in all Judea, and in Samaria, and unto the uttermost part of the earth" (Acts 1:8).

"Know ye not that your bodies are the members of Christ (the anointed One)?" (I Cor. 6:15).

The baptism of the Holy Spirit anoints the church, the body of the anointed One, for her priestly service unto God. The Christians are to bring the words and graces of God to mankind. They are the "seed of Abraham" through whom all the nations of the earth are to be blessed (Gen. 22:18).

The presence of God, healing for the body, the knowledge of how to receive forgiveness of sins through the offering of Jesus Christ on the cross, moral direction, peace, wisdom, the remission or retention of sins: all these divine blessings, guidances, and judgments come to the world *only* through the priestly services of Christ working through Christian people. The baptism of the Holy Spirit sanctifies the believer for his priestly service and endues him with the power to bring the presence, power, and grace of God to people who are bound by the power of the devil.

The promise of the Father. Perhaps the word *Pentecost* is more familiar to us than are the names of the other Levitical convocations, with the possible exception of *Passover. Pentecost* is an anglicized form of a Greek word referring to *fifty*—the fiftieth day after Passover Week. Jesus rose from the dead during the Passover Week. He visited the earth for a period of forty days after His resurrection. Then He ascended into heaven. Following His ascent was a period of ten days of waiting. Jesus had commanded the apostles to stay in Jerusalem and wait for the "promise of the Father." Finally the fiftieth day arrived, the day of the Hebrew feast of Pentecost.

Naturally there were present at Jerusalem many thousands of devout Jews from all over the Roman Empire who, in obedience to the law of Moses, had come to the holy city to observe the convocation of Pentecost. It was upon this memorable day, while the faithful of Israel were gathered together by the Word of the Lord—some in obedience to Moses and some in obedience to Jesus of Nazareth—that the mighty anointing of the Holy Spirit of God fell as a hurricane from heaven, introducing the glory of God into the room where they were sitting.

Suddenly from heaven the spiritual fulfillment of the convocation of Pentecost came down upon them, bringing power to carry out the plan of redemption. The course of world history was changed radically on that day of days. How Abraham must have rejoiced to see his God fulfilling magnificently the promise made to him two thousand years before, as he held the knife over his "slain" and "resurrected" son: "In your seed shall all the nations of the earth be blessed."

Heavenly dynamite. Pentecost! The very name draws our spirits toward the world of the Spirit of God. The word should inspire to the core a true Christian. For upon that day was given to the church the dynamite of the Spirit to so empower the Christian camp that it can blast the kingdom of Antichrist until everything that exalts itself against the name of the Lord Jesus Christ shall be reduced to ashes.

"But you shall receive power (Greek, *dúnamin)* after that the Holy Spirit is come upon you." Here is the baptism of dynamite for service. The tongues of flame abiding upon them signified that the word of judgment had been put into the mouths of Christ's heralds. We see the effects of the word of judgment in the ministries of anointed saints whose words caused people to be gripped in an agony of conviction as the Holy Spirit convicted of sin, righteousness, and judgment.

Mrs. McPherson, Mr. Smith-Wigglesworth, Dr. Charles Price—these names and others of the same breed have been sufficient to stir the writer many a time and to encourage him to turn away from the useless strivings of the flesh and to wait upon the Lord for the enduement of power from on high.

Pentecost! Pentecost! Pentecost! How desperate is the need for Pentecostal power in the world today. Sin-burdened, sick, frustrated people need the gospel of the Lord Jesus Christ, a gospel of power which brings miraculous healings and other supernatural workings of the Spirit of Christ. Let us cry unceasingly to the Lord for "bread" to feed the friends who have come to us "in their journey." Harvest time is here *now.*

At this time (1975) there is a widespread moving of the Holy Spirit among the communicants of the great historic denominations. Episcopalians, Methodists, Presbyterians, Catholics—all are experiencing the speaking in tongues and miraculous healings. The current moving of the Spirit has been termed "charismatic." The speaking in tongues should prove to be a blessing to their individual and corporate worship.

The Christian "in the Spirit" speaks directly to God (I Cor. 14:2). Speaking in tongues makes possible an ease and fluency of worship. There are times when spiritual demands become greater than the ability of the Christian to frame and utter words sufficient for the burden. How blessed it is to be able to let go and allow the Holy Spirit to take up the burden and carry it through to the answer. Of course, the speaking in tongues always must be subject to the will and judgment of the Christian. And the Christian himself always must be subject to the will and judgment of the Holy Spirit of God, being united with Christ in His death and resurrection.

If we have experienced the speaking in tongues and other spiritual enablements, and have learned to yield to the gentle influences of the Spirit of Christ, let us go on. A door has been opened to us into a place where the Spirit does not come in spurts but is an abiding presence, a continual fountain of resurrection life. Let us go through the door which has been opened before us by the Pentecostal experience and enter into the life lived in full communion with and absolute obedience to the Holy Spirit.

Turn you northward! The person who has come to Pentecost is neither in Egypt nor in the land of promise. He ought not to look back toward Egypt (life controlled by fleshly lusts). He must press on toward maturity of the Spirit. The land of promise is reached when our whole being is in total accord with the Lord Jesus Christ.

Thus far in our study of the Levitical convocations we have discussed the blood of Passover, the repentance of Unleavened Bread, the inner rebirth of Firstfruits, and the spiritual law of Pentecost. Three more feasts are ahead of us—three convocations that stand between us and the fullness of redemption. Perhaps most of us have not passed this way before. But Christ surely was in that which went before, and Christ surely is in that which lies ahead. We cannot stop in this pilgrimage until maturity has been reached. There remains much land to be possessed. "Ye have compassed this mountain long enough: turn you northward" (Deut. 2:3).

TRUMPETS

> "Speak unto the children of Israel, saying, In the seventh month, in the first day of the month, shall ye have a sabbath, a memorial of blowing of trumpets, a holy convocation" (Lev. 23:24).

> "And if ye go to war in your land against the enemy that oppresseth you, then ye shall blow an alarm with the trumpets; and ye shall be remembered before the Lord your God, and ye shall be saved from your enemies. Also in the day of your gladness, and in your solemn days, and in the beginnings of your months, ye shall blow with the trumpets over your burnt offerings, and over the sacrifices of your peace offerings; that they may be to you for a memorial before your God: I am the Lord your God" (Num. 10:9,10).

> "So David and all the house of Israel brought up the ark of the Lord with shouting, and with the sound of the trumpet" (II Sam. 6:15).

> "Cry aloud, spare not, lift up thy voice like a trumpet, and show my people their transgression, and the house of Jacob their sins" (Isa. 58:1).

> "Blow . . . the trumpet in Zion, and sound an alarm in my holy mountain: let all the inhabitants of the land tremble: for the day of the Lord cometh, for it is nigh at hand" (Joel 2:1).

"In a moment, in the twinkling of an eye, at the last trump: for the trumpet shall sound, and the dead shall be raised incorruptible, and we shall be changed" (I Cor. 15:52).

"For the Lord himself shall descend from heaven with a shout, with the voice of the archangel, and with the trump of God: and the dead in Christ shall rise first" (I Thess. 4:16).

Spiritual warfare. It is our understanding that Joel 2:1 (quoted above) describes the burden of the Lord in the heart of the Christian who has experienced Pentecost and is ready to move on with God. "Sound an alarm in my holy mountain"!

The blowing of the trumpet is associated with warfare, in many instances. As we move on with God we enter into an understanding of Him as the *Lord of hosts* (armies). The Old Testament in numerous references refers to God as being a leader of armies. Indeed, the *warrior* is one of the most important roles of God, according to the Bible. Yet we Christians do not seem to have much of an acquaintance with the fighting aspect of God's nature. God is the Lord of armies! The day of the Lord, which we anticipate with such joy, is in fact a military engagement, a battle which is going to involve many personalities and which will be fought with terrific fury until the Lord Jesus has destroyed His enemies.

It appears that we Christians have little or no understanding of what spiritual conflict is all about. At Passover we are spiritual babies, just having been born again. At Pentecost we may have gone a bit further with God. But when we come to the convocation of Trumpets, God begins to share with us His concern for spiritual warfare. The Spirit of the Lord of armies cries *war! war! war! war!* in our soul.

"Blow . . . the trumpet in Zion, and sound an alarm in

my holy mountain: let all the inhabitants of the land tremble: for the day of the Lord cometh, for it is nigh at hand" (Joel 2:1).

"My bowels, my bowels! I am pained at my very heart; my heart maketh a noise in me; I cannot hold my peace, because thou hast heard, O my soul, the sound of the trumpet, the alarm of war" (Jer. 4:19).

Rebels from heaven.   The Lord Jesus Christ always is a fighter against evil forces. One of the prominent characteristics of His ministry is the casting out of devils. The unclean spirits, who were so upset by the presence of the Lord Jesus, are God's enemies against whom God wages war.

The Bible is not too specific concerning the rebellion of spirits in heaven. But there is enough said in the Scriptures for us to infer that there was some kind of revolt against the authority and will of God. How and when is not made clear to us. But as soon as Adam and Eve were placed in the Garden of Eden a personality appeared immediately, counseling them to have no faith in God's Word. It is not true that sin commenced in the Garden of Eden. From the account, we know that sin existed in the life of a person or persons who already were in rebellion against God. The deceptive counsel given in Eden assuredly was a very cunning temptation!

There is a hierarchy of wicked personalities. Paul teaches us that we "wrestle not against flesh and blood, but against principalities, against powers, against the rulers of the darkness of this world, against spiritual wickedness in high (heavenly) places" (Eph. 6:12). These wicked lords of darkness are God's enemies. At the present time they are very active among people on the earth, counseling and urging them to defy God, to lust, to murder, to lie; to take part in occult activities: to idolize things and people; to steal. The words and deeds of people upon the earth in 1975 are one mammoth illustration of the nature of the evil lords of sin and rebellion against the Most High. It is these same evil lords against whom the church is to wrestle in the Spirit.

Why hasn't God destroyed the rebels long ago? We cannot say. But we do know from the Scriptures that God has decided to destroy them through Christ (Head and Body) during a period called the day of the Lord. God has not forgotten one single rebellious thought, imagination, motive, word, or deed which has been formed against Him. But in His wisdom He has settled upon a specific manner in which He is going to execute His judgment. God is not slack. He is infinitely wise, infinitely patient, infinitely good. Sometimes people mistake God's patience for indulgence or forgetfulness. This error can be fatal.

The trumpet of the Lord is sounding an alarm in the church these days. God is calling His people to war. The warfare is not against human beings. The warfare is against wicked spirits in the heavenlies. The warfare is not against *our* enemies of the flesh, it is against *God's* enemies. The unclean spirits are God's enemies. They despise the Lord Jesus Christ. They despise the Word and will of God. They despise the image of God in mankind and they pervert the image in every conceivable manner. The Christian churches should be alert to the fact that the Spirit of God is preparing for the day of vengeance.

The Lord Jesus appeared for the purpose of destroying the works of the devil (I John 3:8). He cast out many wicked spirits as He walked back and forth throughout the land of Palestine. The casting out of devils is the first sign that is to follow Christian believers (Mark 16:17).

We Christians must prepare ourselves for spiritual warfare. Our attention must be shifted away from purely human activities and centered upon the things of the Spirit. There is nothing "wrong" with socials, musical events, contests between churches, etc. Good works of all kinds are essential to healthy church life. But the purpose, call, and driving motive of the body of Christ is not in human activities. The "call" of the body of Christ is to God's war of judgment against the hosts of darkness. The destruction of the works of the devil was the purpose for the manifestation of the Son of God (I John 3:8). The destruction of the works of the devil is the purpose for the manifestation of the sons of God (Rom. 8:19).

The burden of God's war against the kingdom of Satan is nearly absent from the Christian churches. Pleasant, entertaining music is sounding in the churches, not the trumpet of God. The trumpet *is* sounding in the spiritual realm. The trumpet of God *is* sounding in the heart of the Lord Jesus; He is God's Commander-in-chief. The trumpet *is* sounding in the heart of the members of the body of Christ who are outgrowing spiritual immaturity.

The alarm is sounding! Violent trumpet blasts reverberate throughout the world of spirits as the Lord of armies prepares His mighty men for the fierce conflict of the day of the Lord. And the churches slumber on. A little slumber. A little folding of the hands. Business as usual. Don't rock the boat or the membership will fall off. Will the membership fall off when the day of the Lord dawns in fire? If so, perhaps it should fall off now in preparation for that great day of spiritual battle which is coming.

"The Lord is a man of war: the Lord is his name" (Exod. 15:3).

"Who is this King of glory? The Lord strong and mighty, the Lord mighty in battle" (Ps. 24:8).

"The noise of a multitude in the mountains, like as of a great people; a tumultuous noise of the kingdoms of nations gathered together: the Lord of hosts mustereth the host of the battle. They come from a far country, from the end of heaven, even the Lord, and the weapons of his indignation, to destroy the whole land" (Isa. 13:4,5).

Sometimes such passages as the one preceding (Isa. 13:4,5) refer to a historical invasion of Israel by a foreign country. But often there is a double reference, one natural and one spiritual. The immediate application of Isaiah may have been to the overthrow of Babylon by the Medes and the Persians. But the language of the context suggests that the Holy Spirit of God, as is true in many other Old Testament passages, is speaking here not only of an immediate physical conflict but also of the ultimate spiritual conflict which yet is ahead of us.

"The Lord shall go forth as a mighty man, he shall stir up jealousy like a man of war: he shall cry, yea, roar; he shall prevail against his enemies" (Isa. 42:13).

"And the Lord shall utter his voice before his army: for his camp is very great: for he is strong that executeth his word: for the day of the Lord is great and very terrible; and who can abide it?" (Joel 2:11).

"The sun and moon stood still in their habitation: at the light of thine arrows they went, and at the shining of thy glittering spear" (Hab. 3:11).

"And I saw heaven opened, and behold a white horse; and he that sat upon him was called Faithful and True, and in righteousness he doth judge and make war" (Rev. 19:11).

It is impossible to understand the purposes and workings of the Christian salvation, to comprehend what God is doing and intends to do through the body of Christ, without understanding the warrior dimension of God's personality. God's attention is focused upon the day of the Lord; and the day of the Lord is characterized by battle, in many places where that day is mentioned in the Scriptures.

The sum of what we are saying is that the churches must

become much more aware of one of the most important purposes of the body of Christ. That purpose is the waging of war against the enemies of God, not against our enemies, but against the enemies of God. They are wicked personalities who dwell in the heavens at the present time. They are the rulers of the darkness of this world. God has had a controversy with them for a greater period of time than we know. It is they against whom God's anger smokes. It is they for whom the lake of fire has been prepared. And God, the Man of war acting through the body of Christ, is going to break the chains of bondage which these rebellious spirits have wrapped around the inhabitants of the earth.

Judgment. It is interesting to note that Trumpets and the Day of Atonement (*Yom T'ruoh* and *Yom Kippur)* are celebrated by the Hebrews in a mood of introspection and contrition. The other convocations have a more joyful tone. Because these two solemn convocations are a time of heart searching they are known as *Yomim Noroim,* the "Days of Awe."

The Days of Awe are concerned with the personal moral condition of the individual Jew. *Yom Kippur* (Day of Atonement) is the day on which (in Jewish tradition) sin is removed from the heart. In time past the ten days from *Yom T'ruoh* (Trumpets) to *Yom Kippur* were designated as days of penitence. The Days of Awe are associated in the devout Hebrew mind with the day when God judges the earth, judgment day.

"Blow the trumpet in Zion, and sound an alarm in my holy mountain." But we don't know how to blow the trumpet. We are not people of war. We would rather think of peaceful things and assure our hearts that all is well. "Blow it! Blow it! Sound the alarm!" commands the Spirit of God. "Sound the alarm of war!"

"But if the watchman see the sword come, and blow not the trumpet, and the people be not warned; if the sword come, and take any person from among them, he is taken away in his iniquity; but his blood will I require at the watchman's hand" (Ezek. 33:6).

The Holy Spirit of God is sounding the alarm of judgment to come: judgment against the world, against the proliferating sins hatched from the spirit of the age. But also against any wickedness that can be found in the churches. If murder, lust, and covetousness are found in the churches, they will be judged as sin by the Lord. Any Christian who is practicing murderous rage, hate, backbiting, jealousy, evil speakings, in his imaginations, motives, words, or deeds, can expect to be hearing from the Holy Spirit. Judgment is being exercised in the household of God. All actions are being screened carefully, one at a time. The bride of Christ must put away every single action and motive that proceeds from or is associated with the enemy. Every manifestation of the spirit of sectarianism, for example, must be abolished utterly.

If Jesus of Nazareth were to appear on earth today, how would we Christians receive Him? Would we cry, "Away with Him!"? Do the events at the time of the outpouring of the Holy Spirit at Azusa Street in Los Angeles confirm that Jesus is no more welcome today in "Israel" than He was two thousand years ago? Will we Christians repudiate and resist the Spirit of Christ whenever and wherever He appears?

As far as covetousness is concerned, can it be said truly of Christians in America that we are not over-involved with the spirit and things of the world? Are we indeed "strangers and pilgrims on the earth"? God in His kindness has given us all good things to enjoy. But the love of the world is not of the Father. Are we bound by the spirit of the age in which we live or are we following in the steps of the Man of Galilee, of Paul, of James, of John, of Peter? No man can be a Christian without putting his hand to the plow and walking straight on in the path set before him by the Holy Spirit. No man can be a Christian without taking up his cross and following Christ. The Lord Jesus Christ is the same, "yesterday, and today, and for ever."

Sometimes we say, "We must have beautiful surroundings to show the beauty of the gospel. We must beautify the house of God." Is the *place* where Christians assemble actually the *house of God?* The record shows that Messiah Jesus was born in a stable. Had God wanted His Son, Jesus, to be worshiped in surroundings befitting His kingly Person, Christ would have been born in a royal palace, not in the worst room in the inn.

But God is more concerned with the condition of the hearts of the Christians than He is with buildings in which they assemble. We are not advocating that Christian people meet in a dirty building. We must be diligent in everything we put our hand to, and taking adequate care of an assembly hall is no exception.

It appears however that we continue to refer to the buildings in which we assemble as the *house of God,* and we teach our children in Sunday School that the buildings are the house of God. We attempt to glorify God by decorating and enlarging the assembly halls. Yet the hearts of the believers in many instances remain boarded-up, cobwebbed shacks. It is time now for us Christians to straighten out this inconsistency.

At times there may be an inverse relationship between the condition of the assembly building and the condition of the hearts of those who assemble in it. Consider, for example, the Azusa Street mission. Compare the condition of that former stable with the beautiful contrition and consecration of the hearts of the recipients of the early outpouring. Or, look at the Lord of armies being born among the patient beasts, an environment which might cause our dainty church attenders to shriek with dismay rather than to worship God in Spirit and in truth. But they who are in the flesh covet the things of the flesh, and they who are in the Spirit covet the things of the Spirit.

"Yet ye say, The way of the Lord is not equal. O ye house of Israel, I will judge you every one after his ways" (Ezek. 33:20).

The trumpet of the Lord is sounding the alarm in Zion. God has come to judge His people wherever there is sin and idolatry and coldness of heart.

"Cry aloud, spare not, lift up thy voice like a trumpet, and show my people their transgression, and the house of Jacob their sins" (Isa. 58:1).

The Spirit of the Lord is sounding the alarm of danger and spiritual warfare. Let us of the churches beware of desiring to hear smooth things, comfortable things. Let us not require of the prophets that they prophesy deceits and tell us how pleased God is with our lukewarmness and our love of the things of the world. If we are cold and backslidden we want to know about it, and not be deceived with lies and hypocrisies. Too much is at stake, individually and collectively.

We may be waiting for God to pour out His Spirit at some vaguely defined future time, not realizing that it is the sin and indifference in the churches that has cut off the flow of the Holy Spirit of God. Now is the time for revival. Occasionally we have "mercy drops," so to speak. Thank God for the mercy drops, and thank God for the ministries and gifts of power which are being raised up in these days. But it is the will of the Father that the authority, power, and blessing of the Spirit come upon us *every time we gather together.* It is *now* that we should be beseeching the Father in the name of Jesus Christ for "rain in the time of the latter rain" (Zech. 10:1).

It is God's will that we should respond to the present-day alarm of the trumpet by getting ready to fight. The battle is against wicked spirits, the hosts of darkness, who are the enemies of God. Their power is exercised not only in the world but also at times in the hearts and lives of Christian people.

Obeying the Lord's trumpet.   Exactly how does one obey the trumpet of the Lord? Since the fight primarily is a spiritual one—we are not warring against human beings—then we must learn to walk in the Spirit and fight in the Spirit. Walking in the Spirit is a way of living which scarcely is understandable to many of us believers. But it is time now to pray in the Spirit, live in the Spirit, act in the Spirit, and to mortify (put to death) the deeds of the body. Unclean spirits use human weaknesses as beachheads from which they can fulfill their unclean inclinations:

> "Therefore, brethren, we are debtors, not to the flesh, to live after the flesh. For if ye live after the flesh, ye shall die: but if ye through the Spirit do mortify the deeds of the body, ye shall live. For as many as are led by the Spirit of God, they are the sons of God" (Rom. 8:12-14).

The preceding passage perfectly describes the correct response to the trumpet call of the Lord. We are to be led by the Spirit of the Lord in combat against the works of the devil in the earth, particularly against the "deeds of the body"—the lusting, coveting, murdering, etc., that we Christians do.

When we are led by the Holy Spirit we can overcome the law of sin which binds the human body. "If we say that we have no sin, we deceive ourselves" (I John 1:8). Sin dwells in our flesh (Rom. 7:20). We do sinful things to which we do not consent (Rom. 7:19). The Spirit of God is ready to go to war against the evil in our life.

A double wielding.   We must cooperate with the Spirit of God in the battle for control of our body. It is the "sword of the Lord, *and of Gideon.*" The Word of God is "the sword *of the Spirit,"* it is true, but it is wielded in the hands *of the Christian*. This double control and responsibility (the Spirit and the Christian) is a very important principle of living and fighting in the Spirit, and a principle that often is rejected by Christians in favor of, "The Lord will do it by Himself," or, "The Lord depends upon us to do it." Listen to the Spirit of God speaking through Gideon:

> "When I blow with a trumpet, I and all that are with me, then blow ye the trumpets also on every side of all the camp, and say, The sword of the Lord, and of Gideon" (Judg. 7:18).

The Lord wouldn't do it alone, and Gideon couldn't do it alone. The Lord won't overcome sin in our life by Himself and we can't overcome in our life by ourself. We overcome our sins "through the Spirit." Although in a final analysis it can be shown that in actuality God is the One who starts and carries out the entire plan of redemption in an individual, yet in the day-to-day working out a great deal depends upon the will and efforts of the Christian believer. We must learn to live, walk, and fight, *in the Spirit.*

A legal declaration of sanctification by grace alone is part of the answer to the power that sin has in our life; but after we have declared ourselves crucified with Christ and free from the law of sin we go right on with our coveting, sectarianism, and backbiting. Human will power against sinning is part of the answer, and through will power we attempt to resist temptation. But since will power depends upon human effort to overcome evil spirits, and since our will power may not be coupled with divine grace and power, we continue with our adulterous imaginations, hatreds, and jealousies. It takes a never-ceasing yielding to and cooperating with the Holy Spirit of God (the sword of the Lord and of Gideon) if the Christian is going to have the wisdom and strength to drive the sin out of his life.

I do not mean by these words to arouse a spirit of anxious struggling in us. Christians maintain their spiritual poise and deeply settled peace in the midst of spiritual conflict by abiding in Christ. Christ reigns in majesty, having completely overcome the authority of Satan and sin. Christ is working in us each day to bring all of God's enemies into utter subjection under His feet. The victory of Christ is total! final! absolute! We are to rest unflinchingly, consistently, courageously, hopefully, faithfully in that fact. And when we do we are *without condemnation* (see Rom. 8:1).

"For if ye live after the flesh, ye shall die: but if ye through the Spirit do mortify the deeds of the body, ye shall live. For as many as are led by the Spirit of God, they are the sons of God" (Rom. 8:13,14).

A warlike attitude.   When the Spirit of God blows the trumpet it is time for us to follow Him into battle. He is ready to wage war against the sin that dwells in us (Rom. 7:20). He is ready to enable the church to invade the "promised land." The promised land of the Christian is whatever God has given him to possess, particularly his own being (I Thess. 5:23).

If we are unwilling to respond to the trumpet of the Lord with an attitude of combat we will come under the curse of Meroz:

"Curse ye Meroz, said the angel of the Lord, curse ye bitterly the inhabitants thereof; because they came not to the help of the Lord, to the help of the Lord against the mighty" (Judg. 5:23).

The attitude of God is revealed in Deuteronomy 9:3:

"Understand therefore this day, that the Lord thy God is he which goeth over before thee; as a consuming fire he shall destroy them, and he shall bring them down before thy face: so shalt thou drive them out, and destroy them quickly, as the Lord hath said unto you."

God is a commander of armies and a God of judgment, and we must adopt the attitude of war and judgment against sin if we have any hope of going on with God past the Pentecostal experience of speaking in tongues and prophesying. Spiritual combat is the only route at this time to possession of the riches of God.

"If I whet my glittering sword, and mine hand take hold on judgment; I will render vengeance to mine enemies, and will reward them that hate me. I will make mine arrows drunk with blood, and my sword shall devour flesh; and that with the blood of the slain and of the captives, from the beginning of revenges upon the enemy" (Deut. 32:41,42).

We may be comfortable and at ease in Zion, and would rather flee to Egypt (back into the world) than to hear the sound of the trumpet, the sound of alarm (Jer. 42:14). But if we are to go on from Pentecost we must arm ourselves for spiritual war (Eph. 6:12-18). Woe to us if we "hold back our sword from blood" in the day of the Lord's battle (Deut. 7:2; I Kings 20:42; I Sam. 15:8-23).

Moving on. As we are proceeding in our study past the convocation of Pentecost and are beginning to think about the final three convocations, we may be traveling on ground that is new to the reader. Many of us have not passed this way before. However, it is not a new way to some of the saints of old, just new to our generation perhaps. And, surprisingly enough, it does not take a Christian years and years to go through these experiences. A pioneer in a wilderness may take five months to travel the same distance that a person two hundred years later can cover in five hours.

And we do not mean to imply that salvation works in a human life in a series of neatly placed separate steps typified by the seven Hebrew convocations. The seven convocations may be thought of as being seven dimensions of the one salvation.

The outworking of salvation in human beings doesn't seem to proceed in an ordered sequence of grade levels. The Levitical convocations portray seven aspects of one salvation. The order can be switched around. The experiences are elaborated in us somewhat differently depending upon the individual Christian. The feasts are woven into the fabric of our lives piecemeal, all at once, hourly, yearly, in small increments, in unfathomable crises. There is no way to organize these into a doctrinal system or constitution upon which to build a new denomination, a new division in the body of Christ. It is a day to strive for unity, not division, in the church of the living God.

Let us remember also that Christians can experience the spiritual counterparts of the convocations without understanding the doctrinal implications, in fact, while rejecting the doctrine. The love of Jesus, rather than doctrinal profundity or accuracy, is the most important quality of the Christian life.

Spiritual New Year. We have mentioned that the blowing of the trumpet heralds the Jewish New Year celebration. So it is that the trumpet of God, sounding in the spiritual realm, is announcing triumphantly that a *new year* is at hand, a year of jubilee (Lev. 25:9), a beginning of deliverances from the oppressor and a returning to that which had been lost. Jesus Christ on the cross destroyed every last scrap of Satan's legal rights to us and to the rest of the creation. The mortgage has been paid to the penny. Jesus holds the title to the creation. It remains for the church to take possession. The eviction papers are in legal order but the old tenants must be thrown out by force.

Overcoming sin. There are those who will question our

position that the overcoming of sin is a process wrought out over a period of time in, and with the cooperation of, the Christian believer. They will maintain rather that the sin question was settled once for all on the cross, that the Christian need only to take a proper attitude (reckoning) toward the finished work of Calvary, and sin as a result no longer is a dynamic in his life.

There is truth in this doctrine. It is a fact that Christ upon the cross *did conquer Satan completely* (Col. 2:15) and that our old man (sinful nature) was and is crucified with Christ (Rom. 6:6). Clearly, this is scriptural.

Continuing along the same line, we would caution against the believer's wrestling with sin in his own life. It is impossible for us by our own will power, even our will power in prayer, to master the sinful tendencies we observe in our lives. It is correct, of course, to use self-control and temperance in all things as much as we are able, and to resist fleshly appetites. If we do not, we can never make a success of Christian discipleship. But struggling against sin may result in the resurrection of the old nature rather than its death. The cross is God's remedy for our sinful nature. We are crucified with Christ and we are, by faith, to rest in this fact (Gal. 2:20; Rom. 8:1).

However, there are two facts which cause us to believe that reckoning ourselves dead (Rom. 6:11) is not the whole answer to the fact of sin in the acts, words, and thoughts of the Christian. First of all, we Christians who subscribe to Romans 6:11 still find ourselves committing sins, and God is concerned about sin and judges it whether committed by believer or nonbeliever (Rom. 2:13). Second, there is considerable Scripture, in both the Old and New Testament, to indicate that the overcoming of sin is a continuous process in the Christian life (Deut. 7:22; Rom. 8:13; I Cor. 15:25; II Cor. 10:5; Gal. 5:16,17; Eph. 4:22-32; and many, many more).

A great portion of the New Testament passages are an

exhortation to holiness (as is true of so much of the Old Testament writings), which wouldn't make too much sense if, upon the adoption of a reckoning attitude, sin ceased to be an active force in the believer's life. If sin were not a problem in the Christian church, then no doubt the letters of the apostles would be somewhat different in content from what they are.

The fact is, however, that a great deal of the New Testament is devoted to exhorting the Christians to overcome sin, to put it out of their lives because of and through their relationship with Christ. It appears, from what we can observe today, that a scriptural, workable, practical, effective process for the development of holiness has not been widely understood nor used by the majority of the Christian believers. By holiness we mean the doing of the things which are pleasing to Christ, and the not doing, in imagination, motive, word, or deed, of the things of the flesh and of unclean spirits. We have not understood the provision which Christ has made for the development of holiness in us, and many have given up trying because of the seeming impossibility of overcoming sinful tendencies.

The day of the Lord. "Behold, I show you a mystery; we shall not all sleep, but we shall all be changed, in a moment, in the twinkling of an eye, at the last trump: for the trumpet shall sound, and the dead shall be raised incorruptible, and we shall be changed" (I Cor. 15:51,52).

"For the Lord himself shall descend from heaven with a shout, with the voice of the archangel, and with the trump of God: and the dead in Christ shall rise first" (I Thess. 4:16).

"And the seventh angel sounded; and there were great voices in heaven, saying, The kingdoms of this world are become the kingdoms of our Lord, and of

his Christ; and he shall reign for ever and ever"
(Rev. 11:15).

The day of the Lord rises in the heart of the overcoming
Christian. In the words of II Peter 1:19," . . . until the day
dawn, and the day-star arise in your hearts." There is a
personal presence of Christ, a personal day of the Lord. And
it is announced by the trumpet of the Lord "blowing," so to
speak, in our heart.

There also is coming a great historical day of Christ,
which is described in the above passages. That day is the first
resurrection, of which Paul speaks in Philippians 3:11; I
Thessalonians 5:2; and I Corinthians 13:10. It is the day of
the return of Jesus Christ to the earth, and the day of the
revealing of the sons of God (Rom. 8:28-30).

So it is that the trumpet of the Lord announces a
personal day of Christ in our heart, which is the absolute,
undivided reign of Christ over our imaginations, motives,
words, and deeds. Also there is a historical blowing of the
trumpet of God—the sounding of the seventh angel, at which
time Christ shall return to the earth, glorify the church, and
extend His rule out from the hearts of the overcomers until
His will completely covers the earth.

There is a personal day of the Lord and there is a
historical day of the Lord. There is a personal millennium
and a historical millennium. We might add that the only
persons who will rule with Christ during the historical
millennium are those who establish a personal millennium—a rulership of Christ—*right here and now* (I John 3:2,3).

The section we have just completed is the new covenant
interpretation of the Levitical convocation of Trumpets, as
we see it. Trumpets is fifth in a series of seven convocations.
Now we have come in our study to the sixth Levitical
convocation, the most sacred day of the entire Hebrew year,
the Day of Atonement.

DAY OF ATONEMENT

"Also on the tenth day of this seventh month there shall be a day of atonement: it shall be a holy convocation unto you; and ye shall afflict your souls, and offer an offering made by fire unto the Lord. And ye shall do no work in that same day: for it is a day of atonement, to make an atonement for you before the Lord" (Lev. 23:27,28).

"And the Lord said unto Moses, Speak to Aaron thy brother, that he come not at all times into the holy place within the veil before the mercy seat, which is upon the ark; that he die not: for I will appear in the cloud upon the mercy seat" (Lev. 16:2).

"For on that day shall the priest make an atonement for you, to cleanse you, that ye may be clean from all your sins before the Lord" (Lev. 16:30).

"Then shalt thou cause the trumpet of the jubilee to sound on the tenth day of the seventh month, in the day of atonement shall ye make the trumpet sound throughout all your land" (Lev. 25:9).

"And not only so, but we also joy in God through our Lord Jesus Christ, by whom we have now received the atonement" (Rom. 5:11).

"And almost all things are by the law purged with blood; and without shedding of blood is no remission. It was therefore necessary that the patterns of things in the heavens should be purified with these; but the heavenly things themselves with better sacrifices than these. For Christ is not entered into the holy places made with hands, which are the figures of the true; but into heaven itself, now to appear in the presence of God for us" (Heb. 9:22-24).

"Having therefore, brethren, boldness to enter into the holiest by the blood of Jesus, by a new and living way, which he hath consecrated for us, through the veil, that is to say, his flesh" (Heb. 10:19,20).

"But if we walk in the light, as he is in the light, we have fellowship one with another, and the blood of Jesus Christ his Son cleanseth us from all sin. If we say that we have no sin, we deceive ourselves, and the truth is not in us. If we confess our sins, he is faithful and just to forgive us our sins, and to cleanse us from all unrighteousness" (I John 1:7-9).

Day of Atonement placed in the latter section of redemption. The Levitical convocations are seven in number. The Day of Atonement, the convocation having to do with the committing of sins by the people of God, was sixth in order. If we are following a logical sequence or pattern of any kind, why wasn't the Day of Atonement placed first in the order of the convocations? It seems reasonable that the first thing that should happen in the plan of redemption is that sin should be taken care of completely.

But the fact of the matter is that the blood of Passover protected Israel from the judgment that falls upon the gods of this world. The Passover blood is a shield, a wall of protection from the judgment of God. The first Passover was celebrated in Egypt; but the Day of Atonement, the convocation having to do with the purging of sins from God's people, was never celebrated in Egypt! The Day of Atonement could not be conducted until the Tabernacle of the Congregation had been set up.

Isn't this order of placement of the Day of Atonement somewhat out of line with our traditional concept of the relationship between the Christian life and sin, in that we would expect the convocation typifying cleansing from sin to come at the very outset of the series of seven convocations?

God's remedy for the sinful condition of His people is the precious blood of our Lord Jesus Christ. God has made an atonement for us, just as He covered Adam and Eve with coats of skins (Gen. 3:21). God has covered us with the blood of Christ so that the shame of our nakedness does not appear when we come into the presence of God Almighty (Rev. 3:18).

The blood of Jesus Christ, the sacrificial Lamb of God, is applied to our lives in four different ways: (1) as the Passover blood, which protects us from the judgment of God as it falls upon the gods of this world; (2) as the blood of atonement which cancels the debt of guilt incurred because of our sins; (3) as the blood of atonement through which the Holy Spirit of God is enabled to remove the tendencies and repair the consequences of the sin in us, give us the strength to resist sin, and fill us with the resurrection life of Christ so that we are lifted above the spiritual realms where sin abounds; and (4) as the blood of the sacrifice which we drink when we receive the body and blood of Christ in the communion. The atonement which God made for us in the sacrifice of Christ upon Calvary is so comprehensive that it is difficult to describe in one or two words. Our definition of *make atonement* is: *restore completely to divine favor.*

The Day of Atonement is the sixth of the seven convocations. The seven convocations do not proceed in order in our lives like the grades of an elementary school. The spiritual counterparts of the seven convocations are experienced by us at the moment of accepting Christ, and should be working in us each day of our pilgrimage. The several facets of the Day of Atonement—the Passover protection, the cancelling of guilt, the washing away of all unrighteousness, and the partaking of the substance of Christ—are ours at the moment of receiving Christ as our Savior and Lord.

As we move along in the plan of God for our lives the convocations are fulfilled in our personalities to an ever greater degree. Certainly, the full weight of authority and power contained in the body and blood of Jesus becomes increasingly meaningful to us. Our day-to-day Christian walk brings us to an ever-greater consciousness of what the blood of Christ really can do concerning the hold that sin has upon us. We become better able to lay hold upon the body and blood and thereby overcome the accuser (Rev. 12:11).

At this point in our book we are going to dwell for a bit upon the need of us who have been Christians for a while to learn to draw upon the authority and power of the atonement made by Christ, so that we can fight our way through to greater freedom from the "sin which doth so easily beset us" (Heb. 12:1). The "living bird" of Leviticus 14:7 and the "scapegoat" of Leviticus 16:10 show us clearly that God intends that our sins not only should be forgiven but also should be *removed* from us. We Christians need to learn more about how to get our sins removed from us so that we can be made perfect in the sight of God (Heb. 10:1).

Perhaps it is our understanding that sin is purged out of our life at the time of our initial contact with the Lord Jesus Christ. And, though we have come by the way of the cross—many years ago in some cases—yet can we claim with certainty that we have been delivered from backbiting, pride, haughtiness, spiritual coldness, covetousness, hardness of heart, slothfulness (concerning the things of the Spirit), hatred, gossip, jealousy, foolishness, idolatry, lust, envy, lying, boasting, stealing, divisiveness, witchcraft, ambition, self-love, complacency, fear, self-pity? If we, individually and collectively, *do* these things, then it appears that the power contained in the atonement of Christ has not accomplished its perfect work in us, although we have been "saved" (Gal. 5:21).

Perhaps there is a reason why in the sequence of the Levitical convocations, one of the most important set of symbols in the Old Testament experience, the Holy Spirit of God placed the Day of Atonement in the latter section of His representation of the Christian salvation. It may be that a person must be converted and then walk with Christ for a season before God is able to deal with the profound deceitfulness of the heart—to root out the tares from among the wheat (Matt. 13:29). As it is written, "The heart is deceitful above all things, and desperately wicked: who can know it?" (Jer. 17:9). This, of course, is not the primary application of the parable of the tares and the wheat (Matt. 13:37-43).

Christians do sin.   In any case, two facts seem evident: (1) the cleansing of the Tabernacle and of the priests and people occurs during the latter part of the series of convocations, just prior to the convocation of Tabernacles (fullness of the indwelling of Christ and the Father; redemption of the mortal body); and (2) the farther along that Christian disciples walk with Christ, the more conscious they become of the problem of sin in their own life and the need for personal holiness, showing that holiness of life is not completely achieved at the time of the first acceptance of Christ.

When a Christian sins the wickedness may not be of the gross, obvious nature of drunken brawling, armed robbery, or pushing drugs. The wickedness may be of a more deceitful nature. The sinfulness of the household of faith tends to be that of the heart, the murderous hardness, jealousy, pride, spitefulness of the heart. Such was the heart-sin of Israel, the murderer of prophets from ancient times. Whenever "Israel" sees her Beloved she is apt to cry, "Away with Him! Crucify Him! Let the guilt for His murder fall on us and our children!"

Perhaps we shouldn't blame the Hebrew Pharisees too much for the murder of Jesus. It is possible that the Christian churches of today would get rid of Christ somehow were He to appear. We might find fault with His words or deeds, or have Him discredited in some manner or put out of the church, while we are singing, "Have Thine Own Way, Lord." Jeremiah may be as current as the morning paper when he warns, "The sin of Judah is written with a pen of iron, and with the point of a diamond: it is graven upon the table of their heart, and upon the horns of your altars" (Jer. 17:1).

It may be difficult for us Christians to believe that there actually is sin in the churches, when the Christian church is God's own institution in the earth. Perhaps part of the reason we find this fact so hard to accept is that we do not understand the pattern of God's workings. Think about the implications of Leviticus 16:16, for example:

> "And he shall make an atonement for the holy place, because of the uncleanness of the children of Israel, and because of their transgressions in all their sins: and so shall he do for the tabernacle of the congregation, that remaineth among them in the midst of their uncleanness."

A misleading assumption. A misleading assumption sometimes made by us is that the presence of God in our midst means that we are holy. The Christian churches are of God, we reason, are of divine origin, and if we sense the presence of God it must be true that we are walking in holiness in His sight.

A good way to test the accuracy of this idea is to ask the people of the world their opinion of the holiness of the Christian church people, as far as can be determined upon the basis of their daily actions and words. Another way to test the idea is to look about us; or, better yet, to look at our own imaginations, motives, words, and deeds.

"And so shall he do for the tabernacle of the congregation, that REMAINETH AMONG THEM IN THE MIDST OF THEIR UNCLEANNESS." If God refused to have anything to do with people until they were holy, there would be precious little of the presence of God anywhere on this planet.

God doesn't come among us because we *are* holy, but rather to make us holy. The Holy Spirit is not given to us because we are holy, but in order to make us holy. The manifestation of the Spirit is not given to a believer because he is righteous, but rather to make him righteous. A person doesn't receive an apostleship, or a gift of teaching and revealing the Word, or a gift of miracles because he is unusually holy, but in order to create holiness in him and in those who receive of the grace given to him.

It is not unusual for Christians to confuse ministry, especially highly visible ministry, with holiness and spirituality. Then, if the highly regarded, sometimes idolized, minister should manifestly sin along some line, neither he nor his followers can admit the sin and treat it objectively. He is destroyed, and some of his followers along with him. He and they had supposed that God had revealed Himself through his ministry because he was particularly holy. We Christians must come to understand that God has set His holy tabernacle, so to speak, among us in the midst of our uncleanness. Then we will be able to view our sins objectively and to confess them from a position of strength, faith, and stability, rather than to pretend that we don't do them or to get unduly alarmed or to fall away in dismay or despair when our sin is revealed.

"Speak not thou in thine heart, after that the Lord thy God hath cast them out from before thee, saying, For my righteousness the Lord hath brought me in to possess this land: but for the wickedness of these nations the Lord doth drive them out from before thee.

Not for thy righteousness, or for the uprightness of thine heart, dost thou go to possess their land: but for the wickedness of these nations the Lord thy God doth drive them out from before thee, and that he may perform the word which the Lord sware unto thy fathers, Abraham, Isaac, and Jacob.

Understand therefore, that the Lord thy God giveth thee not this good land to possess it for your righteousness; for thou art a stiffnecked people" (Deut. 9:4-6).

Can we face the possibility that the Christian church, the very body of Christ, has members who sin? It may help us to remember that a very large fraction of the whole Bible is directed toward the problem of the sins of Israel. A great part of Isaiah, of Jeremiah, Ezekiel, Hosea, Amos, Micah, and so on, were addressed to the "sinners in Zion." The Lamentations of Jeremiah proceeded from the effect of the judgments of God upon His called-out people, His church.

A substantial percent of the New Testament writings is concerned with sin in the Christian life: for example, Romans 13:9-14; I Corinthians 1:10-13; 3:1-5; 5:1-13; 6:1-20; II Corinthians 12:20,21; Galatians 5:15-26; 6:8; Ephesians 4:22—5:7; Philippians 3:18,19; Colossians 3:5-10; I Thessalonians 4:4-8; 5:22,23; I Timothy 6:3-11; II Timothy 3:1-9; Titus 2:1-15; Hebrews 3:12-19; James 3:1—5:20; I Peter 1:13-15; 2:1; 4:1-4; 4:15-19; II Peter 1:4-10; 2:1-22; 3:11; all of I John; III John 9-11; Jude 7-19; Revelation 2:14; 2:20-22; 3:15-17; 21:8; 22:15.

Perhaps the root of our misconception concerning the relationship of the Christian believer to sin is that we have assumed that the bulk of the Bible admonitions against sin is addressed to people outside the church. The truth of the matter is that the Bible almost exclusively is referring to sin inside the church. The prophets spoke to Israel about sin and the apostles wrote to the Christian churches about sin.

But if there were not one single Bible reference to sin in the Christian life we would know, nevertheless, that sin indeed is a problem because of what we find in our own heart, because of the vigilance we must maintain against our own motives and deeds.

Perhaps the greatest of the many dangers facing the church is not the spiritual deadness, the complacency and indifference toward the things of Christ, the love of the world, the slothfulness, the pride and haughtiness, the backbiting and gossiping, the hardness of heart and lack of forgiveness, the desire to seek the approval of the world over the approval of God. These pitfalls are grievous enough.

But the one great piece of evidence that testifies in thunderous tones to the inner spiritual condition of God's people, a fact that nullifies the edicts of the church and eclipses the world's view of Christ upon the cross, is the existence of division and competition in the multitude of denominations and sects of Christianity. Denominational pride and loyalty give final proof of self-interest, self-love, self-ambition. All such organizational and doctrinal divisions are works of the flesh (Gal. 5:20).

God's provisions for the sins of Christians. We have written the truth as we see it in the Scriptures and in real life. And we sincerely believe it to be as dreadful as we have portrayed it. But we believe just as sincerely that there is a remedy symbolized by the Day of Atonement that is more than equal to the task of purifying the church perfectly.

During the Hebrew convocation of the Day of Atonement, the atonement was accomplished by a sprinkling of animal blood and by public confession of the sins of God's people. In the case of the Christians, the atonement was accomplished by the once-for-all offering of Christ upon the cross, and by the daily application of His precious blood to our lives.

Also involved and absolutely essential is the confessing of sins by Christ's disciples; sometimes confessed to God in private, sometimes to another person for counsel or prayer or because the other person is implicated, and sometimes (in rare instances—only when actually necessary because there are pitfalls in this practice) to a group of individuals, such as in a church assembling.

Confessing sins. Many Protestant Christians do not confess their sins: that is, they do not name them clearly before God. They keep the sins and shortcomings buried in their heart. But the sins continue to publicize their presence in their private thoughts, in their words, and in their deeds: adulterous thoughts, spiteful words, and acts of hatred and revenge, for example.

Sins—every last one of them—must be confessed with the mouth (the basic meaning of *confession*) as soon as they are pointed out by the Holy Spirit. A person has to tell the Lord, and sometimes other people, exactly what it is he has thought, said, or done. We may be in too much of a hurry to start naming our sinful imaginations, motives, words, and deeds one at a time to the Lord. God is not in that much of a hurry. He will take the time to listen now or He will take the time to listen during the day of judgment. As it is written: "Every idle word that men shall speak, they shall give account thereof in the day of judgment" (Matt. 12:36).

Only an overcoming Christian, and one with experience, can engage in this kind of daily judging of his motives and actions without falling into gloom and introspection. Confessing one's sins with authority and power is the act of a conqueror, not of a halfhearted person who continually is falling away from his state of obedience to the Master. Perhaps this is why the judgment upon sin in the life of the believer is delayed symbolically and actually until the person is past initial salvation, past Pentecost, and well into the convocation of Trumpets.

Some Christian teachers have maintained that it is necessary only to acknowledge our sinfulness to Christ, accept His forgiveness, and then forget about the sinful nature. To do otherwise, they counsel, will result in the resurrection of the sinful nature. This approach to sin in the Christian solves the problem for some believers, at least for a season, and can be very helpful to the person who has gotten himself worked into a vain struggling against the adversary, against the spirit of the age, and against his own flesh. The will and virtue of a person fighting "in the flesh" cannot possibly overcome the power of sin. But if, on the other hand, the disciple is under the impression that sin cannot affect him because he has accepted Christ, how then can the Spirit of God point out to him acts of sin which he is committing?

Anyone who studies the revivals of the past can notice that the outpourings of God's Holy Spirit were accompanied by confession of sins on the part of God's people. The fact seems to be that we must walk our daily overcoming life in Christ absolutely in faith and with no tinge of gloom or introspection. But we also must ever be ready to sense the rebuke of the Holy Spirit and to immediately bring the offending thought or word to the Lord for forgiveness. If we are walking in the Spirit of God the act of daily confessing will not depress us, but rather will enable us to live a victorious life in this world.

Why is it that Protestants do not include the practice of confessing sins in their daily walk with Jesus? It may be that they have supposed that the exhortations of Scripture against sin are directed toward the people of the world rather than toward the people of God. It may stem from an ignorance of the context of passages of Scripture.

Both the old and new covenant writings are explicit as to what constitutes sin. Many of such biblical pronouncements can be categorized under sexual lust, idolatry, or hatred. It may be observed that mankind has not changed a thousandth of an inch since the days of Noah and Lot. Lust, demon worship, and murder filled the earth in those days; and lust, demon worship, and murder fill the earth in our days.

The nations of Western civilization resemble Sodom and Gomorrah and are hurtling toward destruction with express-train speed. And America is right in the forefront! God always will exercise His wrath upon sexual lust in all its perverted forms, idolatry, and demon worship. This is equally true in the church and in the world.

Perhaps we Christians interpret God's long-suffering and forbearance as a kind of tolerant amusement at our sins, an "It's all in the family" kind of attitude. If so, then we have no conception of the smoking wrath of God that forever is directed toward these practices, or of the maelstrom of destruction which surrounds us. "For the time is come that judgment must begin at the house of God: and if it first begin at us, what shall the end be of them that obey not the gospel of God? And if the righteous scarcely be saved, where shall the ungodly and the sinner appear?" (I Pet. 4:17,18). "Knowing therefore the terror of the Lord, we persuade men" (II Cor. 5:11).

Misunderstanding of grace. One of the more important reasons for our not confessing the sins in our daily walk may arise from a misunderstanding of doctrine, particularly the doctrine of *grace.*

The word *grace,* it appears, frequently is understood to mean the total forgiveness of sins which occurs at the time of the believer's initial acceptance of the atonement made by the blood of Christ. The application of grace to the older Christian's life often is limited to the idea that God forgives our stumblings and shortcomings. Such seems to be the customary understanding of the concept of *grace* among believers in Christ.

The writer holds firmly to the understanding that salvation is the free gift of God which comes upon our accepting by faith the blood atonement made by Christ. But the doctrine which maintains that an initial acceptance of the atonement of Christ is the believer's only encounter with the problem of sin in his life, or that there is no power in God's grace to overcome sin in us, simply cannot be supported by the New Testament writings.

How could anyone study the letters of Paul, John, Peter, James, and Jude and come to such a conclusion? The truth of the matter appears to be that the disciple must be alert continually to the leadings and workings of the wisdom and power of the Spirit of God as He leads us in the conquest of the spirit of this age, the nature and works of Satan, and the lust of the flesh, the lust of the eyes, and the pride of life.

We are in a war, though we may not realize it. The Christian church is God's holy instrument for judging rebellious spirits, not a civic club or fraternal order. Satan, in many instances, has the Christian church bound hand and foot to the extent that we no longer actually believe many of the facts, claims, demands, and promises of the Old and New Testaments. Yet we may be picturing ourselves as the Church Triumphant against which the gates of Hell shall not prevail.

Perhaps it is closer to the truth to say that the Christian church has been a blind Samson making sport for the Philistines. We may have been making great boasts while "lying in the lap of Delilah." But where is the power of God? Paul says, "I . . . will know, not the speech of them who are puffed up, but the power" (I Cor. 4:19).

It is time now for us to confess our sins. "If we (Christian disciples) confess our sins, he is faithful and just to forgive us our sins, and to cleanse us from all unrighteousness" (I John 1:9). As we "walk in the light" (walk in the perfect will of God as revealed continually by the Holy Spirit and proved by the offering of ourself as a living sacrifice), the Spirit of God points out to us specific sins of imagination, motive, word, and deed.

The distinction must be maintained between *accusations* of Satan and the pinpointing of sin by the Holy Spirit. Satan constantly is planting ideas in our mind and accusing us of things Christ already has forgiven, or of sins we haven't really committed and have no intention of committing. A Christian through experience learns to recognize Satan and to resist his accusations. Such accusations are not sin and do not need to be confessed. Sometimes we have to pray for faith and for strength to overcome the depression, gloom, and fear which such accusations produce.

The sins of imagination, motive, word, and deed which are pointed out to us by the Holy Spirit, and which therefore must be confessed, are those which we more or less accept and dwell upon, which we harbor for a period of time, which for one reason or another we do not firmly disown. These attitudes, thoughts, and deeds are sins and must be named as such before the Lord. Imaginations, motives, words, and deeds must be brought under the absolute domination of Christ, and this takes experience, prayer, faith, and a mighty determination to overcome in Christ. The total subjection of the believer's personality to the rule of Christ is a forerunner of the great day of the Lord when every creature in the universe, willingly and joyfully, or otherwise, shall bow in subjection to Jesus Christ. All resistance to the rule of Jesus Christ is sin.

"For though we walk in the flesh, we do not war after the flesh: (for the weapons of our warfare are not carnal, but mighty through God to the pulling down of strongholds;) casting down imaginations, and every high thing that exalteth itself against the knowledge of God, and bringing into captivity every thought to the obedience of Christ" (II Cor. 10:3-5).

I John 1:9. The Day of Atonement has to do with God's provision for the sins of Israel. Three events which occurred on the Day of Atonement were as follows: (1) the blood of a young bull and the blood of a goat were sprinkled upon and before the mercy seat to make an atonement for the holy place, for Aaron and his household, for the Tabernacle of the Congregation, and for all the congregation of Israel, "because of the uncleanness of the children of Israel, and because of their transgressions in all their sins" (Lev. 16:14-17); (2) the sins of the children of Israel were confessed by Aaron and laid upon the head of a living goat (Lev. 16:21); and (3) the scapegoat was removed from the camp, bearing away "all their iniquities unto a land not inhabited" (Lev. 16:22). The provision for the sins of God's people, portrayed in the Day of Atonement ceremony, included atonement, confession, and removal.

There is a similar pattern in I John 1:9: "If we confess our sins, he is faithful and just to forgive us our sins (on the basis of the atonement which was made once and for all time upon Calvary), and to cleanse us from all unrighteousness."

When the believer maintains that he has no sin there is a strong possibility that he is misapplying the teachings of Paul (II Pet. 3:16; I John 1:8). Most of us Christians, if we will think about our imaginations, motives, words, and deeds, must acknowledge that there are occasions when we do exhibit a sinful disposition. The question is: Is there provision in the Christian salvation for actually cleansing human nature? We believe there is.

The Christian counterpart of the Day of Atonement works each day in our life as we confess our sins. It is not a case of our scrutinizing our motives until we turn ourselves into introspective, tortured, despairing souls. Rather it is a matter of living joyously in the knowledge that Christ has forgiven our sins and that we are without condemnation while the process of deliverance is going on (Rom. 8:1).

The Christian experience is one of power, of love, and of a sound mind, not of guilt and defeat. Spiritual strength is based upon the sure knowledge that in Christ we are without condemnation before God. This strength is necessary if the Christian is to stand up successfully under the searchings and cleansings of the Spirit of God, and under the stress of the warfare against Satan.

When the Holy Spirit points out to a Christian a sinful thought, word, or deed, the believer is to name it specifically, acknowledging it to be sin. Confession, ordinarily, is to be made to God. However, sometimes the occasion requires that confession be made to people as well. When we confess the sin the Lord is faithful and just to forgive the sin and to cleanse it away. The forgiveness and cleansing is the Christian fulfillment of the Hebrew Day of Atonement.

Typical example of delusion. Many devout Christians will not sin knowingly even though they are tempted sorely. Satan's approach to such people may come in the realm of delusion and deception.

For example, let us imagine that a voice speaks to you and tells you that you are especially chosen of the Lord and that all Christians in the city in which you live are supposed to obey you and to give reverence to you. You are "The Apostle," or "The Pastor," or "The Prophet" of your area, especially singled out by God to take charge of the particular geographical region. This is a wild proposition but it is characteristic of the fantasies with which Satan fills the spiritual atmosphere. Notice how this particular delusion is pitched toward the spiritually ambitious person, not the lethargic or disinterested.

The watchful overcoming Christian will reject the voice at once since the explicit words as well as the tenor of the teachings of Jesus forbid an elevation of a member of the body of Christ over his brothers.

But let us imagine further that instead of resisting the voice on the basis of Scripture, you toy with the flattering notion. It is possible, in spite of the Scripture, that God indeed has chosen you for honor of this kind. You always have had the feeling deep down inside that you have a special destiny.

Your common sense will hold you back for a while from overt acts perhaps, but in your heart the concept is growing that you are especially favored of the Lord and cannot be deceived. Even though Christ has warned us to pray, "Lead us not into temptation, but deliver us from the evil one." you have an "in" with God since you are one of His favorites.

Naturally you are above asking a fellow Christian to help you judge the voice since this would ruin it all for you—they would never understand!

Now Satan has brought you quite a way into deception. Satan has no power over a Christian unless he can get the believer to cooperate with him, to listen to his suggestions. If Satan can get the Christian to disobey the Word of God, he can bring the Christian into bondage. This is how he brought death to Adam and Eve.

Overconfidence. The Christian believer is mistaken if he thinks that Satan will not lie to him. The overcoming disciple is mistaken if he believes that he cannot have dreams, visions, premonitions, fleeting glimpses into the supernatural, that are not of God. The sold-out saint is mistaken if he believes that because he is surrendered wholly to God that he will not receive all kinds of pleasurable satanic delusions calculated to appeal to his individual personality. His total consecration to God makes him all the more interesting to the forces of darkness.

Passivity. The disciple is making a great mistake if he throws his personality open, saying in effect, "I am without a will of my own. I will move however God moves me." The believer who takes this attitude will be moved by a spirit, true enough. But it will not be the Spirit of God. He now is open to every spiritual revelation that the cunning forces of darkness can manufacture. The believer has declared himself to be fair game. We wonder how many Christians there are in the world who believe that God will not allow them to be exposed to the counterfeit revelations of Satan. Whatever the number is, that is the number of Christians who are living in deception.

Instead of believing himself to be immune to deception, or presenting himself as a puppet for the Spirit of God to move in the manner of a puppeteer, the Christian must judge all things through the Scripture, through prayer, through ministry and help from fellow members of the body of

Christ, through the counsel of devout and experienced elders of the church, and through a consistent life of cross-carrying obedience to the Spirit of God. The Christian must be super-cautious concerning any "voices" that speak to him. He must use his will and judgment in doing God's will and avoid a tendency toward passive yielding.

Never does God take away a person's will. It is with the will that man chooses continually to obey God's Word rather than the flatteries or threats of Satan. The will is associated with the powers of choice and judgment in man. Our will is guided by the Bible and strengthened through constant prayer and through being decisive at appropriate times.

We *will* serve the Lord. We *will* follow Jesus. We *will* read the Word of God and we *will* be guided by it. We *will* resist the devil. We *will* resist temptation. Of course, we are not teaching that man can save himself through his will power. We are saved by faith in Jesus Christ. But we *are* teaching that the will of man is of great importance in the plan of salvation and that it is impossible to pursue the overcoming life until the will is strengthened in prayer and is razor-sharp. "A double-minded man is unstable in all his ways" (Jas. 1:8). If Adam and Eve had used their wills and served God in the manner He commanded they would still be enjoying the garden. God wants Christian men and women, not puppets.

Now, back to the believer who is entertaining the suggestion that he is especially favored of the Lord. As we said, your common sense will keep you from rash behavior at first. But the thrilling concept of spiritual preeminence is locked up in your heart. Sooner or later the forces of wickedness by which you are bound will express themselves and you will say or do something that will shock your Christian sensibilities. The shock may cause you to enter a state of confusion.

Satan may move in at this point with powerful pressures of guilt and fear. You may feel forced to continue in the delusion because of the incorrect notion that since you are yielded to God's will it is impossible for you to be deceived. If you submit to the fear and confusion and continue to assent to the delusion that you are an especially chosen person, although this deception already has borne evil fruit in your life, you are starting down a long dark road to total deception and demonic bondage. In our opinion, the best exposition (next to the Scripture) and analysis of Christian deception and what to do about it was written by Mrs. Penn-Lewis.[7]

Rather than submitting to the fear and confusion, you may wish to be delivered. Deliverance from the power of demons always is available to people through the blood atonement which Jesus Christ made on the cross. Get down before God and confess with your mouth that you have believed yourself to be especially chosen and now you doubt that the voice that told you this was of God.

Confess the situation, whatever it is in your case, and ask God to judge it. Do not be proud. Never fear that you will lose something of God by doing this, or that God will be insulted and draw away from you. Never! That is exactly what Satan wishes for you to think so that you will keep away from Christ's delivering power. When you confess your sins, doubts, fears, or questions, God will receive you. He knows all about the battle.

Anything that God has given you can stand all the examination that can be brought to bear upon it. The wisdom that comes from above is gentle, easy to be entreated. It is Satan who desires that ideas be buried in the darkness of your mind and heart, and who floods you with fear when you try to bring things out into the open. Satan cannot stand light but God dwells in the light. When you confess your imaginations, motives, words, and deeds, you

---

[7] Jessie Penn-Lewis, *War on the Saints*. Fort Washington, Penna.: The Christian Literature Crusade.

are bringing them to the light of God so that they can be judged.

Confess the thoughts and deeds of preeminence, or of lust, or of murder, or of whatever you are suspicious of and troubled about in your own heart and life, and ask God to judge them. If it appears to be too much for you to handle, get a mature Christian (of your own sex unless it is your own wife or husband), and confess to him or her and ask for prayer and counsel. "Confess your faults (sins, offenses) one to another, and pray one for another, that ye may be healed" (Jas. 5:16). God is faithful and just to forgive us our sins and to cleanse us from all unrighteousness.

From now on resist the wicked thoughts and deeds, resting in the strength of Christ as you do so, and Satan will *flee*—not walk away gracefully—will flee from you. "Resist the devil, and he will flee from you" (Jas. 4:7). Never, never, never give up. God does not change His mind. We are in a warfare. Keep on keeping on in the right way, remembering that God "hath delivered us from the power of darkness, and hath translated us into the kingdom of his dear son" (Col. 1:13). If you are bound tightly and hopelessly in the realms of darkness, why don't you try laughing at Satan and at the forces which bind you. Jesus has far and away more authority and power than is necessary to set you absolutely, completely free in every respect, body, soul, and spirit. If you haven't realized before that Jesus has all authority and power in heaven and upon the earth, please be assured that it is true. All that remains for the accomplishment of perfect deliverance is the unwavering exercise of your faith in Jesus and in God's Word. If you just can't seem to bring faith to bear on your problem, ask Christ for *His* faith.

Christian judgment. If you are still in doubt, confess your confusion to a mature Christian of your own sex. As the two of you pray together any working of Satan will be brought to the light and shown for what it is.

The church, the body of Christ, has been designated by

the Lord as the instrument which He will use to judge angelic and human sin (I Cor. 6:1-3). Whenever two or more Christians assemble and pray about sin, possible or actual, the spirit of Christ is present to discern the origin of the action in question and to forgive and remove all evil associated with it. The blood of Jesus is the basis for the legality of the judgment and the Spirit of God provides the power for the execution of the sentence.

There is, in the spiritual realm, great significance attached to the judgments of Spirit-filled Christians as to the rightness or wrongness of a motive or deed. Whatever Christians, who are walking in the Spirit, bind on earth is bound in heaven; and whatever they loose on earth is loosed in heaven. Furthermore, Christian elders, when they are moving in the Spirit, have the authority to remit and to retain sins (John 20:22,23).

Wary attitude toward "voices,"   Let us suppose that a "voice" tells you that you are a prophet. You cannot from the Bible judge this statement as being from a righteous source or from an unclean source. It could be from God. But it tends to exalt you, therefore the odds are against its being from the Lord.

Put such a "word" into neutral. Ask the Lord Jesus to prove it. Do not accept or reject it. If it is the Lord, sooner or later other people will testify openly that you are a prophet because they will have been blessed by your prophecies. You do not have to make any claims for yourself. "The proof of the pudding is in the eating" is an old folk saying that applies in this case. Your power in prophecy will speak for itself.

Forgiving others. Perhaps a member of your church acts spitefully toward you. In revenge you speak a word to him or her that is loaded with venom. Then the Spirit of the Lord reproves you for acting vengefully. You must confess immediately to the Lord the words that were said and the manner and spirit in which they were spoken.

Do not attempt to sugarcoat the act or to justify

yourself or your words. The truth is that you have sinned and there is no way to make the deed palatable to God. The fact that the other person deserved your spite is quite beside the point. God will not for a minute countenance our judging of another. We think, speak, and act in a holy manner because we are God's children, not because other people treat us fairly.

When you confess these vengeful words and motives to Jesus He may or may not require that you ask the other's forgiveness. The requirements for deliverance vary with the individual circumstances. We always must be led by the Spirit of God when we are judging the sin in our life (Rom. 8:13,14).

Sometimes it is better for us to say nothing, and pray, than to go about confessing to people that we hate them. Sometimes, however, asking a person's forgiveness and going out of the way to obtain peace and reconciliation is the surest road to happiness and blessing, and God's favor, for all parties concerned. If neither side can forgive the other then it is impossible for the unforgiving persons to have their sins forgiven. They have been cut off from the benefits of the cross. They are walking in darkness. Their load of oppression and bondage will increase as the cancer of hatred eats into their spirit, soul, and body. The end result will be death and hell. The same kind of stuff we give out we get back in increased measure. "But if ye do not forgive, neither will your Father which is in heaven forgive your trespasses" (Mark 11:26).

Continuing confession. We cannot make blanket confessions and get rid of our fleshly wickedness all at once. It would be a relief if we could. Rather, it is a continual cleansing as the Holy Spirit begins to probe the recesses of the heart. The Spirit of God leads us in such a manner that the sins come to our attention one at a time, in many instances, similar to the manner in which the Spirit of God led Joshua against the cities of Canaan one at a time.

The thing to do is to confess the sins that you are aware of now and get them straightened out. Then the Holy Spirit will direct you to another "city," so to speak. Your sins must be forgiven and cleansed through Spirit-led confession. We are not suggesting here that every day of one's life, an individual is to make a ritual of confessing sins or that the Holy Spirit will show a new sin each day. The point being emphasized is that it is a continuing process in the life of the overcomer and that when sin in one's life has been revealed it is to be dealt with promptly and accurately. The process takes a while. It may be necessary to remind us at this point that the Christian walk is a way of joy and confidence.

Romans 8:1 is a good reference to keep in mind: "There is therefore now no condemnation to them which are in Christ Jesus, who walk not after the flesh, but after the Spirit." Depression and gloom are not gifts of the Father. He commands us to "Rejoice in the Lord always" (Phil. 4:4). We may have one or two "Gethsemane" experiences along the way, but these are extraordinary. We go with strength and confidence into the battle against the work of the enemy in our life. "For this day is holy to our Lord: neither be . . . sorry; for the joy of the Lord is your strength" (Neh. 8:10).

The "sixth" and "seventh" experiences. The Day of Atonement is the sixth of the Hebrew convocations. Perhaps it is significant that it was on the *sixth* day of creation that man was made in the image of God. The image of God is a holy, compassionate moral character. Holy strength of character has not been the image of the Christian church members, in some instances. But as we begin to confess our sins, and as we behold the glory of God in the face of Jesus Christ, a strong, holy, compassionate character, in the likeness of the strong, holy, compassionate character of the Father and Christ, begins to be formed in us. We are destined to be in the express image of Christ—body, soul, and spirit. God will never quit until the perfect molding has been accomplished.

Perhaps it is significant too that of the doctrines mentioned in Hebrews 6:1,2, the last-mentioned doctrine, the one that we leave to "go on to perfection," is the doctrine of *eternal judgment*. We believe that the "perfection," of Hebrews 6:1 is the "rest" which is treated at length in Chapters 3 and 4 of Hebrews. It is our opinion that the doctrine of eternal judgment corresponds to the Day of Atonement; and that "perfection," or the "rest" of God, corresponds to the convocation of Tabernacles which follows the Day of Atonement.

This would make *perfection* the seventh doctrine, and Tabernacles is, of course, the seventh convocation. Some Bible students believe that the number *seven* denotes perfection in the numerical symbolism of the Scriptures. Also, it was on the seventh day that God "rested" from His work.

Judgment of rebellious spirits. It is helpful for us to keep in mind, as we are allowing the Spirit of God to deal with the sin in our life, that the judgment of God primarily is against evil spirits. The lake of fire is "prepared for the devil and his angels" (Matt. 25:41). We are not implying that people also will not end up in the everlasting fire. Some certainly will! But only those who cooperate with Satan and refuse to accept the glory and forgiveness of Jesus. Nevertheless, God's judgment is directed toward evil spirits and it is they, not people, for whom the lake of fire has been prepared.

There is a deep spiritual significance to the whole business of confession and atonement. Every act of rebellion, or confession, and every application of the blood of Jesus echo between heaven and the earth. It appears that the unfolding plan of God directly affects heaven as well as earth, and that whatever makes an impact upon one world sends reverberations throughout the other (Matt. 16:19; John 20:23; Heb. 9:23,24; I Pet. 1:12; Luke 10:18,19; Rev. 12:5-12).

Remember that the holy of holies, as well as the rest of the Tabernacle of the Congregation, was cleansed during the Day of Atonement. Since the Ark of the Covenant portrays (among other things) the heart of the overcomer, according to our viewpoint, one could say that the cleansing of the holy of holies symbolizes the cleansing of the heart of the Christian—the heart of the Christian being, in a very real sense, a mercy seat from which God reigns.

It appears that the tabernacle in heaven was cleansed through the sprinkling of the blood of Jesus, for it is written:

"It was therefore necessary that the patterns of things in the heavens should be purified with these (the blood of calves and of goats); but the heavenly things themselves with better sacrifices than these. For Christ is not entered into the holy places made with hands, which are the figures of the true; but into Heaven itself, now to appear in the presence of God for us" (Heb. 9:23,24).

Moses saw the "heavenly things," the pattern for the Tabernacle of the Congregation, when God called him up into the mountain (Heb. 9:23). Moses saw, in symbolic form, the Christian church, the body of Christ, the eternal tabernacle of God. All the fullness of the Godhead dwells in Jesus Christ, and His body is the completeness of His being. Christ is the temple of God and His church is the fullness of Him. There is no other temple of God. John saw no temple in the new Jerusalem (Rev. 21:22) because the bride of Christ is the true tabernacle of God, and is the new Jerusalem (Rev. 21:2,3,9,10).

Whatever else had to be cleansed in heaven by the blood of Christ, one thing is certain: Christ (Head and Body), is the eternal dwelling place of the living God Almighty. Therefore, the body of Christ, being made up of sinful human beings, must be cleansed thoroughly from its outermost parts to its innermost parts. The blood must be sprinkled upon and before the mercy seat, meaning that the blood of Christ must be brought into the innermost depths of the heart of the Christian believer. Otherwise he cannot be a part of the body of Christ, the temple of God.

The source of sin. Sin came full-blown into the Garden of Eden, not in the form of a human being, but in the form of a serpent. The rebels from heaven possessed ancient cunning when Adam and Eve were naive babes, fresh from the hand of God. Adam was not the father of liars nor was Cain the first murderer. Jesus said to the Jews:

> "Ye are of your father the devil, and the lusts of your father ye will do: he was a murderer from the beginning, and abode not in the truth, because there is no truth in him. When he speaketh a lie, he speaketh of his own: for he is a liar, and the father of it" (John 8:44).

If we would recognize that it is the principalities and powers of darkness rather than mankind who are the authors of sin in the world and in the churches, we might take a more compassionate attitude toward people and, at the same time, act more effectively when dealing with sin.

This is not to excuse people from the responsibility for their actions, because every person is obliged to accept Christ and to resist the devil. It is rather to localize and focus upon the root of the problem so that we may be able to attack the source rather than the symptoms. Our purpose also is to explain that God's anger and judgment is against rebellious spirits and that we wrestle not against flesh and blood, as Paul says, but against the lords of darkness in the realm of spiritual personalities.

The Bible does not portray clearly the details of the rebellion in heaven. Ezekiel 28 and Revelation 12 are two of several references which allude to the dreadful revolution in heaven. Notice in Revelation 12 that the removal of the dragon from heaven is associated with the overcoming by the brethren. In other words, Satan's power is being destroyed both in the heavenlies and also in the lives of the Christians. It seems that the doing of God's will in the earth is related to the condition of things in the heavenlies.

The blood of the Lamb and the testimony of the Christians are a mighty force in heaven and upon earth. We believe that heaven listens intently as the believer passes judgment upon his own actions, measuring them against the Word of God and declaring them to be sinful or righteous, as the case may be. If an action is sinful the blood of Jesus can atone for the sin, the Christian can go free, and the Holy Spirit can judge the prince of this world (John 16:11).

It is interesting to note the thinking of the Hebrews concerning their "Days of Awe." This is the term used by them to describe the serious nature of *Rosh Hashonoh* (modern equivalent of the convocation of Trumpets) and *Yom Kippur* (Day of Atonement). The Hebrew belief, which dates back to the second century, is that God judges the world on *Rosh Hashonoh* and the fates of all men have been decided by the time of *Yom Kippur.* These two convocations are the days of judgment.

Year of Jubilee.   First John 2:2 teaches that Jesus "is the propitiation for our sins: and not for ours only, but also for the sins of the whole world." The revealing of the sons of God (Rom. 8:18-21) will bring the blessing of the atonement to the whole earth (which is not to say that all men eventually will be saved, for it is apparent that some men reject the Son of God, thus sealing their own eternal doom). The great earth-wide deliverance to come is portrayed in the celebration of the year of jubilee.

"Then shall you cause the trumpet of the jubilee to sound on the tenth day of the seventh month, in the day of atonement shall you make the trumpet sound throughout all your land.

And you shall hallow the fiftieth year, and proclaim liberty throughout all the land to all the inhabitants thereof: it shall be a jubilee to you;

And you shall return every man to his possession, and you shall return every man to his family" (Lev. 25:9,10).

Two overlapping years. The year of jubilee, which was announced every fiftieth year on the Day of Atonement, typifies the great day of deliverance for the earth at the appearance of Jesus and the sons of God. The feast of Trumpets and the Day of Atonement mark the beginning of the Hebrew agricultural year, just as Passover marks the beginning of the ceremonial year. The Hebrews had and still have two overlapping years running concurrently, just as we Americans today have a calendar year and a fiscal year which overlap. The Hebrews seem to regard the new year which occurs at the time of the Day of Atonement as *the* New Year, just as Americans regard the calendar year which commences on January 1 as *the* New Year, while July 1, the beginning of the fiscal year, is not as widely celebrated.

So it is, in a manner of speaking, with us Christians. We have a "year" that begins with "Passover" and a "year" that begins with the "Day of Atonement" in our experience of God's salvation. We commence a whole new way of life at our "Passover" when by faith we sprinkle the blood of Jesus upon our life and flee from "Egypt" (the world; the spirit of the age) in the sacrament of water baptism. The "Passover" experience begins our life and walk with God.

A new beginning. But when we come in our experience to the Christian counterparts of the Hebrew convocations of Trumpets and the Day of Atonement, it is as though we have come to a new beginning. It is not that we have come to a new Christ, or a new Holy Spirit, or a new cross. A Christian should never remove the old landmarks, no matter how advanced in God he thinks he may have become.

Passover was repeated annually after it was instituted in Egypt and still, thirty-five hundred years later, is observed each year by the Jews. This is God's way—to have us do a thing over and over and over until it becomes an integral part of our personality. In fact, it appears that many of our churches would profit from celebrating communion more often than they do because during the celebration of the communion, which is our equivalent of the Passover, we bring to mind the death of our Lord upon the cross and our union with Him in death and resurrection. The repetition carves the death of Christ upon the cross into our personality, and also imbues us with the concept that we must continually eat the flesh of Christ and drink His blood. So by talking about a "New Year" with Christ we are not suggesting that we are to forsake or forget our experience in Christ up to this time.

The first observance of Passover occurred on the last day the Jews spent in Egyptian bondage, and the first week of Unleavened Bread was observed during the first seven days of the exodus. The remaining five convocations took place at a later time because the celebration of them depended upon the existence of farms, the Tabernacle of the Congregation, and the Levitical priesthood, none of which the Israelites had at the time they departed from Egypt.

The land of Egypt is symbolic of the spirit of the age in which we live, and Pharaoh typifies Satan. We observe Christ, our Passover, on the last day of our bondage to Satan and his kingdom of darkness. Then we come out of "Egypt" under the mighty hand of God. Therefore Passover begins the "first month of the year" to us (Exod. 12:2).

The year which begins with Passover contains the seven convocations, the last of which (Tabernacles) takes place in the middle of the seventh month. The year starting with Passover is a year of *redemption,* or *salvation.* It is a time, symbolically speaking, during which the Lord God brings a person all the way from the bondage of Satan and complete personal corruption to a wholly transformed creature in Christ, recreated in spirit, soul, and body—a perfect salvation!

The year which begins with Trumpets commences on the first day of the seventh month. This new year does not go from Passover to Passover, but rather follows the cycle of agriculture. Whereas the year which begins with Passover symbolizes the redemptive revealing of God in Christ, the agricultural year symbolizes the setting up of the kingdom of God upon the earth.

So it is that we Christians begin a new year, as it were, when we come to the convocation of Trumpets. This new year contains the culminating convocations of the work of redemption (Trumpets, Day of Atonement, and Tabernacles). But now, instead of being a year of redemptive acts of God toward men, it is the beginning of the kingdom of God in the earth—a year of doing business in, through, and with Christ.

As we start our "observance of Trumpets" we can begin to actually conquer our environment through Christ; we can begin to become a new creature in our daily living; we can begin to enter into the rest of God. It is the start of our conquest of the land of promise, and our rulership in Christ extends on into eternity.

We Christians believe in complete transformation of our spirit, soul, and body into the express image of Christ. We believe in the fullness of the indwelling of the Father and the Son through the Holy Spirit. We believe that it is God's will to pour out upon the Christian disciples the fullness of the anointing of the Holy Spirit so that we can bear witness to the resurrection of Jesus Christ to every man, woman, boy, and girl in the world. Now it is time for us to look steadfastly toward the living God until total personal transformation, total indwelling, and total anointing are in our possession and operate in our daily lives in the earth. Our progress toward absolute victory may be interrupted briefly by our physical death, or by the hour of darkness which is coming upon the earth during which no man can work. But with the exception of this brief interlude, our service to Christ as kings and priests in the earth will go on throughout the ages of ages, world without end.

Passover is the beginning and Tabernacles is the ending of the plan of redemption, all of which is through Christ and *is* Christ. Such is the year of redemption. But Trumpets, in the context of the year which follows the cycle of agriculture, begins our life which has no conclusion, a fellowship with Christ in the bosom of the Father. Throughout eternity we will be kings and priests of God through Christ, and only He will have dominion over us. One of the great purposes of the working of God in us is to bring us to the place that *only* Christ has rule over us. It takes a lot of doing in a person to bring him to this place!

A real difference.   As soon as we begin to confess our sins (Christian counterpart of the Day of Atonement) we notice that something actually is happening in our personality. It is not the old hoping against hope that somehow, someday, God is going to do something about the imperfections of our nature. A difference in our personality is becoming evident to us and to those around us.

Gradually a reshaping of our deeds, words, motives, and imaginations occurs, and we can tell the difference in our heart. The Holy Spirit of God takes the blood of the cross into the depths of the deceit of our being, bringing the judgment of God upon the evil nature which has roots and branches throughout the infinitely convoluted core of our personality, and we are astonished at the intricate maze of subtleties that can be uncovered in the desperately wicked heart of a person. We realize in our spirit that this is the beginning of the year of jubilee for the earth. The kingdom of God has come to the earth, and it has begun in us.

It is not a new gospel, as we said before. The foundation of Christianity is the Rock, Christ Jesus, and Him crucified and resurrected, and it has been laid well by the Christian ministry. But the experience of confessing sins under the direction of the Holy Spirit comes to us with the force and uplift of a "new year." Victory in spiritual warfare transforms our doctrines which we have upheld so faithfully into the bone and blood and flesh of reality.

Confession of sins is not new.   We do not wish to leave the impression that the Christian church has never experienced the confessing of sins under the leadership of the Holy Spirit of God. Just as speaking in tongues has been in evidence throughout church history whenever Christians have gotten down to business with God, so, to an even greater extent conviction of sin in the believers has been in evidence. This statement can be validated easily.

Also, the writings of the Christian saints will demonstrate, we believe, that their individual histories illustrate the kinds of relationships with God that we are suggesting in this exposition, and that the Holy Spirit made them aware of the condition of their hearts and of their motives and deeds just as He makes us aware of our sins in these days. So, then, there is nothing new about the confession of sins.

The fullness of God has been available to every believer since the outpouring of the Holy Spirit in the first century. True, the church has gone through dark days since then. But it is time now to turn to the Lord and seek Him with all our heart, soul, mind, and strength until He comes and rains righteousness upon us (Hos. 10:12).

Judgment begins at the house of God.   We must purify ourselves through the power of the Spirit and the blood of Christ. In the third chapter of I John we find these words:

> " . . . we know that, when he shall appear, we shall be like him; for we shall see him as he is. And every man that hath this hope in him purifieth himself, even as he is pure."

We Christians hope to be like the righteous Jesus when

He appears. But this is a vain hope unless we obey the Spirit right now. *Every man that has this hope in him purifies himself, even as He is pure.* The Lord can't be much plainer than that!

Judgment always begins with the household of God. The nearer we are to the Lord the stricter the judgment is. We, of all people, will be examined to the most minute sin. The prophets can never speak comfortably to Jerusalem until "she hath received of the Lord's hand *double* for all her sins" (Isa. 40:2).

The world may get by with some things, but the church, never. The Lord is going to present to Himself a glorious church, "not having spot, or wrinkle, or any such thing" (Eph. 5:27). Any teaching contrary to this may lead the disciple into the notion that practical, daily holiness of life is not a necessary part of Christian discipleship. Such a notion can lead only to destruction.

Lazarus, a symbol of salvation.   The Christian who has accepted Jesus as his Lord, has been born again, and has been baptized in the Holy Spirit, but who has not had the opportunity to confess his sins under the guidance of the Holy Spirit, may be compared to the resurrected Lazarus. The raising of Lazarus on the *fourth* day is a picture of the salvation experience, including the baptism in the Holy Spirit (convocation number *four).* Lazarus was raised from the dead by the Spirit of the Lord but he came forth bound hand and foot with graveclothes. We too have been raised from the dead by the Spirit of Christ. But the graveclothes of the sins of the flesh are hindering us from acting as we would (Rom. 7:14-25). The carnal mind is hostile to the new Spirit whom we have (Gal. 5:17). Now Christ commands, "Loose him, and let him go" (John 11:44).

It may be noticed that Lazarus had received new life from Jesus, yet his hands and feet were bound, preventing him from acting and conducting himself as he wished. Jesus had the power to strike off the graveclothes with a word, just as He did the chains of Peter in jail (Acts 12:7). But Jesus commanded the people standing nearby to untie Lazarus.

So it is with us. Jesus has the power to cast off all our bondages with the word of His power. But in His own wisdom He directs people to remove our bondages from us. Sometimes we get quite upset at this process!

Judgment liberates Christians.   We do not have to be afraid of God's judgment upon our life. Daniel tells of three Hebrews who were thrown into a furnace that had been fired up until it gave off terrific heat. But when the three emerged from the furnace the only change in them was that their bonds were gone. They did not come out of the furnace naked, everything of value to them destroyed, as it were. They came out fully clothed, not a hair of their head singed (Dan. 3:19-27). They were bound and thrown in by mighty warriors who were slain by the blistering heat of the furnace. They walked out under their own power.

No fire can harm an overcoming Christian who is willing to be taken *by the Lord* through the fires of judgment (there were *four* men in the furnace). "He shall baptize you with the Holy Ghost (Spirit), and with fire" (Matt. 3:11). "Beloved, think it not strange concerning the fiery trial which is to try you, as though some strange thing happened unto you" (I Pet. 4:12-19).

The Lord Jesus never forsakes us no matter how hot the fire gets (Matt. 28:20; Rom. 8:38,39; Heb. 13:5). "They that trust in the Lord shall be as mount Zion, which cannot be removed, but abideth for ever" (Ps. 125:1). "He will not suffer thy foot to be moved: he that keepeth thee will not slumber" (Ps. 121:3).

Purging the House of God.   The Christian church is the New Testament counterpart of the Tabernacle of the Congregation. God's throne (the ark in the most holy place of the Tabernacle) is being created in the hearts of men (II Cor. 6:16). God has no intention of making a sinful house His eternal home (II Cor. 6:17; I Cor. 6:15-20). The Christian therefore should be diligent in confessing his sins as they are revealed to him by the Holy Spirit (Rom. 8:13).

We have come now to the time in our Christian experience when the Lord desires to drive the money changers, so to speak, out of the house of God (the hearts of the believers, not the buildings in which they assemble). "And he shall sit as a refiner and purifier of silver: and he shall purify the sons of Levi, and purge them as gold and silver, that they may offer unto the Lord an offering in righteousness" (Mal. 3:3).

"He shall baptize you with the Holy Ghost (Spirit), and with fire: whose fan is in his hand, and he will thoroughly purge his floor, and gather his wheat into the garner; but he will burn up the chaff with unquenchable fire" (Matt. 3:11,12). We can stand in the day of judgment if we will anchor our hope inside the most holy place (Heb. 6:19). If we will, we can avail ourselves of the sprinkling of the blood of the righteous Jesus, in this manner cleansing ourselves from our iniquities.

> "But if we walk in the light, as he is in the light, we have fellowship one with another, and the blood of Jesus Christ his Son cleanseth us from all sin. If we say that we have no sin, we deceive ourselves, and the truth is not in us. If we confess our sins, he is faithful and just to forgive us our sins, and to cleanse us from all unrighteousness" (I John 1:7-9).

We are of the opinion that this confession and cleansing is the new covenant fulfillment of the old covenant Day of Atonement.

John the Baptist was the personification of repentance and confession of sins on the part of Israel (Matt. 3:6). John came just before Jesus. In the same manner the Day of Atonement comes just before the convocation of Tabernacles. Tabernacles, we believe, typifies the coming of the

Father and the Son, through the Holy Spirit, to dwell forevermore in the believer (Eph. 2:22; John 14:23).

TABERNACLES

"Speak unto the children of Israel, saying, The fifteenth day of this seventh month shall be the feast of tabernacles for seven days to the Lord" (Lev. 23:34).

"Also in the fifteenth day of the seventh month, when ye have gathered in the fruit of the land, ye shall keep a feast unto the Lord seven days: on the first day shall be a sabbath, and on the eighth day shall be a sabbath" (Lev. 23:39).

"And ye shall take . . . on the first day the boughs of goodly trees, branches of the palm trees, and the boughs of thick trees, and willows of the brook; and ye shall rejoice before the Lord your God seven days" (Lev. 23:40).

"Ye shall dwell in booths seven days; all that are Israelites born shall dwell in booths: that your generations may know that I made the children of Israel to dwell in booths, when I brought them out of the land of Egypt: I am the Lord your God" (Lev. 23:42,43).

"Thou shalt observe the feast of tabernacles seven days, after that thou hast gathered in thy corn and wine" (Deut. 16:13).

"And Moses wrote this law, and delivered it unto the priests the sons of Levi, which bare the ark of the covenant of the Lord, and unto all the elders of Israel. And Moses commanded them, saying, At the end of every seven years, in the solemnity of the year of release, in the feast of tabernacles, when all Israel is come to appear before the Lord thy God in the place which he shall choose, thou shalt read this law before all Israel in their hearing" (Deut. 31:9-11).

"Behold, God is my salvation; I will trust, and not be afraid: for the Lord Jehovah is my strength and my song; he also is become my salvation. Therefore with joy shall ye draw water out of the wells of salvation" (Isa. 12:2,3).

"In the last day, that great day of the feast, Jesus stood and cried, saying, If any man thirst, let him come unto me and drink. He that believeth on me, as the Scripture hath said, out of his belly shall flow rivers of living water. (But this spake he of the Spirit, which they that believe on him should receive: for the Holy Ghost [Spirit] was not yet given; because that Jesus was not yet glorified.)" (John 7:37-39).

"And I heard a great voice out of heaven saying, Behold, the tabernacle of God is with men, and he will dwell with them, and they shall be his people, and God himself shall be with them, and be their God" (Rev. 21:3).

The convocation of Tabernacles typifies perfection. The convocation of Tabernacles portrays the resting of God in us and our resting in Him. Tabernacles is the seventh feast, the last feast, and, as we might expect, depicts the consummation of redemption. If one subscribes to the symbolism of numbers in the Bible, it is interesting to note that Tabernacles, a festivity lasting seven days, is the seventh feast and is in the seventh month—a trinity of sevens. There seems to be no doubt that God intends for the convocation of Tabernacles to be associated in our mind with perfection.

Redemption has a definite completion. Salvation, the redemption of the human being, has a definite commencement and a definite completion. Jesus is the finisher as well as the author of our faith (Heb. 12:2). God says, "It is done. I am *Alpha* and *Omega*, the beginning and the end" (Rev. 21:6).

There is no part of the plan of salvation that is vague. It is a good thing that salvation does have a definite fulfillment and that we do have something definite at which to aim. Sometimes the race becomes tiring indeed (Heb. 3:14; 12:12).

It is our point of view that the whole concept of salvation having a definite consummation needs the careful attention of the church. Of course, we are not teaching that Christians will not find new wonders from the depths of God forever. It is clear that our God is so much greater than all of our visions of greatness that there are no words in any language that can begin to convey to us any idea whatever of the extent of the glory of God. Therefore the definite consummation and fulfillment of which we are speaking has to do only and specifically with the plan of redemption.

The Levitical convocations seem to reveal that God's workings in the creation of the church, His living temple, start in a definite manner and finish in a definite manner. A specified completion of salvation certainly is a new idea to many of us. But the Christian experience is one of growth from a seed to maturity. And if there were no point of maturity, no time at which the Christian is fully redeemed, then some of the Scripture would not admit to a simple, direct interpretation. For example:

"Till we all come in the unity of the faith, and of the knowledge of the Son of God, unto a perfect man, unto the measure of the stature of the fulness of Christ" (Eph. 4:13).

"Unto a perfect man"! "Unto the measure of the stature of the fullness of Christ"! There is nothing vague about these words, no uncertain drifting toward a misty nothingness. These are the words of a builder who has seen the blueprint. Salvation has a certain divine beginning and a certain divine conclusion, and a certain divine in-between. The whole work is of God from start to finish. "I am *Alpha* and *Omega*, the beginning and the end."

God, a master builder. God is a builder, a creator. Any person who has ever built or created anything knows that every little bit of effort and material that goes into the work takes its significance from the completed piece. The builder works on and on with the finished product in his imagination. His motivation arises from his anticipation of the joy he will derive from the possession and sharing of his creation. The whole logical process of creating is interrupted if the piece can never be completed.

The finish line. What joy can be had from knowing that no matter how hard or how long you persevere at something you can never complete it—never arrive at the goal? What runner can drive his body to the last searing thrust when he knows that there is no finish line? No wonder great numbers of Christian believers do not get too excited about the concept of the perfecting of the church and of themselves as individual parts of the great body of Christ. They do not believe the goal actually is attainable. Why try!

Paul's attitude toward perfection. Paul does not speak as though the goal of the Christian life were unattainable:

"Not as though I had already attained, either were already perfect: but I follow after, if that I may apprehend that for which also I am apprehended of Christ Jesus. Brethren, I count not myself to have apprehended: but this one thing I do, forgetting those things which are behind, and reaching forth unto those things which are before, I press toward the mark for the prize of the high calling of God in Christ Jesus.

Let us therefore, as many as be perfect, be thus minded" (Phil. 3:12-15).

These are not the words of a builder with no product in mind. These are not the words of a runner on a track with no finish line. These are not the words of a man with no attainable goal. Nor are these the words of most of our churches. One is more likely to hear, "Do your best, but everyone knows that nobody is perfect!"

Sometimes we seem to feel that the goal of the Christian life is an external event in time or place, such as the coming of the Lord Jesus Christ, or our going to heaven. The Jews missed their Messiah by looking too far away.

Perhaps if we look more closely at the words of Paul in the third chapter of Philippians we might gain understanding concerning the goal of the Christian life. And, since the convocation of Tabernacles portrays the consummation of redemption, we might gain understanding of this last and most joyous of the Hebrew convocations.

The goal of the Christian experience. In verses 4 through 6 of Philippians 3, Paul recites his accomplishments as a Hebrew, telling of his pedigree, as it were. And then he states: "Those I counted loss for Christ" (v.7).

Right here is the sum and substance of the whole thing. It is right at this point that we can miss the entire concept of the logic, sequence, and scope of God's plan of redemption. The goal of the Christian life is not an external event in time or place, such as the second coming of our Lord or our going to heaven. These two events assuredly are going to occur literally, and many Christian churches regularly and in good faith announce that these are the goals of the Christian life. But they are not! The fulfillment of the convocation of Tabernacles, the consummation of salvation, is the winning of a Person—the Lord Jesus Christ.

Our confusion may arise over the location of the point in our Christian experience at which we believe that we have Christ. Some set the point at the born-again experience, and in a sense they are correct. But Paul had been born again, at the time of the writing of Philippians. Some set the point at speaking in tongues, and this also is a receiving of Christ. But Paul had experienced the speaking in tongues at the time of the writing of Philippians.

Paul had known to the full all of our fundamentalist and Pentecostal experiences, perhaps some others besides, and was able to look back upon several years of extremely fruitful ministry, by the time the third chapter of Philippians was written.

Well then, what does Paul mean, "That I may win Christ" (Phil. 3:8)? In terms of the doctrines that are commonly taught in our churches, Paul's words are mere platitudes or meaningless gibberish. His words do not square with our teaching or understanding of the Christian plan of salvation. Either Paul's concept of salvation is incorrect or our concept of salvation is incorrect.

Some of the words that Paul uses are repeated by us. But the framework of logic and understanding in which he uses them, and the framework of logic and understanding in which we repeat them, do not appear to match. The voice is Jacob's but the hands are Esau's. We use Paul's words to support our notions. When we get our doctrine in line with the burden of the Holy Spirit, the writings of Paul will be entirely comprehensible to us and will flow naturally and in an unforced manner in the course of our teaching. We will not have to bend Paul's words around our doctrine, taking favorite verses out of their strands of logic and using them in a cut-and-paste, promise-box fashion. We need the whole counsel of God.

God has set a goal before us Christians. That goal is the full possession of Christ. We should be directing our attention toward the goal at this time. We may be stagnating in a lagoon of doctrinal correctness when the Lord Jesus is saying to us, "Speak unto the children of Israel, that they go forward" (Exod. 14:15). If we are Christians we possess

Christ in a measure. But there is more of Christ—a definite more, not a vague, do-good, never-get-there kind of more— that we are to gain here and now. And the Holy Spirit is encouraging us to go forward and possess the good land, the definite, attainable land, which He has promised in His Word. Now, back to Philippians 3:8:

> "Yea doubtless, and I count all things (Paul's religious merit points) but loss for the excellency of the knowledge of Christ Jesus my Lord."

"Excellency of the knowledge"! We Christians know about Christ but we do not know *Him*. We haven't set knowing Jesus—really knowing Him—as the goal of our experience. It is possible for a church attender to know all about the ways of the "house of God," about the vocabulary and customs of his group, and still not know the God of the house of God. One can be well acquainted with *Bethel* (the house of God) and still not be well acquainted with *El-Bethel* (the God of the house of God).

There can be a wide gulf between people who have been into a church and people whom God has called to His side, even though both groups attend the same worship services. The one group is basically different from the other. God comes to a person as to Abraham of old. God calls him out of all that is familiar, reveals Himself to him, and then tests, prods, and deals with him endlessly, night and day. The person is drawn to the limits of consecration many times. God is in all his thoughts. He may become an enigma, a "speckled bird," to the other church people. They in turn are little comfort to him in his quest for God, and their routines in the church doings may seem trivial to him, and, at times, abominable. When revival comes, a whole church may be brought closer to Christ; or, a fervent believer may find it necessary to leave the organized group, even at considerable inconvenience and loss to himself.

Those persons who are in essence more involved in the church than they are in Christ may tend to remain with the organization because it is more understandable and significant to them. At such a time of tearing apart there may be much grief of mind and heart on both sides, and sometimes misunderstandings and even hard feelings for a season. But the separating of the bride from her family, so to speak, is inevitable because it is a necessary part of the plan of the Father to draw out for His beloved Son a holy and utterly devoted bride from the peoples of the earth.

"For whom I have suffered the loss of all things," Paul continues. The "all things" is referring to Paul's religious acquisitions which were the chief joy of his Pharisaical life. "And do count them but dung, that I may win Christ," he finishes.

Let us repeat this idea because we hold that it is the basic concept of the convocation of Tabernacles. Winning Christ is our goal; not things, not experiences, not "secrets" of a successful Christian experience, not ways of getting God to do what we wish, not religious accomplishments, not what we can get from God, not spiritual power, not power in prayer, not a big church, not going to heaven, not coming down from heaven, but Him! Him! Him! Him!

Everything else is idolatry. It is God Himself—the possession of Christ in the heart, not the coming of Christ in His external kingdom although that event will occur in time, but the possession of God Himself—who is the goal of the Christian life.

When we possess Jesus Christ we possess everything that God ever has been or has done, and everything that God ever will be or will do. It has pleased the Father to include in Jesus all of the substance and nature of His own holy being—a perfect and complete revelation and fulfillment of all who God is. It is not that Jesus and the Father are the same person. Rather, it is that because of the unfathomable love of the Father for the Son, the Father has given all of

Himself to the Son. He who has the Son has everything, including the divine Godhead. He who does not have the Son has only a certain fearful looking for of judgment and fiery indignation which shall destroy those who oppose the will and presence of the Son.

The reason why it is so difficult for us to follow Paul's thinking in Philippians 3 is that we believe we already have Christ. We have been born again, so we have Christ. We have spoken in tongues, so we have Christ. We have gone to church all our life, so we have Christ. We have wrought miracles and have done many wonderful things, so we have Christ.

If a person believes that he already has attained to something, or is in possession of something, he is not going to lay all else aside and, at the expense of no little inconvenience and self-denial to himself, devote his time and strength to the attainment of it. This confusion about the goal of the Christian life may explain why Christians come to a halt in their spiritual progress. The fact is, we do not have Christ in the measure indicated by Paul in Philippians 3, in the measure typified by the convocation of Tabernacles. There remains much of the promised land to be possessed. Let us go forward in the wisdom and strength of the Holy Spirit of God. Let us press on to the fullness of the rest of God, and not be unbelieving, fearful of heart, and ready to compromise and share our domain with the world, the flesh, and Satan. The goal is the total possession of Christ. The world, the flesh, and Satan have no part in Him.

> "And be found in him, not having mine own righteousness, which is of the law" (Phil. 3:9).

Two kinds of communicants. Notice that Paul in Philippians 3 contrasts the possession of Christ with his former life as a "Pharisee of the Pharisees." This contrast brings to mind a conflict that exists in the Christian churches of today—a division which can be observed from the time of Abraham.

We are referring to the difference between people who are seeking the spiritual inheritance by their own works, and people who are seeking the spiritual inheritance by faith in God's works.

These two approaches to God are in opposition to each other. They cannot be reconciled. Spiritual fellowship is impossible. To use a figure of speech, there are two nations struggling in the womb of the churches. Each one is termed *Christian.* One group attempts to make spiritual progress and to build up the church by means of human wisdom and effort. The other group is an elect whom God has called out from the world, and whom the world hates.

The two groups are intermingled in the pews of our churches, yet they could not be more opposed to each other, from a spiritual point of view. They are the modern counterparts of Isaac and Ishmael, Sarah and Hagar, Jacob and Esau. The one is of the earth and minds earthly things. The other has a force drawing them eternally toward the heart of God. One group is content to live in the flesh. The other is endeavoring to learn to live and walk in the Spirit.

It is not that one group is good and the other is bad. It may be recalled that Esau in some respects was a more honorable man than Jacob. Jacob lied and stole, with the help of his mother.

But there is a qualitative difference between the good people of the earth and the elect in whose hearts God has placed the divine compulsion. There will be a continual rending and tearing as long as the fabric of the churches contains these two kinds of material. Isaac and Ishmael are forever being pulled and pulling in different directions. Paul has made his choice: "I have suffered the loss of all things, and do count them but dung."

"But that which is through the faith of Christ, the righteousness which is of God by faith: that I may know him" (Phil. 3:10). *That I may know Him,* Paul says, after his years of Christian experience and ministry! Hopefully, God will give many of us Christians such single-mindedness of purpose, such a burning desire. Each one of us can choose to be among God's elect, if we wish; we can choose to be numbered among those who seek Christ with a whole heart (Josh. 24:15).

The first resurrection.   "And the power of his resurrection."

It appears that we have a point of doctrine turned upside down. We think of heaven as something to be attained and the first resurrection of the dead as being a completely external event which is going to promote all believers into a position of rulership with Christ, independently of the living of the overcoming life in this world.

The truth, as we see it, is pretty much the reverse. Going to heaven is the birthright of all Christians. Unless we fall away and go back into sin, we will go to heaven when we die. There is no attaining to it. Heaven is not the land of promise. Heaven is a marvelous paradise in the spiritual world, and a very real place. It is a change of scenery for us while God is preparing His great temple.

But the resurrection from the dead, particularly the first resurrection of which Paul is speaking in Philippians 3 is something to be attained. Indeed it is! "Blessed and holy is he that hath part in the first resurrection" (Rev. 20:6). These are God's rulers, the overcomers, the mighty royal priesthood whom God is preparing to reign with Christ.

These are the judges, the sons of God, whose coming the Hebrew prophets have foretold. In our opinion, the way the rapture has been taught, in some instances, seems to have destroyed much of the scriptural concept of the day of the Lord and the coming of the sons of God by suggesting that the flocks of God's sheep are to be borne gaily through the clouds whether or not they are living overcoming lives. What an unreasonable, unscriptural concept—no wonder we Christians live the indifferent spiritual lives we do!

Revelation 2 mentions that the overcomers shall rule over nations with a rod of iron. There is a spiritual law which dictates, "If we suffer, we shall also reign with Him." We learn to suffer with Him here and now; and we learn to overcome and to govern our own hearts with a rod of iron here and now.

The burden of the Lord today concerns the sons of God and their ministry of judgment during the day of the Lord. If we would be on clear scriptural ground, perhaps it would be a good idea to use the term *first resurrection*, rather than *rapture.* The term *first resurrection* brings us into the mainstream of the concepts set forth by Paul and John, and by the Hebrew prophets as well, and helps us conceive of the day of the Lord as a time of maturity and overcoming strength, a revolution and spiritual victory brought about through the birth of the male child of Revelation 12. The male child, we believe, represents the overcoming saints, the firstfruits of the earth to the Lord.

The concept of the rapture, as it is often taught, suggests a flight to escape the judgments upon the sinners of the world. But what about the sinners in the churches? The teaching of the rapture, if we are not careful, can lead the Christians into a false sense of security, especially regarding the events of the day of the Lord. In contrast to this, the teaching of the need to attain to the first resurrection, to the need to overcome now if we would rule later, leads to renewed consecration and a redoubling of efforts to seek the presence and will of the Lord Jesus Christ in our own life. Isn't this true?

"And the power of his resurrection." Are you seeking and experiencing the power of His resurrection?

The cross and the crown.   "And the fellowship of his sufferings."

If we will reign with Christ we must accept the sufferings which God sends our way (not the sufferings which Satan sends). Wasn't one of the sources of Jesus' sufferings summed up in these words: "He came unto his own, and his own received him not" (John 1:11)? We have said that the convocation of Tabernacles represents perfection—the consummation of salvation. There seem to be few Christians who are aware that a consummation exists, let alone who are attaining to it. Loneliness is one of the crosses which must be borne at times by those who press on in Christ.

The cleavage between Joseph and his brothers represents the cleavage which occurs between the multitudes of Israel and those whom God calls to Himself. They are dreamers of dreams, these called-out ones, and they are foolish enough to believe that their brothers will listen gladly to their dreams of authority. They may end up in a pit, cast out by their own (church) families. Sometimes the world, as in the case of Joseph, is quick to perceive their abilities. And in the end the overcomers will serve to sustain the family of God. These are the hundredfold Christians and they are a firstfruits to God and to the Lamb. (Make sure that you do not separate yourself from your own brothers in Christ through your own foolishness and pride. It probably is true that Joseph could have handled his revelations better than he did.)

The rejection by one's spiritual family occurred in the life of Jesus. The common people heard Jesus gladly. The world to this day recognizes the extraordinary abilities of Jesus of Nazareth. But His peers in Israel, those who should have embraced Him as the Israelite of the Israelites, cried for His blood. Here is a cruel cross—to be cast out by your own!

It is not that your gifts and ministries become inaccessible. Your service must remain entirely fruitful for those people for whom it has been designed. Jesus' ministry remained a perfect communication to all people to whom He was sent by the Father. It is rather you yourself, your motivations and reactions, that may become incomprehensible; therefore suspect, to your brothers. So you may have to walk alone some of the time. Yet you are not alone, you are sharing the suffering of Him who rose early to be with His

Father, and who listened always to the voice of the Spirit rather than to the world, Satan, or His own desires for pleasure or comfort, or the self-seeking Israelites.

If we would obtain resurrection life we must learn what it means to share the sufferings of Christ. The cross and the crown go together. There is a daily crucifixion of the self-life, and sometimes physical suffering. In the fourth chapter of II Corinthians Paul describes the continual crucifixion and resurrection of the Christian:

> "We are troubled on every side, yet not distressed; we are perplexed, but not in despair; persecuted, but not forsaken; cast down, but not destroyed; always bearing about in the body the dying of the Lord Jesus, that the life also of Jesus might be made manifest in our body. For we which live are always delivered unto death for Jesus' sake, that the life also of Jesus might be made manifest in our mortal flesh" (vs. 8-11).

The above is a description of the manner in which resurrection life is created and developed in us while we are yet in the mortal body. It is to the process of continual dying and continual living brought to the full that Paul is referring when he talks about knowing the power of His resurrection and about attaining to the resurrection from the dead.

When resurrection life has been fully developed within us, and we have learned to live in it, move in it, obey it, rest in it, be empowered by it, then, and only then, will we be ready to be clothed upon with our "house which is from heaven." Isn't this what Philippians 3:9-11 is saying?

The nature of the first resurrection. The fullness of the "Tabernacles experience" includes the eternal indwelling of the Godhead in us, we having been clothed over with a glorious "house" containing a limitless amount of abilities and energies. The indwelling and the clothing-over comprise the first resurrection. Movements to and from heaven are no more essential to the first resurrection than driving across town is essential to owning an expensive automobile, or flying to Alaska is essential to owning an airplane.

Movement into the air is not of the essence of the resurrection from the dead, although such movement is associated with the resurrection from among the dead because at the last trumpet the overcomers are going to be gathered together with Jesus in order to prepare for the judging and release of the earth. The essence of the resurrection is the inner development of the life of Jesus, and, when this has been accomplished, the extension of the eternal life into the human body (Rom. 8:11). Now, back to Philippians 3:10,11:

> "Being made conformable unto his death; if by any means I might attain unto the resurrection of the dead."

But Paul, you "have" attained! You are the apostle to the Gentiles! You of all people will go up in the rapture. Quit rocking our doctrinal boat. You don't fit our doctrines.

If we will not press on to the inner resurrection which is available now, we have no reason to believe that we will gain a resurrection body at the appearance of Christ. The resurrection body will clothe only a resurrected personality. God has no intention of clothing an infantile, self-centered, fleshly self-life with an eternal, all-powerful body having the capability of overcoming all limitations of time and space. Let us not deceive ourselves along this line. What a man sows he will reap.

"Not as though I had already attained" (v. 12):

Come on, Paul, You are just being modest. You can't mean what you are saying. If you are struggling to attain Christ, to arrive at the resurrection, where does that leave us? You are just saying the socially acceptable platitudes that we all expect from a distinguished religious leader.

"Either were already perfect": Notice here that resurrection and perfection are linked together in Paul's mind.

> "But I follow after, if that I may apprehend (grasp) that for which also I am apprehended of Christ Jesus."

God has called us to a glorious resurrection rest in Him, both the inner man as well as body—the two eventually must go together. But we have to fight our way by faith into our possessions, under the leadership of the Spirit of God. The fullness of the Tabernacles experience, as we have said, is the indwelling, or resting, of the Father and the Son through the Holy Spirit in a transformed Christian personality.

The body will then be "eternalized," shall we say, by being clothed over with a heavenly body of truly magnificent capabilities, with tendencies toward holiness rather than toward sin. The inner perfecting and clothing-over is the true nature of the first resurrection from the dead, and is the reward of the overcomer only. Changing one's location by flying through the air is of little spiritual significance. Anyone who wishes to fly through the air may do so at his pleasure in the future life.

We are not teaching that the dead in Christ will not rise to meet the Lord in the air at His coming. The Scripture teaches plainly that we will (I Thess. 4:17). What we are teaching is that the rising in the air is not the fundamental nature of the resurrection from the dead about which Paul was so concerned. It is, rather, an ascension; and the ascension is not typified in the major Old Testament types.

The Lord Jesus is the firstborn from the dead. Our resurrection will be patterned after His. It may be observed that His resurrection was characterized by renewal of life and by extraordinary abilities. A study of II Corinthians 4:7 through 5:5 may enable the student to gain some understanding of the resurrection from the dead.

A definite mark. "Brethren, I count not myself to

have apprehended: but this one thing I do, forgetting those things which are behind, and reaching forth unto those things which are before" (Phil. 3:13).

What could a man with the background of Christian experience and ministry of the apostle Paul have been straining forward to reach? Whatever it was, it obviously is the goal of the Christian life. And since the convocation of Tabernacles typifies the consummation of salvation, we might say that Paul was reaching forth toward the "Tabernacles" fulfillment, so to speak.

> "I press toward the mark for the prize of the high calling of God in Christ Jesus" (v. 14).

Perhaps the most important idea emerging from the thoughts we have presented on the last few pages is this: there is a definite, attainable goal, or "mark," toward which the Christian is to be pressing. True, we are to be awaiting with joyful expectancy the glorious appearing of our Lord Jesus Christ. But at the same time we must be pressing toward the mark, as Paul says. That *mark* is the fullness of the indwelling of Christ in us, who is the resurrection and the life.

> "Let us therefore, as many as be perfect, be thus minded: and if in any thing ye be otherwise minded, God shall reveal even this unto you" (v. 15).

Isaiah 12.   In the seventh chapter of the gospel of John we find these words:

> "In the last day, that great day of the feast, Jesus stood and cried, saying, If any man thirst, let him come unto me, and drink. He that believeth on me, as the Scripture hath said, out of his belly shall flow rivers of living water" (John 7:37,38).

What connection does the statement about "rivers of living water" have with the convocation of Tabernacles, for it was at the great day of the feast of Tabernacles that Jesus said this. Perhaps the connection is that the fulfillment of the convocation of Tabernacles is the setting up of the throne of God in the heart of the Christian. The Holy Spirit flows from the throne of God (Rev. 22:1; Ezek. 47:1). When God is enthroned in the heart of the overcomer the river of life will flow out for the healing of the nations.

The concept of the inner river of life is found in Isaiah 12, a passage of Scripture which the Hebrews associated with the convocation of Tabernacles: "Behold, God is my salvation."

Let us repeat the fundamental message of Tabernacles. The fullness of salvation is not another spiritual principle or secret to add to our collection. God Himself *is* our goal. God *is* our salvation. All else is idolatry.

"I will trust, and not be afraid." The word *trust* is significant here. The experience of Tabernacles is characterized by a restful trust in the Lord, an abiding in Christ, a fearless and secure repose upon the rock of ages. This kind of calm resting in the strength of Christ is more important to the overcoming life than are Christian duties, although the doing of good works is very important, as the Lord leads.

"For the Lord Jehovah is my strength and my song"; not, the Lord *gives* me strength—*gives* me a song. He Himself *is* the strength; He Himself *is* the song. The marriage to God, the possession of God Himself, is the ultimate attainment of the Christian experience. All of the other aspects of salvation are means toward this end. He who is married to the Lord Jesus Christ has inherited everything. He who has rejected Christ has lost everything.

"He also is become my salvation. Therefore with joy shall ye draw water out of the wells of salvation."

What, or who, are the "wells of salvation"? Consider:

"Out of his belly shall flow rivers of living water" (John 7:38).

"My Father will love him, and we will come unto him, and make our abode with him" (John 14:23).

"I in them, and thou in me, that they may be made perfect in one; and that the world may know that thou hast sent me, and hast loved them, as thou hast loved me" (John 17:23).

From the above passages it sounds as though the Christians are the "wells of salvation"! The convocation of Tabernacles is fulfilled when God and Christ take up their abode in the heart of the Christian overcomer.

Tabernacles is associated with obedience to the Word, or law, of God. Notice that John 14:23, a statement referring, we believe, to the Christian fulfillment of the Hebrew convocation of Tabernacles, indicates that there is a dependency relationship between obedience to the Word of Christ and the indwelling of the Godhead: "If a man love me, he will keep my words: and my Father will love him, and we will come unto him, and make our abode with him."

And in Deuteronomy 31:10,11 ". . . In the feast of tabernacles, when all Israel is come to appear before the Lord thy God in the place which he shall choose, thou shalt read this law before all Israel in their hearing"; (see also Neh. 8:13-18). The hearing and keeping of God's law is linked with the convocation of Tabernacles. After all, the ultimate expression of the law of God occurs when the Father and the Son through the Holy Spirit rule absolutely in the heart of the saint.

Completion of the harvest season. The convocation of Tabernacles signals the completion of the harvest season: " . . . and the feast of ingathering (Tabernacles), which is in the end of the year, when thou hast gathered in thy labors out of the field" (Exod. 23:16). The completion of the harvesting of the Christian by the Lord is the redemption of the human body. The redeeming of our body is a very important part of salvation by faith in Christ Jesus. Listen to Paul:

> " . . . ourselves also, which have the firstfruits of the Spirit, even we ourselves groan within ourselves, waiting for the adoption, to wit, the redemption of our body" (Rom. 8:23).

Redemption of the human body.   We Christians have not been adopted as sons until our body has been redeemed. In fact, the redemption of the human body *is* our adoption as a son of God, the consummation of the Christian salvation.

From our point of view, the churches have not paid nearly enough attention to the redemption of the body as a part of salvation by faith. Christian teachers have not explained the close relationship and interaction between the pursuit of the overcoming life now and the receiving of bodily redemption at the appearing of the Lord Jesus (Rom. 8:11; II Cor. 4:17; Phil. 3:11; I John 3:3, for example). The redemption of the body (remember that it is the *body* in which the Spirit of God dwells—I Cor. 6: 13-19) has not been pointed to as the climax of the maintenance of victorious faith in Christ.

It appears that the redemption of our body has been regarded by the churches as being an external event over which we have little or no control, such as the planet Earth slowing down and finally falling into the sun. Such inevitability is not the case at all. Physical death is not a "natural" state of man, although Satan would enjoy having us think so. Physical death is a curse upon mankind and is the perpetual, direct, and certain consequence of sin. Death (spiritual and physical) is an enemy which is to be destroyed on the basis of Jesus' finished work on Calvary, whenever the overcoming faith and holiness (conformity to the express image of Christ) of the body of Christ reaches the necessary level. Neither spiritual nor physical death are natural states of being. Death is the product of the work of the enemies of God and man. Death (separation from the life of God) was destroyed legally on the cross, and will be destroyed practically and actually by the Spirit of Christ working through the joyous obedience and faith of His body.

Christian! Begin to get in your being a sense of the attitude of war, enmity, and casting out which our mighty Christ maintains toward death—that archenemy of mankind.

May we add that we do not support those who allow themselves to be deceived to the point where they claim to have redeemed bodies now. Even to suggest such a thing is to be deluded and snared. Anyone who thinks he has a redeemed body now can prove it easily by passing through the wall of a house, or by flying through the air.

But it is equally a delusion and snare to relegate the redemption of the mortal body of the Christian to an external event which will include all Christians regardless of their state of spiritual maturity, an event unrelated to the maturing faith of the overcomers.

The Jews made a similar mistake in their concept of the coming of Messiah. The busy priests who were watching for Messiah to come as a conquering hero, missed Him. The humble of Israel who had a love affair with God in the heart, found Him (Luke 2:25,26).

An increase in available glory.   The writer subscribes without equivocation to the teaching of I Thessalonians 4:15-17. We look for the Lord to descend from heaven with a shout, and for the dead in Christ to rise, and for us believers to be caught up together with them in the clouds to meet the Lord in the air. We know that this event is going to happen literally.

At the same time we are beginning to wonder if the stress on the doctrine of the rapture, which in so many minds is associated with a fleeing from world problems and personal problems rather than with an overcoming faith in Christ, may be causing us to be deaf to the voice of the Holy Spirit of God in our time.

The Christians of today who are hoping for a rapture which will enable them to flee from their problems may miss Him. But they who, like Simeon and Anna of old, are more occupied with the worship of God than they are with the organizational life of "Israel," surely will find Him whom their soul desires above all else. Most assuredly there is going to be a rapture. The Bible terms it the *first resurrection,* and it is going to occur exactly as described in I Thessalonians 4:15-17. But if our understanding is correct, the Holy Spirit of God in Christ is teaching us that many church members of today are not prepared spiritually to be translated into glory. We are to be prepared further by receiving more virtue and strength from the living Christ. This virtue and strength is available now to the disciple of Jesus. Let the prophets judge.

When we halt for a moment our many activities and pray long enough to enable us to hear the voice of the Holy Spirit, it seems He is commanding us to wash our garments and to get ready for an increase in strength and victory; for further experiences and lessons with the great Teacher from Nazareth. The "Tabernacles" convocation of the old covenant will have been fulfilled in the new covenant when our human body has been redeemed. The redemption of the mortal body by the donning of the body from heaven is the consummation—the completeness and fullness of the Christian salvation.

The most joyous convocation.   Tabernacles was by far the most joyous occasion of the Hebrew year. One can imagine a Jew coming out of his house each year and living for a week in a booth made from the branches of trees. Perhaps this was God's way of repeatedly bringing to the attention of the Israelites that their most important contribution among the nations of the earth is not to be in the area of government, economics, or the arts or sciences, as significant as their contributions in those realms may be. The most important and significant gift that Israel brings to the family of mankind is the Law and presence of the living God. Also, living in the booths pointed to the day when God dwells in Israel and Israel dwells in God; God rests in Israel and Israel rests in God. The prophets testified of that day to come, and Jesus and the apostles taught us how God is bringing His will to pass in human beings.

The feast of Tabernacles, the completion of the harvesting of all the fruits of the earth, was celebrated by the Hebrews with the greatest joy and rejoicing. When God and Christ, through the Holy Spirit, come to us in their fullness in the day of the Lord, we will experience such joy, peace, and rest—and fullness of glory—that it will take a redeemed body to contain it all.

Our many possessions and activities shrink in value to us when they are compared with His presence. Our idols are placed in perspective and can be seen for what they really are. He is the living God and must be the focus of our attention at all times. He will be the focus at all times if we love and serve Him as He deserves to be loved and served.

> "That they all may be one; as thou, Father, art in me, and I in thee, that they also may be one in us: that the world may believe that you have sent me. And the glory which thou gavest me I have given them; that they may be one, even as we are one: I in them, and thou in me, that they may be made perfect in one; and that the world may know that thou hast sent me, and hast loved them, as thou hast loved me" (John 17:21-23).

> "Jesus answered and said unto him, If a man love me, he will keep my words: and my Father will love him, and we will come unto him, and make our abode with him" (John 14:23).

> "And I heard a great voice out of heaven saying, Behold, the tabernacle of God is with men, and he will dwell with them, and they shall be his people, and God himself shall be with them, and be their God" (Rev. 21:3).

THREE HOLY CONVOCATIONS

We have mentioned before that the seven convocations were divided into three major convocations: (1) Passover, Unleavened Bread, Firstfruits; (2) Pentecost; (3) Trumpets, Day of Atonements, Tabernacles. When we were describing the Person and work of the Lord Jesus Christ we stated that the first group portrayed Christ as the great High Priest of God; the second group (Pentecost) portrayed Christ as the great Prophet of God; and the third group portrayed Christ as the King of kings and Lord of lords.

> "Three times in a year shall all thy males appear before the Lord thy God in the place which he shall choose; in the feast of unleavened bread, and in the feast of weeks, and in the feast of tabernacles: and they shall not appear before the Lord empty: every man shall give as he is able, according to the blessing of the Lord thy God which he hath given to thee" (Deut. 16:16,17).

Now that we are portraying the redemption of the individual believer, let us look at these three major convocations as three reapings of the Christian person. First, the Christian is reaped unto the Lord Jesus Christ. Second, the Christian is reaped unto the Holy Spirit. Third, the Christian is reaped unto the Father. Let's see if this analysis is helpful to our understanding.

It may be somewhat enlightening to think of these three reapings as three deaths and three resurrections which the Christian experiences. These three deaths and resurrections are typified by the three hangings of the Tabernacle of the Congregation: the *gate* leading into the courtyard; the *door* leading into the holy place; and the *veil* leading into the holy of holies.

The first reaping.   The first reaping is unto the Lord Jesus Christ, so to speak. It is typified by the gate of the courtyard. It is typified also by the first major convocation (Passover, Unleavened Bread, and Firstfruits), and by the Red Sea.

We experience the first reaping when we accept the Lord Jesus Christ as the atonement for our sins and put no confidence whatever in our own ability to satisfy God by our own righteous behavior. We forsake our own self-righteousness, and cast ourself upon the righteousness which is of God by faith in Christ.

This first death is the death of our "old man." It is followed by the judgment of God upon the gods of this world who have kept us in bondage. Calvary is the judgment of God upon the gods of this age. The first death in this context is followed by a first resurrection—a resurrection unto the righteousness of God.

We walk out of darkness into the light of God's presence. We are born again. We get baptized in water, in obedience to God's Word, dramatizing the fact that the power and authority of hell has been left behind and we now are God's servants.

The first reaping occurs instantly, because by faith we reckon ourself death with Christ and by faith we reckon ourself alive with the resurrected Christ. Our spirit is raised up to sit with Christ in God. It is an instant death and an instant resurrection, and from this time forth we walk in the righteousness of Christ freely imputed to us. We are clothed over with His own righteousness.

The second reaping.   The second reaping is unto the Holy Spirit. It is typified by the door of the Tabernacle. It is typified also by the second major convocation—Pentecost, and by the giving of the Law upon Mount Sinai.

We experience the second reaping when we receive the baptism with the Holy Spirit and set out to walk in obedience to the law of the Spirit of life. We forsake our own fleshly lusts and seek to live in the discipline of the Spirit, putting to death the deeds of the body, as the Spirit leads.

The death of the door has to do with our confessing and resisting our sins. It is followed by the judgment of God upon sin which is in us. The second death, in this context, is followed by a second resurrection—a resurrection of the power of the Holy Spirit working in our life.

We come to know the Holy Spirit in two ways: first, as the One who gives us gifts and ministries so that we can contribute and receive the manifestation of the Holy Spirit, thus building us up into the unity of the faith, unto the perfect man, unto the measure of the stature of the fullness of Christ. Second, we come to know the Holy Spirit as the One who brings forth in us the fruit of Christ-likeness: love, joy, peace, long-suffering, gentleness, goodness, faith, meekness, temperance. The Spirit who dwells in us yearns over us with a godly jealousy, and He fights against Satan, against the spirit of this age, and against our flesh.

The second reaping occurs slowly, taking place over a period of time as the Holy Spirit leads us into various circumstances. We do not die out to sin all at once, except in the theoretical sense. In actual experience it is a daily dying and a daily renewing of life, as the Holy Spirit brings us down to the death of the cross, and then imbues us with divine life so that we can overcome evil with good. The Holy Spirit brings to us the virtue of the broken body and shed blood of Christ so that we can keep on overcoming, no matter how much evil hits us. This second resurrection occurs slowly, proceeding out of our daily dying. Death, life! Death, life! Death, life! will it never end? Yes, it will, if we do not give up but remain faithful to the dealings of the Lord in us.

The third reaping.   The third reaping is unto the

Father. It is typified by the veil of the Tabernacle. It is typified also by the third major convocation (Trumpets, the Day of Atonement, and Tabernacles), and by the crossing of the River Jordan.

We experience the third reaping when we press on past Pentecost to know the fellowship of Christ's sufferings and the power of His resurrection. We decide to become the servant of the Lord, and to present ourself before Him forever in order that He may use us in His kingdom as He will.

This third death is the death of our self-will. It is followed by the judgment of God upon us as a person. The third death is followed by the resurrection of the body, at the appearing of our Lord Jesus Christ in glory.

We walk now in the image of Christ. We are fighters against the enemies of the Lord. We are a part of God's great "servant," described in the book of Isaiah. We become a king unto God, ruling over our allotted portion of God's creation. We become a priest unto God, interceding before Him and bringing the knowledge of the Lord to those in need.

The third death occurs over a period of time, as we are brought into the sufferings of Christ. These are not the sufferings which come as a judgment against our sins. These are sufferings of the kind the Lord suffered—the sufferings of the righteous person who is being made perfect. For example: our good is evil spoken of; our judgment is taken away; we are humiliated without reason; we suffer wrong at the hands of our brethren; God deals with us endlessly, night and day, trying every thought, every word, every motive. We see wrong and are forbidden by the Lord to criticize. We become blind and deaf in the Lord, and all our springs are channeled into Him. He becomes our life, and we no longer have the "rights" to self-seeking that others enjoy.

But the fullness of the third resurrection is instantaneous—in a moment, in the twinkling of an eye, at the last trumpet. If we go all the way through this third death, according to God's satisfaction, our reward in glory will be beyond our ability to conceive. The sufferings may be great; prolonged. But compared with the glory which is going to be revealed in us, the sufferings are not worthy of mention. Let us press on!

The idea of the three great reapings is very important. This concept appears many times in Scripture, such as the thirtyfold, sixtyfold, and hundredfold of the parable of the sower in Mark 4; the fruit, more fruit, and much fruit of John 15; the three levels of Noah's ark; and so forth. Paul was caught up to the third heaven. Hosea says, "After two days will he revive us: in the third day he will raise us up, and we shall live in his sight" (Hos. 6:2).

The three reapings are seen most clearly in the Tabernacle of the Congregation, where we have the courtyard, the holy place, and the holy of holies. Notice that the three areas are levels of holiness. We are to be growing in holiness every day of our Christian life.

The first area is that of initial salvation, or redemption. Everyone at this level has been washed in the precious blood of the Lamb and will be saved in the day of judgment. The courtyard was surrounded by the Linen fence of righteousness. It was lighted by the sunlight, indicating that Christ was crucified in the open where He can be seen by the lost.

The second area is that of the ministry of the church. This is a priestly level, and is the place where the ministries and gifts of the Holy Spirit are operating for the purpose of building up the body of Christ. The holy place of the Tabernacle speaks of the partaking by the church of the broken body and shed blood of the Lamb of God; of the manifestation of the Holy Spirit; and of the Spirit-filled prayer and worship which ascends from the body of Christ to the Father in heaven. The second area was lighted by the lampstand indicating that the ministry in here is not where it can be observed by the lost, or understood and appropriated by any who are not of the church.

The third area is that of perfect holiness, of the fullness of God's glory, of the fullness of power and authority, and of the express image of Jesus Christ created in His saints. The third level was lighted by the glory of God shining forth from between the cherubim which overshadowed the mercy seat. The throne of God and of the Lamb are here.

The first area leads into the second, and the second area leads into the third, if we follow on to know the Lord.

"Come, and let us return unto the Lord: for he hath torn, and he will heal us; he hath smitten, and he will bind us up. After two days will he revive us: in the third day he will raise us up, and we shall live in his sight. Then shall we know, if we follow on to know the Lord: his going forth is prepared as the morning; and he shall come unto us as the rain, as the latter and former rain unto the earth" (Hos. 6:1-3).

"Behold, I cast out devils, and I do cures today and tomorrow, and the third day I shall be perfected" (Luke 13:32).

V

THE PERFECTING
OF THE CHURCH

To this point in our study we have discussed the physical description of the seven convocations, that is, how they were observed literally. Then we mentioned the way in which the convocations portray the Person and work of our Lord Jesus Christ. Next, we set forth the doctrine that the seven feasts typify the process of redemption working in the life of the individual Christian, as he or she is brought from the lowest pit of bondage all the way to the throne of God and of the Lamb. What a redemption! Glory to God!

The remainder of the study has to do with the manner in which the feasts of the Lord symbolize the perfecting of the Christian church, the body of Christ; and finally, how they symbolize the setting up of the kingdom of God upon the earth.

The process of the redemption of the believer, and the perfecting of the Christian church, are very closely related in that the church is made up of the believers. The destiny of the saint and the destiny of the church are identical. There are some thoughts, however, which we might want to consider. It is interesting to note that individual disciples are always free to press on and to work with the Holy Spirit on their own time schedule. In the meanwhile, the Christian church as a whole is moving ahead on many fronts. When you look around you can see Christians making headway as they move toward maturity in Christ. Not all groups of Christians are at the same point; some are further along in holiness and/or spiritual understanding. But the Holy Spirit is working with each group that will cooperate with Him.

When we are thinking about the church of Christ we are thinking about the temple of God. The church of Christ is being created by the Lord as a dwelling place for God in the earth. God's desire is to dwell in the earth among His creatures. It is impossible for Him to just build a house and live in it, God being *who* He is and *what* He is, and we being who we are and what we are. Nevertheless, it is God's intention to live and rule in the earth among His creatures, and His purposes and workings are moving toward this end.

God is perfectly at rest in His beloved Son, the Lord Jesus Christ, because Christ is righteous and holy, always doing those things which please God. But God wants more persons in His great temple. Therefore He has "broken" Christ, so to speak, and shed His precious blood, in order that He may build a bride for His beloved Son, resulting in a helpmeet for the Lord Jesus and an enlargement of God's temple, His dwelling place in the earth.

The church begins as more or less organized groups of believers. These are the local churches. When God is finished, every single believer will have been created in his individual place in the temple of God, the wife of the Lamb, the holy city, the new Jerusalem. This is the destiny of the church and of the individual disciples.

THREE HOLY CONVOCATIONS

We have mentioned previously that the seven Levitical convocations were grouped into three major gatherings: Unleavened Bread, Pentecost, and Tabernacles. These three major convocations portray the development of the church, the body of Christ. Passover and the week of Unleavened

Bread portray the church as the assemblies of the redeemed, covered with the precious blood of God's Lamb, baptized in water, and basking in the light of His acceptance and His righteousness, imputed to each one through means of the obedience and the shed blood of the righteous Christ. The assemblies of the redeemed are the first stage of the development of the church of Christ, and there are hundreds of thousands of such assemblies throughout the earth today, of various persuasions and backgrounds.

The second major gathering was Pentecost. The corresponding element of the Tabernacle of the Congregation was the holy place. The holy place was dominated by the golden lampstand. If the seven lamps ceased to burn, the other two furnishings, the table of showbread and the altar of incense, could not be seen. The golden lampstand (the symbol of Jewry from ancient times) is, at least for now, perhaps the most significant symbol of the church of Christ to be found in the entire Bible.

Pentecost, of the Levitical convocations, and the lampstand, of the Tabernacle of the Congregation, speak of the Christian church at its second stage of development. The lampstand portrays the twofold aspect of the work of the Holy Spirit in the church of Christ: (1) the ministries and gifts, the manifestation, of the Spirit; and (2) the fruit of holy moral conduct which grows in the Christian person as a result of the abiding of the Holy Spirit in him. Gifts of power and revelation added to righteous and holy conduct constitute the light of the world.

During the celebration of Pentecost, two large loaves of the finest wheat flour, baked with leaven, were waved before the Lord. The two loaves represent the unimaginable power and authority which has been given to the church of Christ; and the fine flour represents righteousness and purity of conduct and motive. The leaven represents Christ Himself who is growing within the church.

The third major gathering was Tabernacles. When the

church has reached the desired level of maturity, then the Father and the Son through the fullness of the Holy Spirit will take up residence in the church. This will occur to a certain extent at the beginning of the millennium, when our Lord descends from heaven. But it will reach its most complete fulfillment at the time that the holy city, the new Jerusalem, descends from God out of heaven, at the beginning of the new heaven and earth reign of the Lord Jesus Christ.

We will now review the seven feasts as they concern the church, keeping in mind that there is a great deal of overlap between the redemption of the believer and the perfecting of the church, in that the church is composed of the redeemed believers.

PASSOVER

When we consider the exodus of Israel from the land of Egypt, we begin to see a picture of the church of Christ coming out of the slavery to the god of this world. The blood of the Lamb covers the church, and the judgment of God passes over the church, as the Lord God executes judgment upon the unclean evil lords of the darkness of the present age. Although such an escape occurs every time a soul is saved, the most complete fulfillment of the symbolism of the exodus will occur as the Lord Jesus rains destruction upon the earth in the day to come, and then gloriously removes His church from the cruel bondage of the Satan-controlled spirit of the world in which we live.

It is helpful to realize that Israel is one, whether we are studying the Old Testament or the New Testament. The called-out people of God, the Seed of Abraham, God's kings and priests, are one church. The children of Israel were the church under the fall (early, seed) rains, and the Christian church is the church under the spring (latter, harvest) rains. The things which happened to Israel were for our instruction and admonition, upon whom the end of the age has come. The coming out of Israel from Egypt, under the mighty hand of God, was our coming out. First the church came out literally, as a figure; and now the church is coming out from the age in the spiritual sense. Under the former rain the church was protected by the blood of a lamb. Under the latter rain the church is protected by the Lamb of God, Christ Jesus.

UNLEAVENED BREAD

When Israel followed Moses through the Red Sea, the power and authority of Egypt was left behind. Pharaoh and his host attempted to pursue God's servant, but were drowned in the process. The leaven of Egypt, to speak in a figure, was destroyed by the power of God's judgment.

The church today follows Christ through the waters of baptism. Water baptism is a portrayal of the destruction of the power and authority of the spirit of this age, as far as the one being baptized is concerned. The church takes her place with the Lord Jesus Christ upon the cross, and her spirit is raised up to sit with Christ in the heavenlies. Satan attempts to pursue the church, but Satan can never follow the church through the cross of Christ. The cross is his end. His power and authority were destroyed completely in the heart of the earth, as God's mighty conqueror, Jesus Christ, was used of the Holy Spirit as the Redeemer—the One who through the enabling wisdom and power of the Holy Spirit paid the price of redemption for every person. Satan cannot overturn the authority of that transaction by any means whatever.

FIRSTFRUITS

The church of Christ comes up out of the waters of baptism, as did Israel from the Red Sea, and stands at the beginning of the wilderness, ready to follow her Lord through the time of purification, just as was true of Esther. The church is born again through means of the waters of baptism, now being free from the leaven (power and authority) of the spirit of the present age.

The church is the firstfruits, after Christ, of the earth. She is God's first reaping of mankind. The church has access to the heavenlies and holds the keys of the kingdom. In spirit she is at the right hand of the Father in Christ. Whatever she binds on earth is bound in heaven; whatever she looses upon the earth is loosed in heaven. She has the authority of Christ when she is moving in the Spirit of God. She is the light of the world, the ambassador of Christ, Jacob's ladder, the body of Christ in the earth, and in heaven as well.

The kingdom of God is within the church, and it is in the church that the laws of the kingdom will first be kept in the earth. The church is the beloved of the Lord Jesus, and has His entire attention. She is Mount Zion, the holy dwelling place of God in Christ.

The life of the church is the broken body and shed blood of the Lord Jesus Christ. The body and blood of Christ is the food and drink whereby the church lives. There is a tremendous amount of evil in the world, evil which the church cannot overcome by her own goodness. When enough evil encompasses the church she goes under in bitterness and sin. But the body and blood of Christ is the "good" by means of which the church is able to overcome the evil which is in the world.

Although the church is comprised of saved flesh-and-blood people, yet there is another totally different aspect of the church. The church starts out as the assemblies of the redeemed. But because of the continual eating and drinking of the body and blood of Christ, and through many ministrations of the Holy Spirit of God, a miraculous transformation begins to take place in the church. She is built up upon the substance of Christ, just as Eve was built up upon the substance of Adam. The new creation which is built upon the church is not flesh and blood—it is of the substance of Christ Himself. The true church, that which is from heaven and is created from the body and blood of Christ, comes out of the assemblies of the redeemed just as a beautiful butterfly emerges from the cocoon.

There are two aspects to the church. There are the assemblies of the redeemed, and then there is the one church, the body of Christ, the wife of the Lamb. She is the wife of the Lamb because her food and drink is the body and blood of God's Lamb. She is born from above; she is not of this earth, in the sense in which we are speaking at this point.

Although the church starts out as groups of saved people, of various beliefs and cultural backgrounds and practices, the true church is not these various groups of the saved. The true church is created from these believers through means of the workings of the Holy Spirit, using the substance of Christ. When God has completed the fashioning of the bride of the Lamb, the heavenly Eve, she will be a marvelous creature indeed, being in the express image of her Lord, Jesus Christ. She will be beautiful, holy, righteous, a perfect helpmeet for Christ in every last detail. She will not be finished until after the millennium, because it is at the creation of the new heaven and earth, the Bible instructs us, that she will descend from God out of heaven. Until that moment she is undergoing purification.

Christ is so extraordinarily perfect and mighty—far, far more so than any of us have the remotest conception—that the bride, in order to be a helpmeet, cannot be as groups of imperfect flesh-and-blood people. Rather, the bride will be a spiritual creation, built from His body and blood, and will be of His being, of His nature, of His substance, of His wisdom, of His Spirit, of His very life!

The first three feasts, Passover, Unleavened Bread, and Firstfruits, bring her to the first stage of her perfecting. She is now ready for the workings of the Holy Spirit, which will result in her transformation into the bride of the Lamb, the holy city, the new Jerusalem.

PENTECOST

The church of Christ was born in Pentecostal fire and power (Acts 2). Pentecost represents the Holy Spirit coming upon the church, the body of Christ. The two loaves of fine wheat flour, waved by the anointed priest during the feast of Pentecost (Leviticus 23), portray the complete power and authority of Christ given to the church in order that it can bear witness to Him and do His work in the earth.

One of the most significant types of the Holy Spirit found in the Bible is Eliezer of Damascus (Genesis 24). Abraham sent him, his chief servant, to obtain a bride for Isaac. This is a portrayal of the Holy Spirit obtaining a bride for Christ, the Son of the Father. The Holy Spirit has been charged by the Father to create the bride of Christ. The Holy Spirit has complete responsibility for the fulfillment of this mission. It is time now for Christian people to realize the awesome authority of the Holy Spirit, and to begin to obey Him. Creating the church is His job. We only get in the way unless we are led by Him.

It is the writer's point of view that the Holy Spirit needs to be much more prominent in the church of Christ. It seems sometimes that we do not understand the role of the Holy Spirit, and look upon Him as some kind of spiritual phenomenon that we should try to use to accomplish our notion of what is good for our local church or for our own experience. It is not that way at all in the spiritual realm. The Holy Spirit, and He alone, is charged with the building up of the church of Christ. Our job is to become responsive to the will of the Holy Spirit. His job is to present the bride, without spot or wrinkle, to the Son. That is His charge from the Father, and the Spirit will never rest until the bride is perfect.

In line with His commission to build the bride, the Holy Spirit of His own will assigns gifts and ministries to the members of the body of Christ. The Holy Spirit works unceasingly with the goal in mind of bringing the bride to maturity. In the days to come, the Holy Spirit will become increasingly prominent, because the latter stages of the maturing of the bride cannot in any manner be touched by the efforts of the flesh of men, no matter how well intentioned.

The Holy Spirit has been given absolute power and authority over the church, to bring it to Christ as a perfect helpmeet. The Holy Spirit is active in all that the church does and says. To indicate just a few representative passages: the Holy Spirit enables the church to remit or retain sins (John 20:22). Through the Holy Spirit Christ gives commandments to His apostles (Acts 1:2). Believers are to be baptized with the Holy Spirit (Acts 1:5). Christians are given the power to bear witness of the resurrection of Christ, through the Holy Spirit (Acts 1:8).

The Holy Spirit is the director of the building and activities of the church (Acts 13:2). The Holy Spirit tells the church of things to come (Acts 20:23). The Holy Spirit appoints overseers of the church (Acts 20:28). We Christians are the temple of the Holy Spirit (I Cor. 6:19). The Holy Spirit helps us in prayer (Jude 20; Rom. 8:26). We are born of the Spirit (John 3:6). The Holy Spirit is a well of living water in the Christian (John 7:38,39).

The Holy Spirit is the Spirit of truth (John 14:17). The Holy Spirit judges through the church (Acts 5:9). The Holy Spirit is the law of the Christian church, the law of the Spirit of life (Rom. 8:2). The Holy Spirit is going to be the One who makes alive our mortal body at the appearing of Christ (Rom. 8:11). The Holy Spirit is the One who enables us to put to death the deeds of our flesh (Rom. 8:13). The Holy Spirit leads the sons of God (Rom. 8:14). The Holy Spirit is a pledge upon the greater glory which is to come (Rom. 8:23). The Holy Spirit helps our weaknesses (Rom. 8:23). The Holy Spirit assigns to every man the gifts of revelation and power (I Cor. 12:11).

The Holy Spirit is the substance of the new covenant (II

Cor. 3:6). The Holy Spirit is the transformer of the believer into the image of the glory of the Lord (II Cor. 3:18). It is the Spirit of God by whom we Christians minister to people (Gal. 3:5). The fruit of the abiding of the Holy Spirit in us is righteous and holy conduct (Gal. 5:22,23). If we sow to the Holy Spirit, obeying Him in all things, we will reap everlasting life (Gal. 6:8). God dwells in us through the Holy Spirit (Eph. 2:22). The Holy Spirit strengthens the inner man of the believer (Eph. 3:16). The Holy Spirit seals the Christian unto the day of redemption (Eph. 4:30). The Word of God is the sword of the Spirit (Eph. 6:17).

It is through the Holy Spirit that we are baptized into the body of Christ (I Cor. 12:13)!

The preceding references may give us some small idea of the extent to which the Holy Spirit is to be prominent in the creating of the body of Christ, the wife of the Lamb, the church of the living God, the new Jerusalem.

We have seen, then, that the Holy Spirit is the One who has been charged by the Father to obtain a bride for the mighty Son of God, Jesus Christ. The Holy Spirit will be preeminent in the affairs of the church if we will allow him; otherwise, nothing of eternal value will be achieved through our efforts.

The holy place of the Tabernacle of the Congregation portrays the church, the people who have been called out of the spirit of the age in order to be made kings and priests unto God. In other words, the holy place represents Israel—the people of God, the church of Christ, the holy nation—the peculiar treasure unto God of all the peoples of the earth.

During the present age the Holy Spirit is adding persons to the church, the body of Christ. After believers have been added, it is the purpose of the Holy Spirit to build them up into a perfect man, into the measure of the stature of the fullness of Christ.

There are three aspects of the work of the Holy Spirit in

building up the body of Christ, and these three aspects are portrayed in the three furnishings of the holy place: (1) the table of showbread; (2) the lampstand itself; and (3) the altar of incense. Previously we noted none of these three could even be seen if it were not for the light proceeding from the seven lamps of the lampstand.

The table of showbread, with its twelve loaves of unleavened "presence bread" and its cups of wine, represents the body and blood of Christ. The light from the lampstand illumines the body and blood of Christ upon the table, so that the church can eat and drink the life substance of her Lord. In this way the church receives the eternal divine life, and is able to share this life with the peoples of the earth, as the Christians offer prayer and counsel to those in need. Christians are able to impart the life of Christ to the extent that they themselves possess it, just as Jesus Himself gave life to those in need.

The lampstand represents the light which the church shines abroad. That light is nourished by the anointing of the Holy Spirit, who is the oil—the fuel of the light—which the church provides.

The Holy Spirit is as seven lamps which burn brightly before the God of the whole earth. The Holy Spirit shines forth from the body of Messiah, bringing wisdom, understanding, counsel, might, knowledge, the obedient fear of the Lord, judgment, righteousness, justice, power to break every yoke. When the Holy Spirit shines through the Church, the life of the broken body and shed blood of Christ is in that shining. There is divine life; all the power that the oppressed need to be set completely free. Christ (Head and Body) is the lampstand of God. The Holy Spirit is the oil; the fuel, so to speak. When the double portion of the anointing is upon the church, the power of hell must give way.

The altar of incense portrays the communication of the church with God through Christ. The burning incense yielded a holy perfume. As the substance of Christ is worked into the nature of the church, and the fire of God comes down upon the church, the result is a holy perfume coming up before God. That perfume is the prayers and adoration of the church. The adoration of the church, and its petition, must proceed from the righteous and holy nature of Christ which has been worked into every fiber of the church. The prayers and adoration of the flesh may serve some good on occasion. But the prayers and adoration of the substance of Christ within the church is one of the most powerful forces in God's creation. It moves the hand of God as few things do.

The Levitical convocation of Pentecost represents the second stage of the life of the church. First came redemption from the hand of Pharaoh; next, the presence of the Holy Spirit building up the church into the measure of the stature of the fullness of Christ. We have come now to the third and final stage in the development of the church into the perfect helpmeet of the Lord Jesus Christ.

TRUMPETS

When we come to the role of Trumpets in the perfecting of the Christian church, there are two different aspects which must be considered carefully. One aspect has to do with the part of Trumpets which is occurring now. The other aspect has to do with the part of Trumpets which is coming at a later time.

There is no greater mistake which charismatic or Pentecostal believers can make than to assign the fulfillment of Trumpets in its entirety to a later date, and to remain in the belief that the next move of the church after Pentecost is the rapture, that there are no more significant experiences in Christ after speaking in tongues. Surely, the testimony of Paul in Philippians 3 reveals that speaking in tongues is not the last experience before the historical rapture of the church!

The truth is, as we see it, that there are two different

aspects of the fulfillment of Trumpets. One is that which is to come, announcing the appearing of our Lord Jesus Christ with the holy angels. That will come at the end of this age and the onset of the millennium.

It is the other aspect of Trumpets that we want to be sure that we do not miss. It is that part of Trumpets which is going on right now.

Of course, overcomers in Christ of every age have pressed through into all of these experiences. But now, a large group of the church has experienced Pentecost and is ready for Trumpets. What does Trumpets signify, that we are to experience today?

The trumpet of God is sounding in the church of Christ today, announcing to us that God is ready to go to war against the sin in His people. The trumpet prepares us for spiritual warfare, for overcoming, for conquering our environment in the name of the Lord Jesus.

Little by little the Holy Spirit reveals to us the nature of the warfare of God. Sin becomes more sinful, and we receive strength to resist. We begin to become acquainted with the Christ of the Twenty-fourth Psalm, the Lord, strong and mighty in battle. We begin to cry out to God, "Your kingdom come, your will be done on earth as it is in heaven"! (see Matt 6:10). We begin to pass from concern over our own plans, our own salvation, our own experiences, our own blessings, and become more concerned with the will of God. We receive the desire to become the servant of the Lord.

The burden of the Lord Jesus for the possession of the heathen and of the uttermost parts of the earth becomes our burden. We become much more conscious of the relationship of the church to the heavenlies; the church to us is no longer just an earthbound, human organization. We become increasingly concerned over the filling of the earth with the glory of the Lord, as God promised Moses.

We enter into a much deeper death in Christ than we have before experienced. Our chief desire is to know Him, and the power of His resurrection, and the fellowship of His sufferings, that we might attain to the resurrection out from among the dead. We begin to groan for the redemption of our body, so that we might serve God more fully.

Finally our highest desire becomes that of receiving the fullness of the Father and the fullness of the Son into our being. We long for complete transformation into the express image of Jesus Christ.

These are some of the aspects of that part of the feast of Trumpets which we can experience now.

Pentecost is kind of a turning point. Before Pentecost our chief occupation is with ourself, how God saves us, what we are going to get out of it, how we are going to build the kingdom of God, etc. But after Pentecost, as we begin to move toward Trumpets, we become much more occupied with God's purposes, not only in us but also in the earth. Our own sins of deed, word, motive, and imagination come to our attention and, through the wisdom and power of the Holy Spirit, we confess them and then resist the enemy. We follow Christ into death, loving not our own lives unto the death, and choose to live only in and for His glory. He becomes our goal.

Then there is the coming aspect of Trumpets. Christ will descend from heaven; those who are asleep in Jesus will rise; we who are alive and remain will be caught up with them to meet the Lord in the air, and we shall ever be with the Lord. Our bodies will be changed in a moment, in the twinkling of an eye, at the last trumpet. This present wicked and rebellious age will be finished and the new age of the kingdom of God will commence. The faithful will receive their rewards and the righteous will shine forth in the kingdom of God.

The saints will rule over all nations, under Christ, with the rod of absolute power and authority. The church will be the light of the world, and the peoples of the earth will come of their own will to learn of the Father from the church. The lion will lie down in peace with the lamb, and there will be nothing which hurts or destroys throughout all the earth.

The church will still be learning of her Lord and growing in His graces and virtues. We know the millennium is not a perfect age. For although Satan has been bound, yet the nations remain susceptible to temptation. As soon as Satan is released, he is able to persuade the nations to rebel against God, even though they have been instructed by the church for a thousand years.

We see then that there is an immediate aspect of Trumpets and a future fulfillment, both of which have significance for the building up of the church, the body of Christ. We need to pay close attention to the purposes which the Holy Spirit has in the fulfillment of Trumpets in these days, if we are to be ready for the great earth-wide blowing of the Trumpet at the appearing of our Lord and Savior, Jesus Christ. If we are not faithful in the lesser, we will not be faithful in the greater. If we are not faithful in the blowing of the trumpet which is occurring now, then we will not be faithful in the greater which is to come.

DAY OF ATONEMENT

The Day of Atonement also has both a future and a present fulfillment for the church of Christ. The future fulfillment of the Day of Atonement is the millennium. The present fulfillment of the Day of Atonement is our dealing with the sins in our own life, as the Holy Spirit enables us to do so.

To understand the Day of Atonement we have to understand its two great dimensions: the forgiving of sin's guilt, and the destroying of sin's hold upon us. We have discussed previously in our study how that the slain goat (Lev. 16) has to do with the forgiving of the guilt of our sins, and the living scapegoat has to do with the removal of our sins from us.

The first dimension, that of the forgiveness of our sins, was wrought upon the cross of Calvary. The second dimension will have its greatest fulfillment during the millennium when the power of Christ redeems the earth from the bondage of sin during the great millennial jubilee.

But what of us now? Romans 8:13 tells us that if we live after the flesh we will die; but that if we will put to death the deeds of the body we shall live. Our job as Christians, then, is to be receptive to the leading of the Holy Spirit as He mounts the attack against the sins which we commit. As soon as the Holy Spirit makes known to us where the problem is, then we are to confess our sins (I John 1:7-9). The response of Christ is to forgive us our sins and to cleanse us from all unrighteousness. The entire book of I John informs us, as do many other passages in the New Testament, that it is the will of Christ that we get the victory over sin and quit committing sin. It is the job of the Holy Spirit to give us the wisdom and strength to put to death these sins which we are committing as Christians.

The church faces the Day of Atonement as a creature who has been redeemed through the precious blood of Christ, has partaken of His broken body and shed blood, and has received the Holy Spirit. Next, the church must come face to face with the Holy Spirit in the matter of sins of deed, word, motive, and imagination. Her Lord, Jesus Christ, has made the atonement for her. Now she must avail herself, not only of the forgiveness of guilt, but also of the destruction of sin's power over her. The bride of Christ must overcome sin in all forms. Both Christ and His bride love righteousness and hate iniquity. The church is not quite at that point as yet, but will get there through the provision which God has made in the Day of Atonement. This counterpart of the Day of Atonement is going on right now in the church of Christ, and it is being announced by the trumpet of the Holy Spirit which is blowing now in the church.

"Cry aloud, spare not, lift up thy voice like a trumpet, and show my people their transgression, and the house of Jacob their sins" (Isa. 58:1).

Once the church has been made ready, the power and authority of the Day of Atonement will be brought to the entire earth. The creation will be redeemed from the awful bondage of sin and death and will be released into the glorious liberty of the children of God. What a day of days that will be!

Again, let us remind the reader that if we would be ready for the Day of Atonement which is to come at the millennium, we must allow the Holy Spirit to fulfill the Day of Atonement in us right now. He will, if we will cooperate with Him.

TABERNACLES

The same thing is true of Tabernacles, which we believe to be true of Trumpets and of the Day of Atonement. There is a part of Tabernacles into which the church is to press right now, and then there is a future glorious fulfillment of Tabernacles which exceeds in joy, magnificence and beauty, anything which the disciple of Christ can envision in his most sublime moments.

Let us think for a moment about the current fulfillment of Tabernacles. Jesus said, "If a man love me, he will keep my words: and my Father will love him, and we will come unto him, and make our abode with him" (John 14:23). If we have been alerted by the trumpet of the Lord sounding in the spiritual realm in these days, and we proceed on to the Day of Atonement by confessing our sins and overcoming them through the assistance which the Holy Spirit gives, then we will begin to experience a much fuller abiding of Christ in us than we have known. The more we press on into the overcoming of sin, into obedience, into the death to our self-life which the Lord requires, the more we will be blessed with His abiding presence.

Paul had set his hand to knowing the Lord in His fullness. That ought to be our goal also, that we might come to possess Christ in a greater way than ever before. God through Christ desires to live and move and have His being in us, but we have to be made ready through the various ministrations of the Holy Spirit.

Trumpets, the Day of Atonement, and Tabernacles are at hand, ready for us to press in. Perhaps this is the first time in history when so large a group of the church of Christ is at the place where this kind of progress in Christ can be made. In time past individuals have pressed on through, but today it is numbers of people who are ready to move on with God. And God is always ready! It is we Christians who must address ourself to the Holy Spirit in a diligent, faith-filled manner, in order we may move on with Christ.

What of the future fulfillment of Tabernacles? It is so stupendously glorious that we can only hint at what it will be like. It is the new heaven and earth reign of Christ. The bride, the church of Christ, will be as a city which is surrounded by a great wall constructed from the most precious minerals. This wall typifies the resistance against sin which has been created in the church.

The street of the city is transparent gold, speaking of the absolute clarity and transparency of the refined nature of the members of the body of Christ. In the city is the throne of God and of the Lamb. Out from the throne flows the Holy Spirit in uncrossable depth and width. Along the banks is the tree of life, which is the substance of Christ within the church.

There is no need for the sun by day or the moon by night, for there is no night there. The inhabitants do not need rest, for God is their rest. The glory of God is their light. They see His face, wonder of wonders, and minister before Him. God's servants rule over the kingdoms of the earth, and the nations of the saved walk in the light of the city. The kings of the earth bring their glory and honor to the new Jerusalem.

There is no unclean thing within the city, being kept out by the massive walls and gates. Here is the tabernacle of God among men. Here is the end product of the ministrations of the Holy Spirit. Here is the eternal helpmeet of the Son of God, the Lord Jesus Christ. Here is the dwelling place of God and of the Lamb unto the ages of ages. Here is the result of the travail of the soul of Jesus Christ. Here is every good, every perfect, every acceptable, every righteous, every beautiful, every pure, every glorious thing brought to the fullness of radiance and usefulness. Here is the complete and total vindication of all that God has promised.

What a time of joy will be here when God descends from heaven in the holy city. All of the plantings of God have now been reaped and processed. It is the time for the turning back of all things to the Father by the Lord Jesus. Then will come the eighth day of the feast of Tabernacles, the first day of the week of eternity which has no end.

With such a goal in view, how can the church of Christ do other than to cry, "Lead on, Lord Jesus, no matter what the cost!" The church is still in the early stages of its perfecting at this time. But God has shown us what it will be like when He is finished.

All things will be inherited by those who overcome. Let us see to it that we are counted among those to whom the Lord Jesus can say, "Well done, good and faithful servant. You have believed God and have believed that I came from God. Enter into the 'all things' promised to Me and to you by My Father."

VI

THE SETTING UP
OF THE KINGDOM OF GOD

We have mentioned the manner in which the seven Levitical feasts typify the Person and work of the Lord Jesus Christ; the redemption of the believer; and the perfecting of the Christian church, the body of Christ. Now we will discuss briefly their portrayal of the setting up of the kingdom of God in the earth.

The church of Christ and the kingdom of God are closely related, and the church is part of the kingdom. There are some special facts about the church which we should note, however. For example, the church is the wife of the Lamb. Also, the church holds the keys of the kingdom and has the power to bind and loose in the spiritual realm, and to remit and retain sin. The church has the power and authority of judgment, in other words. It is through the church that God is going to set up His kingdom in the earth.

The kingdom of God is the world-wide establishing of righteousness among all peoples, including the judgment and deliverance of the peoples of the earth. It is the setting up of the rule of God. The church, on the other hand, is a called-out group of people who are being formed into the body of Christ. In the days in which we live, each person who receives Christ is born into the kingdom of God, and then is to be baptized by the Holy Spirit into the one body of Christ (I Cor. 12:13).

The purpose of the two thousand-or-so years from the ascent of Christ until He returns to the earth is the creating of the body of Christ by the Holy Spirit, taking her from the peoples of the earth. It appears that the church will make great progress in the grace and knowledge of the Lord Jesus Christ during the millennium, and then will descend from heaven to earth after the final judgment of God. "So shall we ever be with the Lord," the Bible says; and no doubt our constant association with Him in the work of His kingdom will make us a great deal more like Him than we are now.

The kingdom of God also is being established now in its firstfruits, the church; and everyone who will believe and be baptized will be saved (Mark 16:16), meaning that he will not be destroyed in the day of God's wrath. But, as Jesus tells us in John 17, the world-wide acceptance of Christ will not take place until the church has been made one in the glory and love of God. This unity, glory, and unmeasured anointing has not taken place yet. But it will all come to pass exactly as Jesus prayed, praise the Lord!

Now, let's take a look at how the three major convocations, and then the seven individual feasts, represent the setting up of the kingdom of God in the earth.

THREE HOLY CONVOCATIONS

The grouping of the seven Levitical convocations into three major convocations, Unleavened Bread, Pentecost, and Tabernacles, portrays the three stages in the setting up of the kingdom of God in the earth. However, they must be regarded in the reverse order, Tabernacles, Pentecost, and then Unleavened Bread, if we would see the setting up of the kingdom from God's point of view. It is true also of the Tabernacle of the Congregation that the order of the holy furnishings must be reversed if we would understand them from God's point of view. God sees the furnishings as commencing with the Ark of the Covenant and working out toward the bronze altar of burnt offering. In setting up the kingdom of God, God began with the holy of holies and is working toward the courtyard.

God began His kingdom with the holiest of all, the Lord Jesus Christ. The Lord Jesus is the tabernacle of God. It is interesting to note that the seven feasts portray the working of Christ, if we look at them in reverse: (1) He came to earth as the tabernacle of God, the One in whom the Father dwells; (2) He made atonement for us; (3) He rose from the dead, in fulfillment of the feast of Trumpets; (4) He shed forth the Holy Spirit, corresponding to Pentecost; (5) the church began to receive of His broken body and shed blood, thereby making her a firstfruits of God among the peoples of the earth; (6) the example and teaching of the church has had the impact of removing the leaven of sin, to a certain extent, in the earth—there is no doubt that the earth would be a fermenting mass of iniquity today if it were not for the righteous influence of Christ through His church; and (7) Christ is coming as our heavenly Moses to remove His people from the evil bondage of the spirit of this present age.

The Lord Jesus Christ is the tabernacle of God, and God began His kingdom with Him. It is our understanding that included in this category should be the saints, the overcomers, who press on through to know the Lord, as mentioned by Christ in the second and third chapters of Revelation. The saints are part of the church, of course, but they press on through to Christ when so many are dawdling about in the rudiments of salvation. There is a reward for seeking Christ with the whole heart! And it is to whomsoever will.

The second stage in the setting up of the kingdom of God is that of Pentecost—of the church, in other words. The church of Christ is part of the kingdom of God, but is a firstfruits of the kingdom and holds the keys to the kingdom. The laws of God, which laws in fact constitute the nature of His kingdom, are kept first by Christ, then by the overcomers, then by the entire church, and finally by the whole earth. That is the order in which the kingdom is being established. God is creating the church first; and then through the church will extend the kingdom of God until every soul on earth has been brought under the rule of God through Christ.

The third stage in the setting up of the kingdom of God is portrayed in the first major convocation, that of Unleavened Bread. When God is finished, all leaven will have been removed from the peoples of the earth. Not a trace will be found. Sin will no longer be a factor in the earth. So total will be the destruction of sin that there will be no more need of redemption. Silver typifies redemption in Bible symbolism. You will look in vain for a mention of silver in the new heaven and earth reign of Christ, as it is described in Revelation 21 and 22. The reason for the absence of silver is that no redemption occurs at that time. No redemption occurs during the new heaven and earth reign of Christ because sin (leaven) has ceased to be a factor. Hallelujah!

These three stages in the setting up of the kingdom of God in the earth may be found in I Corinthians 15:23-25:

"Christ the firstfruits; afterward they that are Christ's at his coming. Then cometh the end, when he shall have delivered up the kingdom to God, even the Father; when he shall have put down all rule, and all authority and power. For he must reign, till he hath put all enemies under his feet."

We have seen, then, that the three major convocations, looked at in reverse order reveal the general pattern of the setting up of the kingdom of God in the earth. However, as we look at the great kingdom-wide acts of God we will look at them in the usual order, for we can understand them best that way from our standpoint as human beings approaching the living God through Christ.

PASSOVER

The cross of Jesus Christ is the kingdom-wide fulfillment of the convocation of Passover. Passover marks the beginning of the work of redemption for all peoples, and also the end of the first creation. The protection offered through the blood of God's Lamb is for everyone. Whosoever will accept the blood of Christ for a "token upon his house" will be saved from the wrath of God when He "passes over" to destroy the gods of this age.

"Believe on the Lord Jesus Christ, and thou shalt be saved, and thy house" (Acts 16:31). The blood shield comes over us when we call upon the name of the Lord Jesus. It is God's will that no person be destroyed but that all come to repentance and accept the protection of the blood of the cross. Jesus Christ was offered once upon the cross for all peoples, and all the work of redemption in the kingdom of God refers back to the Lamb of God who was slain for us.

The four horns upon the fours corners of the great bronze altar of burnt offering speak of the spreading of redemption and of the kingdom of God to the four corners of the earth. Truly, if Christ be lifted up He will draw all men unto Himself. God meets mankind at the cross and only at the cross.

The entire kingdom of God (past, present, and future) is founded upon the cross of Christ—upon the fact of the transfer of all power and authority to Him through means of His payment of the price of redemption with His blood. Here is the legal basis for the setting up of the kingdom, and for the exercise of the power of God in the setting free of people from the bondage of sin and death.

The convocation of Passover will have its most complete kingdom-wide fulfillment during the new heaven and earth reign of Jesus Christ. Every person on earth at that time will be a saved person, having received the benefits of the blood of the cross. Please notice that we are not saying that everyone eventually will be saved, for that is not true. What we are saying is that everyone who is left upon the earth to enjoy the goodness of God during the new heaven and earth reign of Christ will be a saved person. It would be wonderful if everyone would accept Christ and be saved, and that certainly would please God. Unfortunately, some will not accept the Lord Jesus, and because they will not accept Christ they seal their eternal doom.

UNLEAVENED BREAD

The descent into death of Jesus Christ is the beginning of the kingdom-wide fulfillment of the feast of Unleavened Bread. Unleavened Bread reminds us that the leaven of the first creation was abolished in Jesus Christ. All of the rebellion and pride which originated in heaven and then came into the earth was removed through Christ, as to its authority over people, when He said, "It is finished!" The "it" refers to the leaven of the old creation. There is no place in the kingdom of God for the old leaven of rebellion, malice, and wickedness.

The physical body of Christ lay in the tomb of Joseph of Arimathea during the convocation of Unleavened Bread. Jesus Himself, in spirit, had carried away the leaven of this age into the heart of the earth. The crucifixion of Christ signifies the end of the first creation of God. The whole world died in Christ, not just the Christians. Everything is over—finished! God is going to start all over again, and Christ is the first of the new creation.

When the believer in Christ enters into the water of baptism he is entering by faith into the death of Christ. When he comes up out of the water of baptism he is dramatizing that as far as he is concerned the first life is over; the leaven has been left on the cross. When Christ came out of the tomb of Joseph of Arimathea, the leaven of the old creation had been left in the heart of the earth, in the realms of darkness and eternal death.

When any man, woman, boy, or girl is baptized into Jesus Christ, it is the same as the Israelite crossing through the Red Sea. The power and authority of Satan cannot follow him or her through the water of baptism any more than Pharaoh was able to follow his former slaves through the Red Sea.

"Who hath delivered us from the power of darkness, and hath translated us into the kingdom of his dear Son: in whom we have redemption through his blood, even the forgiveness of sins" (Col. 1:13,14).

The convocation of Unleavened Bread will have its most complete kingdom-wide fulfillment during the new heaven and earth reign of Jesus Christ. There will be no leaven of sin anywhere in the earth. Sin will have been completely destroyed by the Lord Jesus Christ working in, through, and with His saints.

FIRSTFRUITS

The resurrection of Jesus Christ is the kingdom-wide fulfillment of the feast of Firstfruits. In the death of Christ, God the Father brought to an end His whole creation. When Jesus Christ rose from the dead on the very day of the observance of Firstfruits, He was the first—the beginning—of the new creation of God. The crucifixion and entombment of Christ was the crucifixion and entombment of the entire creation. The resurrection of Jesus Christ was the birth of a new universe in which every creature and created thing finds its place in Christ.

Every person who rejects Christ succeeds only in rejecting himself from the kingdom of God. The kingdom of God, which will last for ever, was born when Jesus Christ rose from the dead. Jesus Christ Himself is the first of the firstfruits. Then come the saints of Christ who also are a firstfruits (Rev. 14:1-5). Next, the whole church itself is a firstfruits of the earth (Jas. 1:18). Finally, the whole world will be harvested (John 17:21).

The convocation of Firstfruits will have its most complete kingdom-wide fulfillment during the new heaven and earth reign of Jesus Christ. There the wife of the Lamb, who is the firstfruits unto God of the peoples of the earth, will stand perfect and complete in all the will of God, having been made so through the ministrations of the Holy Spirit of God. She will have been created upon the body and blood of Christ just as Eve was created upon the rib of Adam.

PENTECOST

The kingdom-wide fulfillment of Pentecost commenced when the Holy Spirit came, as recorded in Acts 2:1-4. Since that time the Holy Spirit has been active in the world, ready to work with every person who will accept redemption through Jesus Christ.

Pentecost represents a turning point in the workings of God. Prior to Pentecost, the grace of God has had to do mainly with the salvation of individuals, saving them from the destruction of the wrath of God poured out upon the gods of this age. But after Pentecost the believer moves toward the rule of the kingdom of God, the keeping of the laws of God, and the serving of God's purposes. Before Pentecost we are saved people. After Pentecost we begin to become the servants of the Lord.

We understand from the Scripture that the ministry of the Holy Spirit is going to increase as we draw toward the coming of the Lord Jesus Christ. It appears that the testimony of the two witnesses in Revelation 11 portrays the double portion of the anointing which will come upon the Christian church just prior to the return of the Lord Jesus. The testimony of God will be empowered by the Holy Spirit, we believe, until every man, woman, boy, and girl upon the earth has seen and heard the gospel of the kingdom of God, and the power of that kingdom.

By speaking of *seeing* the gospel of the kingdom of God we mean that signs and mighty wonders will follow the testimony of the good news of the kingdom, as it was in the first century, except in greatly increased power and glory. The good news is that the kingdom of Christ is about to be set up upon the earth, and that whosoever will believe on the Lord Jesus Christ and be baptized will be saved from the wrath of God which now is close at hand.

Although the testimony of the church will be overcome in order to make way for the culmination of evil in the earth (II Thess. 2:7; Rev. 11:7; 13:7), at the return of Jesus Christ to the earth the Holy Spirit will be poured through the saints in such a fullness of divine glory that eternal resurrection life will be as a deep and wide river which will flow out to the ends of the earth (Ezek. 47:1-12).

We have noticed, from comparing the Old Testament types, that the millennium is the great fulfillment of the year of jubilee (Lev. 25). The year of jubilee was instituted during the Day of Atonement, every fiftieth year. The word *Pentecost* means *fifty*. We know therefore that during the millennium, which is the kingdom-wide fulfillment of the Day of Atonement, the Holy Spirit is going to be poured out upon the earth to an extent which we cannot conceive at this time. During the millennium, which will be a jubilee of redemption for the peoples of the earth, particularly for the church but also for others, the Holy Spirit will be as a river, an ocean, a flooding of the earth with the glory and presence of the Spirit of God. As God spoke in the Old Testament, the earth will be filled with the glory of the Lord as the waters cover the sea.

One of the results of this unprecedented downpour of the Holy Spirit will be the conversion of the peoples of the entire earth. The river of life will flow out from the saints, and the "fish" will be many. The tree of life (the body and blood of Christ) will be growing along the banks of the river of life, a symbolic portrayal of the Spirit of God coming out of the members of the body of Christ, and the substance of

Christ in those same members being food and drink for the spiritually dead of the earth. Also the leaves of the tree, which represent the Spirit of power and revelation in the church, will be for the healing of the nations.

The convocation of Pentecost will have its most complete kingdom-wide fulfillment during the new heaven and earth reign of Jesus Christ. The Holy Spirit will be a "pure river of water of life, clear as crystal, proceeding out of the throne of God and of the Lamb" (Rev. 22:1). The Holy Spirit will not be given as is true today, where we have just a small amount—a sealing, and then a measure of the Spirit for our ministry. Nor will it be as during the millennium, where the outpouring of the Holy Spirit is for the resurrection and release of the spiritually dead of the earth. Rather, during the new heaven and earth reign of Christ the Holy Spirit as the river of life will flow pure and clear throughout eternity, world without end. Every person who is permitted to enter into that city will be able to drink until he is satisfied and as often as he likes. The Holy Spirit will be present eternally to fill us with the life of God.

It will be remembered also that the Holy Spirit is our law, and the giving of the Law to Moses on Sinai is a type of the giving of the Holy Spirit to the church. The Holy Spirit is the law of the Spirit of life. The law of God finds its fullest expression in the holy city where the law has been resolved into its highest form, which is the beauty of holiness. The beauty of holiness is the law of God brought to perfection. The beauty of holiness reaches its peak expression in the new Jerusalem, which is the creation of the Holy Spirit.

The directions for the Tabernacle of the Congregation were given at the same time as the law of Moses, and therefore must also be considered as a type of the giving of the Holy Spirit to the church of Christ. In the new heaven and earth reign of Jesus Christ, the tabernacle of God is with men. The holy city itself is the tabernacle of God. Therefore the holy city is the most sublime expression of the Holy

Spirit, and the most complete fulfillment of the Levitical feast of Pentecost.

TRUMPETS

The kingdom-wide fulfillment of Trumpets will occur when the great trumpet of God sounds, heralding the return of the King, Jesus Christ. That trumpet will summon the saints to ascend in resurrection power; will announce the take-over of the kingdoms of this world by Christ; will signal to the wicked the coming of the wrath of God and the onslaught of the armies of the Lord against the evil forces in the earth; and, most joyously of all, as far as the peoples of the earth are concerned, will proclaim the advent of the millennial jubilee—the release of the creation into the glorious liberty of the children of God (Lev. 25; Rom. 8:21).

When the trumpet sounds, God's kingdom begins in the earth. Of course, when Jesus cast out devils along the shores of Galilee, the kingdom of God was among us. Today we have the power and authority of the kingdom of God reaching from the future back in time into the day in which we now live, performing works of kingdom power and glory, in the name of Jesus Christ.

But the full expression of the kingdom of God belongs to the age to come. The feast of Trumpets was New Year's Day, the beginning of the agricultural, or civil, year. It was the business year, whereas the year which began with Passover was the ecclesiastical, religious, liturgical, ceremonial year, as you will. Business in the kingdom of God commences with the feast of Trumpets. "When the trumpet of the Lord shall sound, and time shall be no more," the Lord Jesus is returning to the earth to set up and operate His millennial kingdom.

The convocation of Trumpets will have its most complete kingdom-wide fulfillment during the new heaven and earth reign of Jesus Christ. The new heaven and earth reign of Christ is the time when Christ has put every enemy under His feet, and turns the kingdom back to the Father. The kingdom of God, then, will rule unto the ages of ages. The feast of Trumpets in its grandest expression represents the time when God rules in the earth and in the heavens without one dissenting spirit in the entire universe. All creatures will love God and will be at rest and in total joy, peace, and thankfulness in the will of God.

DAY OF ATONEMENT

The kingdom-wide fulfillment of the Day of Atonement is the day of redemption, which is the hope of the church, and also the hope of the remainder of the peoples of the earth. The day of redemption will bring release to the entire created universe. You may recall that there were two goats used during the observance of the Day of Atonement (Lev. 16). One goat was offered for a sin offering. Its blood was sprinkled upon the mercy seat and before the mercy seat, to make an atonement for the children of Israel.

The slain goat portrays the Lord Jesus Christ who, through His own precious blood, made an atonement for all the peoples of the earth. The price has been paid for every man, woman, boy, and girl. It remains for the individual person to accept the blood by faith as the redemption payment for his or her sins. Through the blood of Christ the whole creation was redeemed—bought back from the ownership of sin. The blood of Christ is the legal basis upon which Christ is going to release the world from the bondage of sin and death.

But there is more to the Day of Atonement than just the change of title. There must be a real deliverance, not just a removal of guilt. This is where the living goat comes in (Lev. 16:21). The sins of the children of Israel were laid upon the head of the living goat, and it was sent away and let loose in the wilderness.

We can see in the ceremony of the leading away of the living goat that our Lord Jesus Christ not only forgave our sins, but also removed the sins from our presence. Our iniquities were placed upon Him, and He carried them away out of the camp. God is showing us by this that He not only forgives us our sins but also removes our sins, and the results of those sins from us.

What is true now for the church will be true throughout the whole earth during the millennial jubilee which is just over the horizon. When Jesus comes He has the power and authority not only to forgive sins but also to remove sin itself from the whole earth. Those who resist and reject Christ will be destroyed at His coming. Christ will appear as "the Lord strong and mighty in battle." Then the whole earth will be glad and break forth into singing, because the kingdoms of this world will become the kingdoms of our God and of His Christ; and He shall reign forever and ever.

During the millennial age which is to come, both aspects of the Day of Atonement will be in operation throughout all the earth. The guilt of sin will be forgiven, and the power and curse of sin will be removed from the earth. This is what Jesus meant when He said, "Your redemption draws near." The Redeemer is coming to destroy the works of the devil out of the earth, and to bring the whole world into the glorious liberty of the children of God. There will be a thousand years of obedience to the laws of the kingdom of God upon this earth, as Jesus Christ rules with His saints.

"The wolf also shall dwell with the lamb, and the leopard shall lie down with the kid, and the calf and the young lion and the fatling together; and a little child shall lead them. And the cow and the bear shall feed; their young shall lie down together; and the lion shall eat straw like the ox. And the sucking child shall play over the hole of the asp, and the weaned child shall put his hand on the adder's den. They shall not hurt or destroy in all my holy mountain; for the earth shall be full of the knowledge of the Lord as the waters cover the sea" (see Isa. 11:6-9).

Isaiah tells us, "He shall see of the travail of his soul, and shall be satisfied" (Isa. 53:11). Right now, Jesus Christ is waiting patiently for His Father to make His enemies His footstool. But in the days to come, the kingdom-wide fulfillment of the Day of Atonement will bring righteousness, peace, and joy to the whole earth and to all the peoples thereof. The saints of God will be glorious in holiness, and the nations of the earth will be learning righteousness from the church. Our great Redeemer at the cross destroyed every last trace of the authority of sin over us. In the future He is going to destroy every last trace of the power of sin in the earth. The last enemy that shall be destroyed is death.

During the millennium, which is at hand, the members of the body of Christ will cross over Jordan, so to speak, and will conquer the land of promise. This time Israel will make a full end of the enemies in the land. The Christian church will enter into the rest of God through means of the conquest of the earth. Christ will change from His Moses ministry into His Joshua ministry. He will become the Lord, strong and mighty in battle. At this time the "manna" will cease and the members of the body of Christ will eat the food grown in the land of promise. This means that the gifts and ministries, the "seeing through a glass darkly," will not be needed by the church. Rather, the church will know the Lord, from the least member to the greatest. We will not need gifts and ministries because we will be able to talk to Him face to face. We will minister to the peoples of the earth as did Jesus; not in prophecy, tongues, or the gifts of healing, but in the fullness of the Spirit of wisdom and understanding, of counsel and might, of knowledge and the fear of the Lord, and of judgment and dominion.

The convocation of the Day of Atonement will have its

most complete kingdom-wide fulfillment during the new heaven and earth reign of Jesus Christ. The Day of Atonement, being the sixth of the convocations, signifies the "day" when the Lord God makes man in His own image. During the new heaven and earth reign of Jesus Christ, we see the image of God in Christ and in the wife of the Lamb. It is written, "In the image of God made He him, male and female made He them." In other words, the total image of God requires both male and female. So it is that the Lamb of God and the wife of the Lamb, taken together, are the fullest expression of the image of God. The work of God will have been completed, having found its most exalted expression when the Lamb and His wife are together as the holy city, the new Jerusalem.

TABERNACLES

The kingdom-wide fulfillment of the convocation of Tabernacles is so glorious that our hearts and minds cannot grasp the fullness of that which is coming to the earth. For the fulfillment of the feast of Tabernacles is the new heaven and earth reign of Christ, as described in the twenty-first and twenty-second chapters of Revelation. We have seen that each of the other six convocations found their highest expression in the new heaven and reign of Christ. But the feast of Tabernacles is the summation of all of the feasts, because it speaks of the indwelling of the living God through Christ. There is no higher experience.

Just as the kingdom-wide fulfillment of the Day of Atonement is the establishing of the kingdom of God throughout the earth (as symbolized by the rule of King David over Israel), so the kingdom-wide fulfillment of the feast of Tabernacles is the eternal reign of God in Christ, in the bride, over the nations of the earth for eternity, as typified by the rule of King Solomon over Israel. Christ is the fulfillment of both David and Solomon.

The glory of God in Christ, through the church, will be so great that there will be no more need of the sun or moon to give light to the new Jerusalem. The dwelling place of God will be forever with people, and He will be their God and will wipe away all their tears. The throne of God and of the Lamb will be upon the new earth.

The city of God, the new Jerusalem, will be the perfection of the beauty of holiness, which is the law of God brought to consummation. It is the end of the harvest season, when all of Christ that has been sown in the earth has been brought forth and harvested. God has found His perfect rest in the body of Christ.

The Holy Spirit is present as the river of life, and all who are in the city can drink of the Holy Spirit as often as they desire. The tree of life, which is Christ, grows along the banks of the river of life. The fruit of the tree is for food, and the leaves for the healing of the nations.

The best part of all is that His servants shall serve Him, and we shall see His face and minister before Him for ever. Can you imagine what it will be like to stand in the very presence of God throughout eternity?

There is no silver in the holy city, because the work of redemption, as symbolized by silver, is now a thing of the past. The eighth day of the feast of Tabernacles (Lev. 23:36) symbolizes eternity, the beginning of the week which will never have an end. Everything has been finished. The rebellion in heaven, which was brought down to earth and spread among mankind, has now been judged and its consequences destroyed. God is now ready to settle down and enjoy His handiwork. All enemies have been brought under the feet of Jesus Christ, and He now turns back the kingdom of God to the Father.

The walls of the city are set with multiplicity of precious stones, and the glory of God coming from within the city shines through these stones filling the whole new earth with a beautiful rainbow of color. The precious stones speak of the various graces and virtues which have been wrought in the saints as they have been recreated into the image of Christ, through the ministrations of the Holy Spirit.

Every person who is written in the Lamb's Book of Life will live in the new earth. Everyone left upon the earth will be saved, and will have a portion of Christ within Him and the blessing of God upon his life. Praise the Lord! This is the kingdom-wide fulfillment of the Levitical convocation of Tabernacles.

The convocation of Tabernacles is the possession of the land of promise—rest, peace, joy, abundance in that land of milk and honey. Everything sown by God in the earth has now been harvested and processed. It is a time of joy, of thanksgiving, of dwelling in the "booth" of the Lord throughout eternity, to contemplate His beauty and to abide in His temple.

The best part of all is the eternal presence of Him who dwells between the Cherubim of glory. All of the Person and being of the Almighty God is present in the holy city for His servants to behold and to love forever. Because of the triumph of Christ in our life, nothing ever again will stand between us and the Father, to cause His face to grow dim. Rather, we shall see Him as He is to our hearts delight and content.

It is finished. Christ is the *Alpha* and the *Omega*, the beginning and the ending. He who overcomes shall inherit all things. God in Christ is at rest, and we are at rest in Him forever and ever, world without end.

"Thus the heavens and the earth were finished, and all the host of them. And on the seventh day God ended his work which he had made; and he rested on the seventh day from all his work which he had made. And God blessed the seventh day, and sanctified it: because that in it he had rested from all his work which God created and made" (Gen. 2:1-3).

"And the Spirit and the bride say, Come. And let him that heareth say, Come. And let him who is athirst come. And whosoever will, let him take the water of life freely" (Rev. 22:17).

"He which testifieth these things saith, Surely I come quickly: Amen. Even so, come, Lord Jesus" (Rev. 22:20).

REVIEW

We began our study of the Levitical convocations by observing how they were celebrated literally. Then we discussed their portrayal of the Person and work of the Lord Jesus Christ. Next, the seven feasts were seen as types of the plan of redemption in the life of the believer. After that, the perfecting of the Christian church was studied. Finally, we have seen that the setting up of the kingdom of God is symbolized by the feasts of the Lord.

In our book we may have emphasized the personal interpretation of the convocations, that is, their portrayal of the process of the plan of redemption of the believer. The reason for the stress upon the salvation of the individual is that we are going through these things now. And if we do not go through with God, then, as far as we personally are concerned, the work of Christ is limited or in vain; the church suffers imperfection; and the kingdom of God is not established. Each Christian believer is of priceless value to God, and He has gone to great pains in His love to provide for our total and complete redemption. We ought to grasp this love and respond by giving our best to Christ in order that He may finish His work in us. Don't you agree?

It was pointed out that the pattern of the feasts suggests that salvation, or redemption, is not a once-for-all happening but rather is a growth to maturity. The somewhat revolutionary idea was introduced that the plan of redemption has not only a definite beginning but a definite ending as well.

The main thrust of Passover was expressed as the application by faith of the blood of the righteous Jesus to ourself and our household as the means of protection from God's executioner who carries out the judgment of God upon the gods of this present age. The Passover experience marks a "beginning of months" to the Christian, being the first step of the Christian life. The sacrament of communion is parallel, in the new covenant, to the eating of the Passover Lamb.

Unleavened Bread was presented as typifying the putting away of every sin, the sincere repentance which must characterize the person who comes to the Lord Jesus Christ for salvation. The act of being baptized in water dramatizes the fact that the believer has died to the world and the lusts thereof. The convert by faith assigns his old nature to the cross with Christ, and his new nature to the throne of God with Christ.

It was mentioned that the concept of a *firstfruits* is commonly found within God's manner of working. Christ is a firstfruits of those who sleep. The Christians are the firstfruits of the harvesting of the earth. In Romans 8:23 it is said that we Christians have the "firstfruits of the Spirit." The amount of the Holy Spirit that we possess at present is but a first installment upon the fullness of the Holy Spirit who one day will flood our whole being, body included. We will live eternally in the fullness of resurrection life, a state which we should be anticipating with great joy.

Pentecost is the Hebrew convocation which has lent its name to a large contemporary branch of the Christian believers. The Hebrews associate the feast of Pentecost with the giving of the Law on Mount Sinai. We may tend to think of Pentecost in connection with power for ministry, and in terms of speaking in tongues.

If we combine the Jewish concept of divine law with the

Christian concept of witnessing of Christ's death and resurrection with divine enablements of power and revelation, we find that the outpouring of the Holy Spirit was and continues to be the bringing of the law of the Spirit of life to the earth, just as Sinai was the bringing of the moral law, the Ten Commandments, to the earth. The Holy Spirit in Christians brings them and their surroundings under the discipline of Christ. Speaking in tongues is an entrance for us into a life which is governed by the Holy Spirit. Christians are ruled by the law of the Spirit of life rather than by the law of Moses.

We stated our belief that the entire Christian era is the time of the "latter rain," mentioned by Joel. It follows therefore that the latter rain (Holy Spirit outpouring) always is available to us and that we do not have more of the Holy Spirit than we do, in many instances, because we prefer our way of doing things to the Holy Spirit's way of doing things.

We Christians, to a great extent, are not willing to live individually or corporately in direct obedience to the Spirit of God. Disobedience and unbelief often has characterized the Israel of God.

The Pentecostal experience is a kind of turning point in the redemption which God has provided. If we have gotten this far we must not look back toward Egypt (life under the control of the spirit of this age and our fleshly desires). Rather, we must press on toward the fullness of resurrection life in the Spirit of God. The Holy Spirit is saying to the body of Christ: "There remains much land to be possessed. You have gone around this mountain long enough: turn you northward."

New adventures in Christ are before us. Let us arm ourselves in the Spirit and invade the land of promise.

The various uses of the trumpet were mentioned. The use of the trumpet as an alarm for war was stressed. The name of God as Lord of hosts (armies) was pointed out. The concept of God being a commander of battle may not be the most delightful idea in the world, since people today are worried about the continual riotings, wars, and rumors of wars. Many groups are seeking to end war. But the Christians stand on the brink of an awful conflict in the realm of spirits. The great war of God is just getting under way.

Each Christian must gird up his mind to the fact of spiritual warfare. The enemies of God—spirits of rebellion, perversity, and uncleanness—are the ones who are producing the spirit of the age in which we are now living. It is not a pleasing state of affairs from God's point of view that the earth is becoming a nauseating cesspool, a viper's pit of lust, idolatry, and murder. God's unspeakably terrible wrath is as a furnace which has been heated to a frightful degree. His fierce anger is ready to be poured out upon the world; and woe! woe! woe! to those who are rejecting and resisting Christ when the wrath of God is poured out upon this earth.

Every Christian by the nature of his being and calling is deeply involved in God's war against evil spirits. The Holy Spirit of the God of armies is sounding the trumpet blast loudly and clearly in our time: "Get ready for the day of the Lord! Let every Christian put on the gospel armor and prepare to cast out devils, heal the sick, raise the dead. I give you authority and power over all the authority and power of Satan. Nothing shall by any means hurt you. Listen to the voice of the Spirit as He points out the sin in your own heart. You cannot fight the battles of the Lord when there is an Achan's wedge of gold hidden in your tent."

It was stated that Trumpets and the Day of Atonement are known to devout Hebrews as the "Days of Awe" because of the solemnity of their import. The seventh month, which contains Trumpets, the Day of Atonement, and Tabernacles, is the conclusion of the old agricultural year and the beginning of the new.

Thus the seventh month speaks to us of the beginning of actual divine conquest and working out of God's judgment in our own life, and the beginning of our reign with Christ over the earth. Passover, on the other hand, being the beginning of the ecclesiastical year, can be thought of in terms of the beginning of our religious life of faith and doctrines. Passover is associated with coming out of Egypt; Tabernacles is associated with entering into the land of promise. Passover is the beginning of redemption; Tabernacles is the maturing of redemption *and* the commencing of eternal, glorious rulership in, through, and with Christ.

The Day of Atonement represents the purging of sin out of the Christian life, and ultimately out of the entire creation of God. Specific confession and the blood of Jesus Christ are involved. Included in the concept of the atonement is the judgment of God against wicked spirits, against the lords of the darkness of this present evil age.

It was suggested that this dimension of the atonement, the cleansing of sin from our personality, is experienced after the Christian life gets under way rather than at the very beginning. The somewhat arresting idea was presented that God has not chosen us because we are holier than other people, but because of His own plans and purposes in Christ Jesus. However, God has every intention of working with us until we do become holy! Of note among the sins of Christians are all forms of murder, lust, and idolatry. Sectarianism and the party spirit is especially weakening to the body of Christ.

The Day of Atonement is a time of very serious heart searching among the Jews *(Yom Kippur)*. However, *Yom Kippur* does have one joyful feature. For the year of jubilee, which typifies the great day of deliverance for the earth at the appearing of Jesus and the sons of God, was announced every fiftieth year on the Day of Atonement. The fact that the year of jubilee occurred on the Day of Atonement appears to signify that the fullness of the blessing and application of the atoning blood of Jesus will not be realized until the manifestation of the sons of God. The manifestation of the sons of God is associated with the redemption of the earth (Rom. 8:21).

Please note that we are not suggesting that the blood of Christ does not completely avail for our needs now, for it most certainly does. Also, today is the day of salvation, and we must do all in our power in our own day to persuade men so. What we are saying, however, is that we are in the time of the birth pangs of the earth. In the days ahead of us we will not be seeing less of the power of God working through the blood of the righteous Jesus, but, in fact, a great deal more! The best is yet ahead! He has kept the good wine until now!

Remember the words of the prophet Isaiah?

"Arise, shine; for thy light is come, and the glory of the Lord is risen upon you. For, behold, the darkness shall cover the earth, and gross darkness the people: but the Lord shall arise upon thee, and his glory shall be seen upon thee" (Isa. 60:1,2).

"Then thou shalt see, and flow together, and thine heart shall fear, and be enlarged; because the abundance of the sea shall be converted unto thee, the forces of the Gentiles shall come unto you" (Isa. 60:5).

The greatest days of redemption and conversion are yet ahead of us, and all that Jesus prayed in John 17 will be fulfilled abundantly. The world will yet come to know beyond the shadow of a doubt that Jesus Christ is God's beloved Son.

The Day of Atonement comes as a "new year" to us Christians because its Christian counterpart, the confessing of our sins, gives us a workable method for dealing with the sins which we commit as Christians. We who have received Christ do not have to fear the judgments of God upon our life. The judgments of God are directed primarily against unclean spirits. If we cooperate with the Holy Spirit by confessing and renouncing the actions, words, and motives which He points out as being unclean, the fire of God's judgment will no more harm us personally than the furnace of Nebuchadnezzar harmed Shadrach, Meshach, and Abednego.

The convocation of Tabernacles portrays perfection—the consummation of the plan of salvation. The Scripture indicates that God is moving the members of the body of Christ toward a specific mark. It was pointed out that it is very difficult for someone to work hard at overcoming obstacles when there is no definite goal in mind.

Perhaps one of the main reasons why church people do not become more excited about the outworking of redemption in their life, the process of spiritual development toward perfection of union with Christ, is that they do not really believe that there is any target at which to shoot. Since the goal of the overcoming Christian life is extremely vague, perhaps nonexistent, why exert effort in this direction!

Two cautions were set forth concerning the doctrine of the rapture, as it is commonly taught: First, does the teaching of the rapture have the desired scriptural effect upon the spiritual development of the Christians? Or does the manner in which we teach the rapture turn the attention of the believers away from the necessary concentration upon learning to walk and fight in the Spirit, and toward external events over which Christians have no control and which do not lift us up toward a fuller knowledge of Christ?

Second, does the way in which we teach the rapture follow the main current of burden and logic of the writings of the Hebrew prophets and Christian apostles, or is it a "private interpretation"?

From our own point of view, it is difficult to harmonize some of the aspects of the rapture as it is sometimes presented, with the burden of the letters of Paul concerning the nature of the day of the Lord. Philippians 3, for examples, seems to us to imply that the "prize of the high calling of God in Christ Jesus" has more to do with the perfecting of our walk in the Spirit than it does with external events.

Please note that in raising the question of the attitude of the churches toward the rapture we are in no manner attempting to detract from the literal interpretation of I Thessalonians 4:13-18, a passage which many Christians associate with the rapture. Rather, we are calling the attention of believers to the fact that we must get ourselves ready for the resurrection from the dead, instead of remaining spiritually indifferent and lethargic in the hope that we are going to be transformed magically into spiritual giants at the coming of Christ.

Whatever God has ordained will certainly come to pass, and it behooves us to live in total readiness. Then we will be prepared for the future. The most important preparation that we can make is to work each day at our union with God through Christ, remaining sensitive and responsive to the guiding of the Holy Spirit.

The possession of God Himself, rather than things, experiences, secrets of spiritual power, is the fulfillment of the feast of Tabernacles. Any goal that we have, other than that of God Himself, is shortsighted, and eventually will prove to be another means toward the great end.

The end of the matter is the "rest of God." God rests in us and we rest in God. God enjoys our presence forever and ever and we enjoy God's presence forever and ever. The Christian experience is an affair of the heart between God and the believer. It is the love song of Christ and His bride.

God is jealous of idols that claim our attention, and He desires to be in all our thoughts. Once God has set His great heart upon us He will act to remove any thing or person or experience which threatens to divert our attention and love away from Himself. God wants to liberate us from our idolatrous bondages. We are foolish children indeed if we turn away from such great love and choose instead to lust after the "weak and beggarly elements" of this evil age in which we are now living. But the Lord knows those whom He has called, and all matters will be proved out in due time.

Firstfruits and Pentecost marked certain points in the grain harvest. But the convocation of Tabernacles was in celebration of the completion of the harvest season. All that the Israelites had worked—barley, wheat, grapes, olives, nuts, vegetables, figs, citrus, etc.—had been gathered and processed by the time of tabernacles.

As far as we Christians are concerned right now, our lives have been partially harvested in Christ. The harvesting (gathering, winnowing, crushing) is still going on. The redemption of our human body is the completion of the harvesting of our life—the culmination of the plan of redemption. Included in the plan for the redemption of our mortal body is the preparation of our spirit and soul for such a fullness of divine revelation and power, and a clothing over with a transcendent body fashioned from resurrection life. Our gathering together with Christ will occur with the resurrection of the body, but is not of the essential nature of the resurrection.

The essential nature of resurrection, whether it be of the spirit, of the soul or of the body, has to do with the restoring to life of that which was dead. All that we are and possess must be brought to the death of the cross. Whatever part of what we are and possess that God chooses to bring back to life, after it has suffered the death of the cross of Christ, is of the resurrection. Ascending to meet the Lord in the air is not of the essential nature of the resurrection, but is rather an act of kingdom power—the power of the righteous age to come. It is important to Christians that they understand clearly the difference between resurrection and ascension, because the foundation for bodily resurrection is being established right now as the Holy Spirit brings us down to the death of the cross; whereas ascension is an act of kingdom power which will occur at the coming of our Lord Jesus Christ with the holy angels.

We shall rise to meet the Lord in the air, and will be gathered together to be with Him forevermore, at the time of the first resurrection. There is a "resurrection of damnation" (John 5:29), an awakening to "shame and everlasting contempt" (Dan. 12:2). It is certain that we will reap what we have sown.

The redemption of the human body is an attainment in Christ to which we Christians should be giving some attention, and the thought of which should be filling us with pure delight and enabling us to stand firm in all our testings. The redemption of our mortal body is the fulfillment of the promise of Christ concerning eternal life. It is the salvation ready to be revealed in the last time (I Pet. 1:5).

Paul wrote, "We groan . . . within ourselves, waiting for the adoption, to wit, the redemption of our body" (Rom. 8:23). Why don't we ourselves feel more of this burden? Perhaps we do not press toward the redemption of our mortal body simply because our mortal body in its present condition is adequate to support the fleshly life which we are living at this time! We Christians may be living primarily "in the flesh." But Paul died daily to the desires of the flesh and the mind, and was revived daily by the resurrection power of Christ. His inner life had been transformed from beholding the glory of the Lord just as Moses' face had been transformed from continually beholding the glory of the Lord.

Paul's mortal body no longer was adequate to support the glorious resurrection life which was flowing in the compassions and purposes of God toward those whom Christ was saving. The stress was increasing daily. The new wine in Paul was in an "old bottle," and the old bottle was cracking.

And so Paul groaned! When a Christian gets into and remains in the center of God's will for his life, and his spiritual personality begins to develop, he will find himself pressing toward Paul's "mark." Paul's mark is the "prize of the high calling of God in Christ Jesus." The prize includes

(1) recreation of the Christian into the express image of Christ in spirit, soul, and body; (2) the indwelling eternally of the fullness of the Father and the Son through the Holy Spirit; (3) power and authority over the domain assigned to the individual Christian; (4) and life without end lived in the fullness of the anointing of the Holy Spirit.

It is our hope and prayer that each person who reads this study of the seven Levitical convocations has received from it a portion of the broken body and shed blood of our Lord Jesus Christ in his soul, and some understanding in his mind. Our desire is that you will be inspired to seek Christ with your whole heart. The rewards of serving Christ are so unimaginably great that you should at once take up your cross and follow on to know the Lord, doing so with exceeding great joy and gladness. Will you do that?

"He that overcometh shall inherit all things; and I will be his God, and he shall be my son" (Rev. 21:6,7).

"O God, hear our prayer as we stand in Christ Jesus before Your great throne. Grant unto us, as dear children, that we may be accepted in Your sight. Help us to lay aside every weight, every sin, and to press on the upward way toward the fullness of Your beloved Son. We thank You for receiving us graciously, and for forgiving us our sins as each one of us, from the heart, freely forgives every person who has sinned against him. Bless this study to the reader, and work Your perfect will in him. In Jesus' name we pray. Amen."

APPENDIX

QUESTIONS WHICH CAN BE USED FOR STUDY

GENERAL

1. Explain two guidelines for interpreting Bible types.
2. Name the seven Levitical convocations, and give one Scripture reference for each of the seven.
3. Name four areas of application of the Levitical convocations.
4. Into what three groups were the seven convocations arranged?
5. Define the term *Levitical convocation*.
6. Briefly describe some of the similarities which can be found when we compare the four major types of redemption.
7. State the approximate months of our calendar during which the convocations were celebrated.
8. Describe briefly some of the new covenant counterparts of the seven convocations, listing references from the New Testament in order to show that your application of the type is taught directly in the New Testament.
9. Give the approximate historical date of the inception of the convocations, and the geographical location where they were first set forth by the Lord.

10. Explain why the seven convocations must be considered as being seven dimensions of the one redemption rather than seven rungs on a ladder.
11. What was unusual about the fact that the Lord enjoined the feasts upon the Israelites while they were in the wilderness? How does this unusual factor apply to us today?
12. Briefly describe the agricultural year of Canaan, and the rain cycle of that area.
13. What is spiritually significant about the fact that the feasts were proclaimed "in their seasons"?

PASSOVER

1. On what date of the Hebrew calendar did God execute judgment upon the firstborn of Egypt?
2. What is the spiritual significance of, "Your lamb shall be without blemish" (Exod. 12:5)?
3. What are some of the similarities and differences between the Hebrew Passover and the Christian communion service?
4. Why do we eat the flesh of Christ and drink His blood?
5. What is the spiritual significance of "roast with fire" (Exod. 12:8)?
6. What is the spiritual significance of "unleavened bread" (Exod. 12:8)?
7. What is the spiritual significance of "bitter herbs" (Exod. 12:8)?
8. Exactly who was it that passed through Egypt to smite the firstborn of humans and animals? Give three Scripture references.
9. Why were the *firstborn* executed?
10. Against whom was the Lord executing judgment?
11. Against whom does the Lord execute judgment today? Give Scripture reference.
12. What did the Passover blood actually accomplish?

13. How does the "Passover blood" work in our lives today? Give New Testament references.

14. Explain the expression, "a lamb for a house," in terms of the new covenant.

15. Explain the new covenant application of "no uncircumcised person shall eat thereof."

16. Briefly describe the manner in which the feast of Passover portrays the Person and work of the Lord Jesus Christ.

17. Briefly describe the manner in which the feast of Passover portrays the redemption of the believer.

18. Briefly describe the manner in which the feast of Passover portrays the growth to maturity of the Christian church.

19. Briefly describe the manner in which the feast of Passover portrays the setting up of the kingdom of God upon the earth.

UNLEAVENED BREAD

1. Describe the Hebrew convocation of Unleavened Bread, with main Scripture references.

2. From the sixth chapter of Romans, explain what water baptism portrays concerning our "old man."

3. Explain what water baptism portrays concerning our new relationship to the resurrected Lord Jesus Christ.

4. If our dual position of death and resurrection life has been portrayed as accomplished in water baptism, in what manner and to what extent are these states of being actually true in our lives?

5. Into what two traps can a disciple fall, in terms of the two spiritual states of being which are portrayed in water baptism?

6. What role does faith play, with respect to the dual position dramatized in water baptism?

7. Briefly describe the manner in which the feast of

Unleavened Bread portrays the Person and work of the Lord Jesus Christ.

8. Briefly describe the manner in which the feast of Unleavened Bread portrays the redemption of the believer.
9. Briefly describe the manner in which the feast of Unleavened Bread portrays the growth to maturity of the Christian church.
10. Briefly describe the manner in which the feast of Unleavened Bread portrays the setting up of the kingdom of God upon the earth.

FIRSTFRUITS

1. Describe the Hebrew convocation of Firstfruits, with main Scripture references.
2. Explain the scriptural concept of a "firstfruits." Give at least three references from the New Testament.
3. How is Christ the "firstfruits" of the members of His body?
4. In what way do we have the "firstfruits of the Spirit"?
5. How should we respond when God "gives" us spiritual or material blessings which we, in actuality, do not have as yet?
6. What is the difference between scriptural faith and mental assent?
7. What is the difference between scriptural faith and presumption?
8. What is your understanding of James 1:18?
9. How is the born-again experience related to the concept of Firstfruits?
10. Sum up the manner in which the first three convocations portray the crucifixion, descent into the heart of the earth, and resurrection of Jesus Christ.
11. Sum up the manner in which the first three convocations apply to our personal experience of redemption.

12. Briefly describe the manner in which the convocation of Firstfruits portrays the Person and work of the Lord Jesus Christ.

13. Briefly describe the manner in which the convocation of Firstfruits portrays the redemption of the believer.

14. Briefly describe the manner in which the convocation of Firstfruits portrays the growth to maturity of the Christian church.

15. Briefly describe the manner in which the convocation of Firstfruits portrays the setting up of the kingdom of God upon the earth.

PENTECOST

1. Describe the Hebrew convocation of Pentecost, with main Scripture references.

2. How is the convocation of Pentecost related to the giving of the Law on Mount Sinai?

3. Which of the holy furnishings of the Tabernacle of the Congregation is equivalent to the feast of Pentecost.

4. What are the similarities and differences between the law of Moses and the law of the Spirit of life?

5. At what points in its development did/does the Christian church come under the different "rains" of the Holy Spirit?

6. Briefly, what is the message of the book of Joel?

7. List some Scripture references, Old and New Testaments, which indicate that the greatest outpouring of the Holy Spirit is yet ahead of us.

8. What are some things which we can do to insure that the Holy Spirit is present in our church activities? Give Scripture references.

9. What is the spiritual significance of speaking in tongues? Give references.

10. What is the end result of the "Pentecostal" experience?

11. How can you explain the fact that there was leaven in the wave loaves?

12. How do the gifts of the Spirit differ from the fruit of the Spirit?

13. Show how the raising of Lazarus is a type of the Pentecostal experience.

14. Explain the expression, "the oil upon the blood."

15. Explain why it can be said that the person who has received the baptism in the Holy Spirit has been "partially harvested."

16. What are some means which we can use to keep our body under subjection?

17. What is the significance of the "anointing oil" upon the body of Christ (Messiah)?

18. Exactly who are the seed of Abraham?

19. What are some things that the Holy Spirit accomplishes in the Christian disciple?

20. What is the meaning of the word *Pentecost?*

21. Why were there so many nations represented in Jerusalem at the time of the first Pentecostal outpouring?

22. Briefly describe the manner in which the convocation of Pentecost portrays the Person and work of the Lord Jesus Christ.

23. Briefly describe the manner in which the convocation of Pentecost portrays the redemption of the believer.

24. Briefly describe the manner in which the convocation of Pentecost portrays the growth to maturity of the Christian church.

25. Briefly describe the manner in which the convocation of Pentecost portrays the setting up of the kingdom of God upon the earth.

TRUMPETS

1. Describe the Hebrew feast of Trumpets, with main Scripture references.

2. On what day of the Hebrew calendar did Trumpets fall?

3. To what did the blowing of the trumpet call attention?

4. What is the Hebrew term for New Year's Day?

5. On what day of the calendar did the Day of Atonement fall?

6. On what day of the calendar did the convocation of Tabernacles fall?

7. Explain the two overlapping Jewish years.

8. List three uses of the trumpet in the culture of Israel.

9. Against whom are Christians to fight? Give Scripture references.

10. How and where did sin originate?

11. How is God going to destroy sin out of the earth?

12. Why was the Son of God manifested? Give Scripture reference.

13. How does the body of Christ fit into God's plan for executing judgment against sin?

14. How can a Christian prepare himself for his part in God's army?

15. What church activities do you believe to be most effective in the warfare against the powers of darkness? Cite Scripture for your belief.

16. Describe any differences, from God's standpoint, between the Christian who is committing a sin and an unsaved person who is committing the same sin. Give Scripture for your belief.

17. In terms of the new covenant, exactly what is the "house of God"?

18. Specifically, what are some things a Christian can do in order to overcome the sins that he or she is committing?

19. What is the "land of promise" of the Christian disciple?

20. Why does spiritual warfare play such an important part in the Christian life?

21. What is the difference between legal possession and actual possession?

22. Are there any differences between what the Old and New Testaments have to say about the committing of sins by God's people?

23. How is II Peter 1:19 related to the convocation of Trumpets?

24. Explain the three deaths portrayed by the three hangings of the Tabernacle of the Congregation.
25. Briefly describe the manner in which the feast of Trumpets portrays the Person and work of the Lord Jesus Christ.
26. Briefly describe the manner in which the feast of Trumpets portrays the redemption of the believer.
27. Briefly describe the manner in which the feast of Trumpets portrays the growth to maturity of the Christian church.
28. Briefly describe the manner in which the feast of Trumpets portrays the setting up of the kingdom of God upon the earth.

DAY OF ATONEMENT

1. Describe the Hebrew convocation of the Day of Atonement, with main Scripture references.
2. Why would we ordinarily expect the Day of Atonement to come at the beginning of the convocations?
3. How do we know that our tendency toward sin was not purged from us at the time of our initial acceptance of Christ Jesus?
4. How is it possible for God to work with His people even though they are not perfect in righteousness and holiness?
5. Did God choose the people of Israel because of their righteousness and holiness? Explain, with Scripture references.
6. List ten behaviors that the New Testament calls sin.
7. What does the New Testament have to say about the role of the confessing of sins in the life of the Christian?
8. What provisions are included in the grace of God, as far as sin in the Christian life is concerned?
9. How can we distinguish between the accusations of Satan, and the sins which we are practicing and which need to be dealt with through the power of the Holy Spirit?

10. Describe the relationship between the Day of Atonement and I John 1:7-9.

11. Why were *two* goats used in the ceremony of the Day of Atonement? What does this signify to us in practical terms?

12. What is one way in which Satan can bring a Christian disciple into bondage?

13. Describe the peril of overconfidence.

14. Describe the peril of passivity.

15. How does a Christian go about judging spirits and "voices"?

16. What part does human will power play in the Christian experience?

17. What should you do once you begin to suspect that you have fallen into deception? Give Scripture references.

18. Do we dare judge something that may be of the Holy Spirit? Give Scripture reference.

19. Describe the personal and historical fulfillments of the year of jubilee.

20. How are the actions of a Christian in dealing with his sins related to conditions in the spiritual realm? Give Scripture references.

21. How does a Christian "purify" himself?

22. Why does judgment begin in the household of God rather than among the unsaved?

23. What is the baptism with fire (Matt. 3:11)?

24. In terms of the new covenant program of redemption, how is the Day of Atonement related to the convocation of Tabernacles?

25. Briefly describe the manner in which the Day of Atonement portrays the Person and work of the Lord Jesus Christ.

26. Briefly describe the manner in which the Day of Atonement portrays the redemption of the believer.

27. Briefly describe the manner in which the Day of Atonement portrays the growth to maturity of the Christian church.

28. Briefly describe the manner in which the Day of Atonement portrays the setting up of the kingdom of God upon the earth.

TABERNACLES

1. Describe the Hebrew convocation of Tabernacles, with main Scripture references.
2. Why is it important and practical that we realize that the plan of redemption has a definite point of completion?
3. Toward what "mark" was Paul pressing? Explain, with Scripture references.
4. Explain the relationship between the twelfth chapter of Isaiah and the convocation of Tabernacles.
5. What is the goal of the Christian experience?
6. The convocation of Tabernacles celebrates the completion of the harvest. What spiritual significance does this fact have?
7. What relationship exists between the feast of Tabernacles and the law of Moses?
8. What relationship exists between the feast of Tabernacles and the "water" of the Holy Spirit?
9. What relationship exists between the feast of Tabernacles and the "light of the world"?
10. What is the significance of the eighth day of the feast of Tabernacles?
11. How would you apply the symbolism of the dwelling in booths?
12. How do you account for the extraordinary joy which accompanied the celebration of Tabernacles?
13. When is the convocation of Tabernacles fulfilled in the Christian life?
14. What relationship exists between the way in which we pursue the Christian life now and the redemption of the body when Jesus appears? Give Scripture references.
15. Briefly describe the manner in which the convocation of

Tabernacles portrays the Person and work of the Lord Jesus Christ.

16. Briefly describe the manner in which the convocation of Tabernacles portrays the redemption of the believer.

17. Briefly describe the manner in which the convocation of Tabernacles portrays the growth to maturity of the Christian church.

18. Briefly describe the manner in which the convocation of Tabernacles portrays the setting up of the kingdom of God in the earth.